KELLY

ALSO BY DANIEL J. BOYNE

Essential Sculling

The Red Rose Crew: A True Story of Women, Winning, and the Water

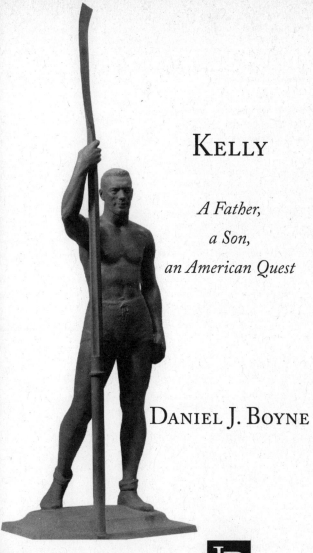

KELLY

A Father,
a Son,
an American Quest

DANIEL J. BOYNE

LYONS PRESS
Guilford, Connecticut
An imprint of Globe Pequot Press

Copyright © 2008 Mystic Seaport Museum, Inc.

First Lyons Press edition, 2012

This edition of *Kelly: A Father, a Son, an American Quest* by Daniel J. Boyne is published with the express written consent of Mystic Seaport Museum, Inc.

Lyons Press is an imprint of Globe Pequot Press.

Text design: Sheryl Kober

ISBN (paperback) 978-0-7627-7929-1

ISBN (cloth) 0-939511-23-1
Boyne, Daniel J.
Kelly: a father, a son, an American quest / by Daniel J. Boyne—1st ed.—Mystic, CT: Mystic Seaport, © 2008.
p. : ill. ; cm.
Includes bibliographic references and index.

1. Kelly, John B., 1889-1960. 2. Kelly, John B., 1927-1985. 3. Rowers—United States—Biography. I. Title.
 GV790.92.K4. B69 2007

Title page: Sculpture of Jack Kelly Sr., by Joseph Brown. Kelly was often described as having the perfect male physique. One of his nicknames was "the Adonis of East Falls."
© TEMPLE UNIVERSITY LIBRARIES, URBAN ARCHIVES, PHILADELPHIA, PA

Printed in the United States of America

10 9 8 7 6 5 4 3 2 1

To Lawrence Barss, an oarsman and a gentleman,
who first shared his stories of the Kellys with me.

TABLE OF CONTENTS

PREFACE

High above the banks of the Schuylkill River, a few miles upstream from the Philadelphia Museum of Art, rests the imposing figure of a giant green man, the bronze statue of an oarsman in a single scull. Captured in mid-action, holding onto his oars and gazing off toward the upstream reaches of the river, the waterborne Olympian looks as if he is trying to decide whether to take another stroke or

Jack Kelly Jr. holds up his son, Jack Kelly III, to touch the statue of his grandfather at the finish line of the rowing course, Schuylkill River, June 26, 1965. © TEMPLE UNIVERSITY LIBRARIES, URBAN ARCHIVES, PHILADELPHIA, PA

let his boat finally come to rest. The stoic expression and chiseled physique suggest the appearance of a Greek hero, riding on the waves below him, or perhaps some sort of a sphinx—half boat, half man, a riddle waiting on his sealed lips.

At the base of the statue, there is a simple inscription that reads:

JOHN B. KELLY

OLYMPIC CHAMPION: SINGLES 1920 DOUBLES 1924

DOUBLES 1920

The story of Jack Kelly Sr. and his long quest for international recognition in rowing is a colorful legend that has been passed along so many times in the sports world that it has become, like his statue, somewhat larger than life. Yet among the general public, the name Kelly registers very little, if anything, unless it is made in reference to his famous daughter, the actress Grace Kelly. Most people are unaware of how this Philadelphia patriarch rose from working-class Irish roots to become not only the most famous American oarsman of all time but also a millionaire businessman whose brick company was one of the largest on the Eastern seaboard. Most are unfamiliar with his noteworthy political career, which paved the way for the Democratic party in Philadelphia, or with his two brothers, George and Walter, who worked beside him in a local carpet mill as children and became famous as well—one as a Pulitzer Prize–winning playwright and the other as a popular vaudevillian. Many do not even realize that Kelly Drive, the long road that runs along the west bank of the Schuylkill River, was named after his equally lauded son, Jack Jr., or "Kell."

This is not a book about Grace Kelly, of which there have been many. But once, when the movie star-turned-princess was asked if she would ever like to write her autobiography, she replied, "No, but I would like to write one about my father, in which I am only a postscript." Although she may have eclipsed her father in international fame, this humble acknowledgment is a tribute to a figure whom many of Grace's biographers have often dismissed as yet another difficult parent of a struggling star, a tyrant who had little regard for his talented middle daughter. Similarly, he has also been accused of using his son Kell as an "instrument of revenge" against the English aristocracy that prevented him from entering the prestigious Henley Royal Regatta. Some of this is myth, and some of it is truth. As I hope this book will illustrate, the negative characterizations are insufficient at best. First, they fail to take into account the significant cultural changes that took place between the two generations of Kellys, including two world wars and the Great Depression. Second, they fail to acknowledge how Kelly Sr. laid the foundation for his children's success, literally brick by brick, despite any shortcomings he may have had as a father. Finally, they lack the perspective that, for better or worse, most successful oarsmen are single-minded by necessity, if not nature.

This last part of Jack Kelly's identity is perhaps the most important key to understanding the duality of his character, for rowing was the cornerstone of Kelly's life and the initial way that he developed the qualities of self-discipline and perseverance that lent him the ability to overcome many formidable obstacles in adulthood. A gifted athlete who could have chosen any number of physical disciplines, Kelly settled on this ancient and odd sport where the athlete cannot see who or what lies ahead, and contact with an opponent is forbidden. Under such restrictions, the oarsman's focus almost by necessity travels inward, requiring intense concentration and a certain moral resolve. This mental and physical training may have given Kelly the ability to succeed at a high level in various pursuits, although it may have also left him blind, at times, to the impact of his success on those around him. Donning a green cap to proudly signify his Irish lineage, Kelly also chose a color that was appropriate in representing many other aspects of his character: his naïveté, in assuming that he could tackle any task put before him; his sense of competitive envy toward his rivals; a serenity that came from achieving financial well-being; and finally, a sense of renewal in witnessing the success of his four children—particularly his son, Jack Jr. Roughly stated, these four qualities represented the four seasons of Kelly's life.

More than a few of Jack Kelly's early biographers and syco-phants have painted him as a Galahad who could do no wrong. This, too, does not do him full justice or render him in the three dimen-sions that he deserves. Like the impressive statue that rests along the Schuylkill River, Kelly was indeed a giant, an almost mythical pres-ence (in the early days of his athletic career, he was even referred to as "The Iron Man"). But he was also very human, made out of flesh and bone, emotional and vulnerable, and as prone to error as the rest of us. More importantly, for this story at least, it was how Jack Kelly dealt with his own shortcomings and the social bias against him that shaped his character. Only by turning these into sources of motiva-tion was he able to achieve his impressive feats in athletics, politics, and business.

Early on in the writing of this book, I was handed a copy of Jack Kelly's memoir, describing what he thought were the important

events in his life. The manuscript is by and large a sportsman's reflec-
tion, a tidy, twenty-page narrative focusing on his rowing exploits. It
also outlines the colorful Kelly family history that came before and
after him. If a person's writing is any indication of their ego, Jack
Kelly Sr. was a fairly modest and even self-effacing man. He clearly
wanted his accomplishments to be recorded, for he viewed much of
his life as a romantic quest. This book tries to reflect that simple wish,
without getting overly sentimental or critical of its subject. As anyone
who has ever tried to row a single scull knows, the boat doesn't move
forward too well if you can't keep it balanced. Nor does a book.

As an athlete and, in particular, an oarsman, Jack Kelly had few
rivals, if any, who accomplished what he did. The one exception was
his son, Kell. Jack Kelly Jr. is more than just a footnote in this story;
he is nearly the entire second act. To the extent that he succeeded
in carrying out his father's mission for him, Kell might easily be
viewed as heroic in his own right, and deserving of a full treatment
of his own. For the sake of narrative closure, however, I have chosen
to end this story at the completion of Jack Sr.'s boyhood dream, at
the Henley Royal Regatta in 1947, and leave the remainder of the
Kelly saga for another time, or perhaps another author more willing
to take up the daunting task of examining the life that Kelly Sr. left
in his wake.

DANIEL J. BOYNE

We must remember that one man is much the same as another, and that he is best who is trained in the severest school.

—THUCYDIDES

PART ONE

Boathouse Row, circa 1938. COURTESY OF DANIEL J. BOYNE

Chapter One

TWO MONTHS BEFORE THE END OF WORLD WAR I, JACK KELLY finally got his chance to fight. Unlike the soldiers around him, however, he would not be engaging in brutal trench warfare, nor pursuing the romantic aerial duels that he had once imagined. No matter. As a medic, he had seen plenty of injured doughboys, and the romance of the war had all but worn off. The US Ambulance Corps to which he had been assigned was stationed at Chateau Guian, a small French village about 75 miles from the front. Every day, hundreds of wounded men would arrive by train, largely victims of mustard and chlorine gas. In makeshift hospitals that had once been health spas, Kelly and his fellow medics often worked around the clock, doing what they could to help their fallen countrymen. It was exhausting work, and when his transfer orders came through, the twenty-eight-year-old Philadelphian was relieved to get a break from the constant sight of human suffering.

Ironically, the opportunity for combat came almost immediately after he was moved farther south in September 1918, away from the front lines. His new assignment was to take charge of a forty-group ambulance unit in Tours—Evacuation Company #67. Shortly after Kelly got settled into his new post, the army camp's athletic director showed up at his tent, asking for him by name. The director was desperate to find someone to box in the Friday night

Jack Kelly Sr., ambulance driver, WWI, 1918. © JOHN B. KELLY III

bouts, and apparently no one would go up against a gargantuan French opponent. Rumor had it that Kelly was a tough Irish kid who knew how to handle himself in the ring, and he had won the ship's boxing championship on his way over the Atlantic. But as soon as he identified himself to the camp athletic director, the man frowned involuntarily and shook his head. He'd been told that Jack Kelly was a big fellow, a heavyweight, and the guy standing in front of him didn't quite measure up.

In his baggy fatigues, Kelly certainly didn't look that impressive, although there was no mistaking him as anything but an athlete. He was six feet two inches yet lanky and lean, and he had a relaxed way of holding himself that disguised his muscular physique. When he posed for photos, he often sank his weight back into his heels, and with his hips thrown forward and his arms crossed, he looked more like a farm boy or a mechanic who had just finished a good day's work. Kelly was also strikingly handsome—not the sort you might imagine to be a seasoned boxer. He had a strong, square jaw, a Roman nose, and piercing aquamarine eyes that rested between high cheekbones and a broad forehead. His thick brown hair grew straight up off his right brow and warred briefly with a cowlick on the left side. His lips were thin, almost delicate.

Standing beside him in photographs, everyone else seemed to strike an unnatural pose for the camera, as if they were uncomfortable in their own bodies. Kelly's shoulders were always dropped and relaxed, and the upper portion of his arms was so long that when he crossed his elbows in front of his body, his forearms completely covered his belt. As the director looked him over, Kelly explained that he was in excellent shape, for back home in Philadelphia he had been training to be a world-class oarsman. The camp director was not impressed. He didn't know much about rowing, except that people probably didn't hit each other with the oars. Besides, Kelly looked too thin.

"You must not weigh more than 170 pounds," he quipped.

"One hundred eighty," Kelly corrected, adding a few pounds for good measure.

"Still too light," the director countered. The French boxer weighed 225 and easily dispatched most of his opponents. Someone more substantial than Kelly was needed to go up against the giant in order to provide some worthwhile entertainment for the troops. Kelly offered that he was unconcerned about the disparity in weight, and eagerly asked how much the winner would get paid. Fifty francs would go to the victor, twenty-five to the loser.

"In that case," Kelly said, "I'm your man!"

The director shook his head again and started to leave when Kelly implored him one last time.

"Tell you what," the man said. "If I don't find a big lug soon, I'll come back and lead you to slaughter—after all, it's your life!"

He returned the following afternoon, having failed to find an alternative to the lanky Irish kid from Philadelphia. Jokingly, he told Kelly to pay up his life insurance, for the Frenchman was a beast of a man who liked nothing better than to humiliate people—allies or not.

But Jack Kelly was no newcomer to the ring.

By all reports, the Frenchman wouldn't go down easily. He was apparently in great shape, and he preferred to work out in public view—a practice that discouraged other fighters from challenging him. He'd knocked out his last three opponents with relative ease, and he was already bragging that he'd make short work of the new American. Knowing all of this, Kelly quickly called eight of his friends together. He told them he needed help, and he'd pay them five francs each to serve as sparring partners in the days leading up to the match. In doing so, of course, he'd have to split the winner's purse nine ways, leaving himself only ten francs if he proved victorious. But Kelly knew it was his only real chance to train properly for the bout.

When the night of the big fight finally arrived, Kelly seemed unnaturally composed. He often radiated a sense of calm, but no one, except perhaps his buddy Bert Bell, knew the real source of this confidence. Kelly hadn't talked much about his Philadelphia background, or how he had dropped out of school after eighth grade to help his parents pay the bills. He hadn't talked about his early boxing career at the Fairmount Inn, nor spoken about his bloody, bare-knuckles fight with the East Falls bully, Pat McCarthy. These memories had come back to him as he prepared for the bout, however, as well as his longing to be back on the Schuylkill River, rowing alone in a single scull.

In contrast to Kelly's air of composure, his French opponent seemed impatient to get on with the fight. As both men stepped into the ring, Jack finally got a good look at him. He was as big as advertised, hairy and brutish, and at least forty pounds heavier. The weight difference would be a huge advantage if the Frenchman could land his punches, and Kelly decided that he would need to evade him as much as possible, countering only when the right opportunity presented itself. As predicted, when the bell rang for round one, the Frenchman rushed straight at Kelly and tried to bowl him over with a wild fury of thrashing blows. Jack parried and dodged, fighting for his survival. His adversary seemed completely out of control, and when most of the giant's punches failed to connect, he grew even angrier and more reckless with his technique. When the bell rang again, ending the round, the Frenchman reluctantly stalked off to his corner, glaring hard over his shoulder at Kelly. He had bragged that he would knock out the American in round one, and this prophecy had failed to materialize.

During round two, Kelly again spent most of his time on defense. He was lighter and more nimble than his oversize opponent, but he realized that the man was still quite fit and dangerous, and he decided to knock him down as quickly as he could. Jack moved quickly around the ring while the Frenchman swatted the

Kelly in football uniform, circa 1917. A consummate athlete, Kelly played competitive basketball, football, and water polo. He also competed in swimming and boxing, and was an active golfer. © TEMPLE UNIVERSITY LIBRARIES, URBAN ARCHIVES, PHILADELPHIA, PA

smoky air, still missing most of his punches. The pace had slowed. Anyone in the audience who knew about boxing would have quickly surmised that it was a classic face-off between a brawler and a polished boxer. A brawler always took the offensive and tried to overwhelm his opponent with a flurry of punches. A boxer studied his opponent, waiting for the right moment to execute a counterattack.

Suddenly, halfway into the second round, Kelly saw his opening and drove a solid left into the Frenchman's ribs. He followed quickly with a right cross to his jaw. The big man staggered and then feebly tried to counter with an uppercut. Kelly jumped back, dodging the weak punch, and shot another hard right to the Frenchman's jaw. He felt the punch connect, and then watched as his opponent's head snapped back. The Frenchman staggered, trying to regain his balance, and then his huge body dropped to the canvas, landing with a dull thud. When the referee finished his ten-count, he still lay there, unable to move. The crowd of soldiers, who had been shouting hysterically the entire time, suddenly fell silent as they realized it was all over. Then their eyes fell on Kelly. Who the hell was this kid, anyway?

Jack calmly walked out of the makeshift arena and collected his fifty francs from the bursar. He counted out the money, removing ten francs for himself, and then divided the remaining sum into eight equal portions. A small crowd of friends and other soldiers had gathered around him, patting him on the back and insisting that he join them for a celebratory drink. Jack smiled, graciously accepting their praise, and talked with them for a while, recalling the fight as best he could remember it. The men were all in a state of euphoria and near disbelief about what had just happened, and hearing the story told again seemed the only way to make it true. He embellished the tale where his memory failed him, but after he had handed out five francs to each of his training buddies, Kelly begged off the invitations for further celebration. He was "in training," he explained, for his real sport—rowing—and could not touch alcohol.

As he lay on his cot later that night, feeling the exhaustion of the boxing match settle into his bones, he replayed the fight in his mind, chuckling softly to himself when he recalled the surprised reaction of the crowd. The upset was worth more to him than the ten francs he earned. Even his commanding officer had been so impressed that he'd asked whether Kelly would be willing to enter some more fights and maybe even consider the AEF (American Expeditionary Forces) championships. It would be worth a lot to him, his C.O. mentioned, if Kelly could help him out. But Jack wasn't sure; he had other, more important things to consider.

He retrieved a letter from the desk beside him that he had received from his mother, a few weeks before his transfer orders came in. In it she expressed her concern about his brother George, who was also serving in the war as a non-commissioned officer. She had not heard from him in weeks, and she was worried. "He is a sensitive soul," she wrote, imploring Jack to find him and let her know that he was safe. He began to wonder how he could locate George and perhaps even get him discharged. Everyone, it seemed, looked to him for help.

Before he went to sleep, as he did each night, Kelly prayed and tried to clear his mind of everything, particularly all the battlefield scenes that sometimes haunted his dreams. In order to block out the images of wounded and dying men, he often played a game in his mind where he imagined himself back home on the Schuylkill, rowing against his most difficult competitors. These were older men who had beaten him before, and Kelly pushed himself hard during the make-believe races, not relenting until he had actually seen himself win. When he finished with the mental exercise, he was completely exhausted and yet satisfied that something important had been achieved. Tonight, as he slowly drifted off to sleep, he took the familiar, childhood territory of the river with him into his dreams. It was a ribbon of green water, glistening in the midday sun, and he was moving just above it, rowing so fast that he felt like a bird flying, without effort.

Chapter Two

IN 1899, FOR FIFTEEN CENTS AN HOUR YOU COULD RENT A BICYCLE in the city of Philadelphia and travel anywhere your legs would take you. If you were an adventurous ten-year-old boy from the nearby village of East Falls, chances are you would eventually follow gravity's lead and let yourself coast down one of the many dirt roads that descended steeply to the Schuylkill River. This aptly named waterway ("hidden creek," in Dutch) occupied the lowest point in the hilly surrounding landscape, and East Falls Drive, which ran along the river for a distance of roughly five miles, provided a scenic promenade from Jack Kelly's working-class, Irish neighborhood to the city waterworks at the base of Lemon Hill.

Lining the banks were great stretches of green space, dairies, and elegant homes with names like Rockland, Ormiston, Woodford, Strawberry Mansion, Belmont, and Sweet Briar. These private estates lay on both sides of the river and composed an area known as Fairmount Park. They were the remnants of an original plan that William Penn, the city's founding father, had envisioned for the nation's first capital. An enterprising Quaker and one of America's early urban planners, Penn wished to develop "the great green town" so that it looked less like a crowded urban center than a collection of gentlemen's farms. His was a romantic, utopian scheme, which had considerable merits and a few critical

Schuylkill River Regatta, Philadelphia, July 4, 1874. © TEMPLE UNIVERSITY LIBRARIES, URBAN ARCHIVES, PHILADELPHIA, PA

flaws. One of these was the lack of affordable housing for the people who would become the driving force behind the city's economy, the immigrant families who made up the working class, like the Kellys.

At age nine, John Brendan Kelly ("Jack") had already begun to work at Dobson's, a carpet factory and woolen mill where nearly all of the Irish in East Falls were employed. His four older brothers—Patrick, Walter, Charles, and George—all worked some portion of time at the mill as well, so that their four sisters—Ann, Mary, Elizabeth, and Grace—could attend secretarial school after completing the eighth grade. Mary Costello Kelly begrudgingly sent her sons to work at the English-owned outfit in order to make ends meet, while her husband, John Henry, was busy getting an insurance concern established. On weekends, however, her youngest son and ninth child was often free to do as he pleased. More often than not, when he wasn't playing with his neighborhood pals, he was down by the river, pedaling his way toward the Fairmount Dam and a place called Turtle Rock.

There were certainly better ways to see the Schuylkill River than on a rented bicycle, from which a good view was often obscured by thick stands of trees. On the narrow, winding road that followed the river, there were also horse-drawn carriages to contend with, although most people now took trolleys or the Reading Railroad to enter the city. For twenty cents you could also board a paddle-wheel steamer and get ferried downstream in fairly short order, despite numerous stops along the way. Ferries, in fact, had plied the Schuylkill River long before good roads and railways had been established, transporting produce and later parties of people who went upstream to picnic or sightsee for the day.

Ever since the lower reaches had been dammed in 1822, the character of the river had changed radically from a narrow tidal stream, used mainly for utilitarian purposes, to a wider, slower-moving waterway, ideal for public recreation. The mighty Delaware, which ran along Philadelphia's eastern boundary before the Schuylkill joined it to form a watery necklace around the city, was far too big and dangerous to serve this purpose, despite the legend of George Washington's historic crossing. But with its little islands, canals, and various tributaries, the Schuylkill presented an opportunity for youthful adventures to rival those of Huckleberry Finn.

Yet, while other boys from East Falls might take a skiff up the nearby Wissahickon Creek to swim or collect apples for the day, Jack was not interested in anything so aimless. Instead, nearly every free weekend beginning in May, he would ride his rented bicycle to Turtle Rock to see the rowing regattas. He loved to watch the single scullers in particular, plying the oars with all of their strength and skill as they moved majestically across the water in silence. The good oarsmen traveled nearly as fast as he did on his bicycle, and he began to follow them to test his speed against their own.

From an early age, the sturdy, thick-haired boy was less a dreamer than a doer, more physically gifted than any of his brothers. More importantly, however, once Jack focused on something, he stuck with it until success was realized. These weekend excursions to the river may have at first been inspired by a simple curiosity about the sleek racing boats and the athletic men who mastered them, but this casual interest quickly blossomed into an obsession. He began to follow the mile-and-a-half races on his bicycle regularly and memorize the names of each competitor. As Kelly learned more about the sport and the skill it required, he also began to make mental notes about technique, training, and racing strategy. He was still too young to row himself, but he made up his mind to become an oarsman when he came of age. During regattas he would often follow several races in one day, covering a total distance of about twenty-five miles on his bicycle. It was an impressive amount of exercise for a ten-year-old, but the physical effort was only an auxiliary benefit, largely unregistered in the boy's mind. For Jack Kelly had an indescribable passion for rowing, and just watching others do it left him feeling exhilarated.

After the races, he would appear at the closely packed cluster of buildings known as "Boathouse Row" to try to catch a glimpse of his waterborne heroes, heavily muscled men like Fred Sheppard, the senior single scull champion from Brooklyn, New York. By the turn of the century, Philadelphia had become a rowing mecca, and it attracted an impressive group of nationally ranked competitors. It was these oarsmen, too, not the baseball, football, or basketball players, who became the first sports celebrities of the day. (It would be several years before names like Babe Ruth or Joe DiMaggio even entered the public consciousness.) But Jack Kelly loved the sport for other reasons than its popular appeal. To him, oarsmen literally walked on the water and seemed to carry themselves on a higher plane than other athletes. They were fitter than most, from the grueling demands of the sport, but they never had to lay a hand on their opponents, to curse or foul them in order to win. They were, in fact, some of the first "gentlemen" that he had ever met.

He also loved the look and the smell of the boathouses, Victorian Gothic-style cottages that reeked of sweat and rubbing alcohol, and the wooden boats fashioned from mahogany and Spanish cedar. To a young boy's eyes, the boathouses were no less romantic than the private country estates that lined the river. Many years later as a grown man, Jack Kelly would still be unable to verbalize exactly what drew him to his chosen sport, which offered so little in the way of financial gain and demanded so much time and physical pain. There was something pure and unfettered about rowing, and the element of water provided an immediate sense of personal freedom—an escape, perhaps, from the realities on land.

⁓

Jack Kelly wasn't the first Philadelphian to fall in love with rowing and make icons out of the oarsmen who plied the Schuylkill River. Forty years earlier, a budding local painter named Thomas Cowperthwait Eakins had also found his way down to the river and decided that a waterman's life was the one for him. Unlike Kelly, however, Eakins was the son of an academic, a writing instructor, and the social circles he traveled in were of an entirely different sort. Yet from its very beginnings, the Philadelphia rowing fraternity was one in which different classes of people could and did mingle. Some of Eakins's best friends, like the sculler and attorney Max Schmitt, boated out of the Pennsylvania Barge Club, alongside those who were less financially sound or socially established.

During Eakins's youth, it was actually possible to make a career out of rowing, if one had enough talent and luck. A successful professional sculler could win prizes of over $5,000 a race, a small fortune in those days. And if one were willing to travel around the country, or even overseas, an exceptional oarsman could sustain a career much like a prizefighter—drawing huge crowds, celebrity, and money. But the professionals, by and large, came from the ranks of the working class, particularly those who spent more of their time around boats than books. And so, either due to lack of skill or parental disapproval, Eakins ultimately sought his fortune in another field.

Failing to make a career out of rowing, Eakins dedicated himself to his other passion, painting, and distinguished himself by becoming one of the first Americans accepted into the prestigious Ecole des Beaux Arts in Paris. After three years of study, he returned home and watched his friend Max Schmitt win the Schuylkill Navy Regatta on October 5, 1870, a well-attended event that was held to showcase some of Philadelphia's rowing talent. The waterborne celebration certainly made a big impression on the artist and native son, whose mind was now filled with new ideas about art, while his heart was still tied to the Schuylkill River. The two passions met in a series of rowing paintings, unparalleled to this day.

The rowing studies were exceptional in many ways. Not only did Eakins's work display an intricate knowledge of geometry and perspective, color, and light, but both his subjects and the way he portrayed them were revolutionary. Instead of choosing noteworthy figures from genteel society, he singled out the best of the amateur and professional oarsmen, often "rough-looking" men like the Biglin brothers from New York, and celebrated them on canvas. Unwittingly or not, Eakins was paying homage to a class of Americans who were aspiring to prove not only their athletic prowess but also their overall worth in the eyes of American society.

One of the few artists of his day to make an extensive study of human anatomy, Eakins also rendered his oarsmen in their unadulterated physical state—grim-faced from the strain of their efforts, with bare arms and legs heavily contoured with muscles. Prior to this, most rowing studies had suffered from being overly sentimental or cartoon-like, Currier and Ives–style renderings that failed to convey the raw emotional power of the sport. Eakins's subjects, usually captured in motion, appeared to emerge dramatically from the evocative natural environment around them. In this fusion of French painting technique and American realism, he elevated the oarsmen to a more noble level than most competitive athletes were regarded at the time, perhaps in his longing to be one of them or perhaps in sympathy with the grueling hard work that they invested to move a boat well over water. He knew from experience what it took to do well, and it was no less a discipline than his artistic studies.

The American painter was documenting the sport at the height of its popularity, and also registering a change in his country's social fabric. It was an odd, transitional period in US history, where ostentatious displays of extreme wealth hid a population of Americans just struggling to survive. The post–Civil War industrial boom had created enormous wealth, but only for a select few, and those who did not have the good fortune of a Carnegie or a Rockefeller lived a very different way, by and large supporting those who did. But things were starting to change, and the artists saw it first, serving as a cultural bellwether. As one art historian, Elizabeth C. Milroy, described it, Eakins, together with the visionary poet Walt Whitman, shared "a determination to break down aesthetic barriers to the acceptance of raw-boned athletic Americans as emblematic of the nation's citizens." Or as Helen A. Cooper put it, "Eakins saw in rowing the American egalitarian spirit in its purest form: a blend of intellect, precision, and stamina that together could attain heroic ends."

And it was into this time of transformation, on October 4, 1889, that John Brendan Kelly was born.

John H. Kelly and Mary Costello had both emigrated from Ireland as the Civil War was drawing to a close. They met and married in Rutland, Vermont, and after brief stints of employment there and in upstate New York, they moved to the Irish community known as The Falls. They brought with them two boys and a girl, and a sense of intense patriotism that was reflected in their first son's name—Patrick Henry. Upon arrival, Mary Kelly, the only child of a poor tenant farmer, kissed the Liberty Bell and proclaimed America as "God's Country." John Henry, a quiet, brooding man who stood six feet tall and weighed two hundred pounds, was looking forward to a respite from his prior employment as a manual laborer.

Their new hometown, however, was something of a disappointment. East Falls, which sat on the fringe of Philadelphia, was a warren of narrow streets lined with two- and three-story tenement houses. While some residents proudly claimed that their tiny community predated William Penn's arrival in 1682 and was first called St. David's, it was isolated from the city by both its geography and overall character. It was, in fact, little more than a working-class slum. Many Falls residents lived their entire lives without having once ventured into downtown Philadelphia.

Midvale Avenue, where the Kellys eventually settled, was one of the primary roads that sloped down to the river, situated halfway between St. Bridget's Church and the local post office. A good Catholic, Mary Kelly produced and raised seven more children, losing only one, and found solace from her trying circumstances by reading constantly. Her new neighbors were often taken aback to see her sitting on her porch, a baby in one arm and a book in the other. She was Irish, sure enough, but somehow different from most

Kelly family, circa 1912. Back Row (left to right):
Charles, Mary, George, Patrick Henry. Middle Row:
John Henry and Mary Kelly. Front Row (left to right):
Jack, Grace, and Elizabeth. (Note: Absent from
photo is brother Walter Kelly.) © JOHN B. KELLY III

of them. She had real book learning and could quote long passages of Shakespeare from memory, or tell you the lineage of English kings. John Henry, who originally hailed from County Mayo,
also appeared to be well educated, endowed with an exceptional
memory and a gift for elocution. While out walking with a friend
one day, he reputedly quoted nearly the entire length of Sir Thomas
Moore's *Lalla Rookh*, an epic poem of over a thousand lines.

Something else, however, set Mary Costello Kelly apart, and
it came out mainly in the way she raised her children. She wanted
them to be good Catholics and follow most of the prescribed rules,

but she also had her own set of expectations and morals, and it was these that she used to raise her large brood. From an early age, they were drilled in this Spartan code, which included being punctual and just, sparing of promises, and keeping one's word at all costs.

"The trouble is that in most families the mother is afraid of her children," she once explained to a neighbor, who had innocently posed a question about favoritism in child rearing, only to find herself treated to a long lecture.

> *I never stood in fear of mine, even though I would have given my heart's blood for them. They are the whole world to me. But I've never been afraid of them. Why should I be? For their own good, they must be taught to respect me as their superior. Not that I demand their respect just because I happen to be their mother. You can demand a show of respect, as long as you are the stronger. But the thing itself must be earned. I will never stop trying to earn the respect of my children.*

Years later, during an interview with *American Magazine* in September 1925, the Irish matriarch also revealed her philosophy about teaching money matters to children. From an early age, she explained, by giving them small tasks, "you can easily make them understand that when they do one thing they are earning the right to do another." And if they wanted something "extra," she elaborated, they not only had to earn it but also understand the work that went into it.

Once, when young Jack asked for a pair of ice skates, his mother made him go to the public library and learn everything he could about how they were made—right down to the details of how leather was tanned, the iron was mined, and the wood was harvested. "I want you to see that a pair of skates has been earned for you by the labor of others, and that you must put your labor in it, too, if you want to enjoy them," she explained. And John Brendan dutifully did as he was told.

Nor were her strong opinions reserved for the members of her own family or her immediate neighbors. Once, a local pastor was delivering a long, public tirade against a parishioner he held in very low regard. When he finished with his loud invective, Mary Kelly replied, "Thanks be to God, Father, there's a higher judge than you!"

On another occasion, when St. Bridget's church was first being constructed, a cleric named Monsignor Walsh was admiring the view from a spot just in front of Mary Kelly's front porch.

"It certainly is an imposing edifice," he remarked, engaging her in light conversation.

Mary Kelly put down her book for a moment, stopped rocking in her chair, and regarded the church with a pregnant frown.

"It's a far cry from Bethlehem, Monsignor," she replied.

Chapter Three

MARY KELLY'S HARSHEST DIATRIBES, HOWEVER, WERE RESERVED for the village overlords, the Dobsons. Most of the residents of East Falls lived in fear of James and John Dobson, two England expatriates who had opened their first mill in 1851 and become millionaires by the end of the Civil War. Woolen blankets, supplied to Union soldiers, were one of the many lucrative products they produced. By the 1870s, when the Kellys moved to East Falls,

Dobson's Mill, early 1900s. © EAST FALLS HISTORICAL SOCIETY, PHILADELPHIA, PA

encouraged by their cousins and the promise of employment, the Dobson's Mill grossed more than $20 million annually.

The employee benefits, however, were substantially less impressive.

The company accepted children for employment at the age of nine, and their average day began at 6:30 a.m. and ended at 6:00 p.m. Weekly pay for these twelve-hour days was a meager $2.50. In addition, many of the workers' houses were leased from the company, effectively turning some families into urban sharecroppers. In the eyes of the Philadelphians living outside of East Falls, the Dobsons were a great success, but to their employees they were nothing but cruel despots. To the many Irish immigrants of the Falls who had originally come across the Atlantic to flee the economic tyranny of the British, employment at the English mill could only have felt like a cruel, ironic fate.

A few episodes in particular would stay fixed in the Kellys' minds for generations to follow.

One revolved around a particularly degrading practice that occurred whenever one of James Dobson's five daughters got married. On these occasions, Mrs. Dobson would hand out pennies to the local Irish children and have them line up and cheer the wedding party as they left the Anglican Church, St. James the Lesser. Once, when Mary Kelly was looking around for her youngest three children, she got wind of the fact that they were watching one of these celebrations. When she found them being herded into place by Mrs. Dobson, she grabbed them and shouted, "To hell with your pennies! No Kellys are going to stand up in front of a Protestant church and cheer the Dobsons, now or ever!"

Another memory was when Patrick Henry ("P. H.") was still a boy and caught pneumonia, severe enough for him to stay home for the week. His job at Dobson's was specialized and somewhat important, for it involved selecting appropriate dyes from the mill's color charts. A few days after P. H. took ill, the person covering his post made a bad error in judgment, a mistake that caused an entire section of the mill to be shut down. Shortly thereafter, a foreman appeared at the Kellys' front door, explaining the dire predicament. Nothing, apparently, could be done without P. H., so the sick boy was rolled up into a blanket and driven over to Dobson's. A few hours later, having resolved the problem, he was returned to his home on Midvale Avenue and allowed to finish his convalescence.

Mary Kelly had every intention of having her nine children succeed in whatever field of endeavor they chose. Her husband, John Henry, thought that each of the boys should inevitably learn a trade, to experience the value of working with their hands. But Dobson's was not what either of them had in mind.

Fortunately, the Kelly family's tenure at the English carpet mill was short-lived compared to most of their neighbors. Their fortune changed first with P. H., who came home one day with a half-baked, pie-in-the-sky idea. One of the big newspapers, *The Philadelphia Press,* was sponsoring a contest to find "the most popular employee of the year." The generous prize was a new house, valued at nearly $5,000. Patrick Henry showed the paper to his mother and explained that if he could somehow win, he would sell the house and use the capital to start his own contracting business.

Mary Kelly scrutinized the rules for the contest, which simply involved getting the most ballots from subscribers. "And why shouldn't you win it?" she asked. "It's the ballots that will win, not popularity." If her first son was surprised by his mother's reply, what she did next must have come as even more of a shock, for the woman who believed in the value of hard work was not above trying to win at all costs. She assembled her nine children and organized them into a small army of door-to-door canvassers, explaining what they were expected to do and how they were to do it.

Jack, being the most athletic of the lot, was assigned the task of waking up before dawn and following different newspaper deliverymen on their routes. His job was to take down the addresses of all the houses that received a paper. These addresses would then be handed over to Ma Kelly, who divided them up and distributed a different block to each child, along with a small pair of scissors. Over the course of the next week, while the contest was being held, they were instructed to go door to door, asking each resident to vote for their older brother. If the mistress or master of the house hesitated or raised an objection, they were to hold up the pair of scissors and offer to clip out the coupon themselves.

It was an audacious plan, but it worked. Few, it seemed, could resist the small scissors, particularly displayed in the hands of a child. And when the votes for the contest were tallied, P. H. had won easily. He sold the prize house and quickly set up his own business, taking brother Charlie and sister Ann with him. Within three years, he would be a millionaire, one of the first in the Falls to free himself from the mill.

With her oldest son on his way to becoming a success, Ma Kelly turned her attention toward the younger members of her brood.

The girls were all expected to finish their education by attending secretarial school, and then move on to jobs as stenographers or bookkeepers. The boys, however, all set their sights higher, despite their lack of education. Walter and George were the family clowns, endowed with their father's gift for inspired oratory, often infused with a ration of lowbrow humor. Walter in particular was a born entertainer, able to draw large crowds of people at street corners with his impromptu skits and speeches. George was more intellectual and introverted, but no less dramatic. Sometimes he would wrap himself up in a white sheet and recite passages from Shakespeare in front of the family at dinnertime. These dramas sometimes became family duels, where Ma Kelly would begin one phrase and George would complete it before she could finish. When she lost her patience with him once and threatened him, he replied, "Go ahead and hurt me, Mary Kelly, but you will be sorry when my name is in lights!"

The entire family exploded with laughter, including George's recalcitrant mother. They were prophetic words for the budding playwright, but at the time they were simply seen as one of the many hilarious moments that offered comic relief for the Kelly family. The melodramatic line would be repeated over and over again by the boys, who found it a useful way to disarm their mother when they broke one of her many house rules. Punishment usually took the form of a swat on the back of the head, and Mary Kelly's wedding ring could inflict serious pain. Yet despite the strict discipline she tried to uphold, or perhaps because of it, the Kelly boys would all find avenues to success, in ways that neither one of their parents could have imagined possible.

When he finished grammar school, Jack took a job as a "telephone boy" during the construction of Wanamaker's department store on 13th and Market Street. His job was to run around the construction site and locate various foremen as they were needed on the phone, negotiating his way up and down the half-finished building. It was dangerous, often acrobatic work, and one day Jack lost his footing and fell three stories from an open window. Luckily, he landed right in the middle of an ash heap, which cushioned his fall and saved his life. When he came home at the end of the day and reported the incident to his mother, showing off his bruises, Ma Kelly was not altogether surprised. Her youngest son seemed to have a special knack for getting himself into trouble and then emerging unscathed.

He had been named after her firstborn, who had died of heat stroke at age ten, but this one seemed to have the vitality of two boys. As Jack grew older and bigger, fueled by two-inch-thick steaks and homemade custards, his appetite for living only seemed to increase, despite constant admonitions to slow down. Jack took most of his mother's advice, and her meals, to heart, but she didn't know exactly how to deal with her overactive, thrill-seeking son. The answer, however, lay close at hand. Organized sports in America were newly minted, with rules and legends yet unwritten. They rapidly took hold of the country's youth, and the Irish community of East Falls proved no exception. Despite a visible lack of resources, Jack Kelly's neighborhood soon became a virtual hotbed of sporting enthusiasts, many of whom would go on to national prominence in various fields, including golf, boxing, football, baseball, basketball, and tennis. A gifted young athlete looking to prove his physical prowess, Jack would try his hand at most of these sports before he focused exclusively on rowing.

Mary and John Henry were soon taken off guard by their son's enthusiasm for various sporting activities, and both questioned whether they would lead to anything useful. They might, in fact, lead him down paths that were dangerous, like the boxing he began to practice at a place called the Fairmount Inn. Jack and his friends had first gravitated toward the roadhouse because it was known as a place where fights often broke out and gambling was rampant. It was also a hangout for professional boxers, men with names like "Terrible" Terry McGovern, "Battling" Nelson, and Tom Sharkey. Kelly and his friends idolized these fighters, just as Jack idolized the single scullers on the Schuylkill River. Sharkey, once a contender for the heavyweight boxing title of the world, had once trained at the Fairmount Inn and then popularized it as a training center for Philadelphia pugilists.

Jack and his pals soon became regulars at the inn and began to enter the junior bouts. The prize money for the winner could be as high as $5, or two weeks' pay at Dobson's Mill. Largely unskilled, Kelly lost his first two fights before he realized that he would have to start training like the professionals—putting in the daily miles of running known as "roadwork" and refining his boxing technique with an experienced coach. Sensing a talented and eager young student, Hughie McGovern, the brother of "Terrible" Terry, agreed to take Jack on. In less than a month under McGovern's tutelage, Kelly won his first tournament and took home a cash prize of $4.75.

Ma Kelly was not impressed and insisted that he return the money. Despite her humble roots, she did not approve of fighting as a respectable way to earn a living. John Henry, however, thought differently and interceded on his son's behalf. He pointed out that it was a good, practical thing for a young man to know how to use his fists. He himself had been recently employed as a stagecoach driver, and his pugilistic skills had come in handy. The dangerous route to which he'd been assigned had been losing money, beleaguered by a rough clientele, many of whom refused to pay their fares. But only a week after John Henry took over, these collection problems suddenly disappeared; no one messed with the big Irishman. And so, in the end, his son was allowed to keep the money from the boxing match. Mary Kelly had no problem with her sons fighting to stick up for themselves; she had actually encouraged them to do this from an early age. Taking money for fighting, however, was another matter, for it might lead to the world of gambling, and worse, eventual injury. She had begun to notice that Jack always managed to get himself into some sort of scuffle, regardless of the arena.

In fact, almost every sport that Kelly participated in seemed to involve some form of violence—fights that were not generally included in the rulebook. The football games between East Falls and the other surrounding townships, for example, frequently ended in all-out fistfights. One famous game was held between the Casey Athletic Club from the north end of town and the Clearfield Athletic Association from the south end. These two teams were such bitter rivals that only a few of the competitions held between them were ever actually completed, the majority of contests ending as pitched battles between the spectators. This particularly memorable game was held on Christmas Day, a rematch from an earlier Thanksgiving Day competition that had resulted in a scoreless tie. So many bets were riding on the intra-town rivalry that a clear decision was called for by the numerous fans, most of whom worked at Dobson's Mill. Entire paychecks were riding on the outcome of the game, and tensions between the fans had greatly escalated. Jack

Kelly was an irregular member of the Casey squad, brought into this game to try to tip the scales in their favor. His last-minute appearance at fullback, however, was strongly objected to by the Clearfield squad, who proceeded to try to embarrass their rivals by stealing their mascot, a live goat. A few nights before the big game, they paraded a wagon through town with a sign that read, WE GOT CASEY'S GOAT.

Even with numerous police on hand, three huge fights broke out among the spectators during the game. The majority of the five thousand fans were drinking heavily, a claim substantiated by the number of flasks collected later on the playing grounds. Nevertheless, Casey prevailed 16–0, and by his own accounting, Kelly had "a good day." After the game, however, as he was heading back to the Casey dressing room, he made the mistake of taking a shortcut through a flock of Clearfield fans. A group of disappointed women proceeded to beat him over the head with their banners, first stripping off Jack's helmet to make the punishment more severe. When Kelly finally fought his way back to the dressing room, he discovered that his football jersey was ripped to shreds and his body was riddled with fingernail scratches.

Basketball wasn't any better organized. Kelly played on different teams, including the Germantown Boys' Club from the village north of East Falls. The rules of conduct on the court seemed to be subject to the whims of the players, and the presence of a referee was generally considered unnecessary. Any number of boys could play on each side, but commonly there were ten—a total which may have reduced the amount of overall running required, but seemed to increase the frequency of "scuffles" for the ball. These games, too, often disintegrated into free-for-alls.

As a novice at the game, Kelly often found himself at the bottom of a large pile of players, all of whom were vying for the basketball. Sometimes, as the human heap disentangled itself, the players took wild swings at one another. During one of his first games, held against St. Anne's in Port Richmond, Kelly was checked so hard that he went airborne, flying into the second row of the stands. The game was tied at 25–25, and now it was overtime. The fans from both sides had slowly worked themselves into a frenzy, and Kelly's dramatic ejection became the catalyst for the game's demise. The stands emptied as the spectators took to the court, and the game turned into a colossal rumble. Once again, Kelly was beaten up by the opposing side, this time so badly that he had to be "introduced to his mother," because his face was swollen and bruised beyond recognition.

In a subsequent game, Kelly decided to use his boxing skills to defend himself, but this tactic nearly got him into even worse trouble. When a player from an out-of-state team decided to take a swing at him, Kelly countered with his left hand and knocked the boy out cold. When the player didn't immediately regain consciousness, several fans got out of their seats and began to surround Kelly, looking for revenge. Fortunately, Jack's friend and boxing pal, Joe Burns, was also in the stands and jumped down beside him.

"Back to back, Jack," Joe Burns shouted, and the two of them made their way out the door, trading a few well-aimed punches with those who tried to bar their way.

Chapter Four

AT AGE EIGHTEEN, JACK KELLY TOOK UP THE TWO PHYSICAL activities that would shape much of his adult life. The first was bricklaying, and the second was rowing. One was work, and the other was play, but in the end both would take up so much of his time that it was often difficult for those around him to tell which was the vocation and which the avocation. While Jack had already been working for his brother P. H. for a few years as a mason's apprentice, he was officially initiated into the Bricklayers Union as a journeyman mechanic in 1910. Bricklaying was a very old and well-respected trade, complete with three classic designations of skill: apprentice, journeyman, and master craftsman. It was also a very masculine line of work—beginning with the dirty, back-breaking task of "hodding" bricks to the worksite in a big wheelbarrow, and progressing to the artistry and engineering skill needed to set a course of bricks in a straight row, then "throwing" and furrowing lines of mortar. It required quick, strong hands and a keen eye, skills that were only developed after holding, setting, and cutting thousands of bricks, the porous clay squares that sucked the moisture out of your hands and left them first blistered, then calloused and hard.

It was also very satisfying work for a person with the right temperament. In the construction business, masons were commonly

P. H. Kelly Co. construction crew, with Jack Kelly Sr. in front row on a barrel, hat in hand, October 27, 1912. © JOHN B. KELLY III

known as quiet types who went about their days with a high level of concentration. The work itself required a certain degree of silence. But once you got beyond the initial hardships, it had some hidden physical benefits, as Kelly would soon discover. In fact, if you were to try to come up with a perfect exercise for strengthening your hands, wrists, and forearms, you would be hard-pressed to find one that was superior to bricklaying. In some ways, it might have seemed like a fine prerequisite for rowing were it not for the physically exhausting aspects of the work.

After a long day of laying brick and spreading mortar, Kelly would make his way down to the Schuylkill River and jump in a boat as a junior member of the Vesper Boat Club. Vesper, which took its name from the evening prayer service of the Christian monastic tradition, was another fraternal organization that had its own hierarchy based on both age and skill. A highly competitive club with a long string of victories, it was an appropriate choice for the young acolyte from East Falls who was looking to demonstrate his athletic prowess in a more structured, subtle venue than both boxing and the ball sports he had been playing.

Kelly's connection to the river had actually come in fits and starts, partly reflecting his limited financial situation and partly due to the difficulty that all novice rowers faced in trying to join a club. For serious oarsmen with unlimited resources, it was simply a matter of finding a place that had the best combination of equipment, coaching, and camaraderie. Many of the older boat clubs in the country had actually begun as social venues, where rowing was simply an auxiliary benefit. On the Schuylkill, Bachelor's Barge and Undine, two of the oldest organizations, both had upstream buildings as well, called "The Button" and the "Castle Ringstetten," or "The Ring." It was here that dinner parties and banquets where often held, away from the hustle and bustle of the city. Most of the serious rowing, however, took place downstream.

Kelly first joined Chamonix, not far from East Falls, and then quickly switched over to another called Montrose. To a young aspirant like Jack Kelly, joining a club was more a question of finding one that would take you in as a member, and both of these clubs were accessible to him, if not entirely desirable. To some extent, you got what you paid for, and the dues were not very high at either of these places. The coaching was commensurate with the participation fees. Once, while they were taking a Sunday stroll along the Schuylkill, Kelly's sister Ann and brother Charles spotted their younger brother making one of his first attempts to row in a four-oared shell. The unschooled oarsmen from Montrose were making a spectacle of themselves, lurching along, with their oars going in and out of the water at random intervals.

"My, sis, what a motley-looking crew!" Charles said, affecting a mock-British accent.

Within a year, however, Jack's finances had improved, and he migrated downstream to Vesper, where he would stay loyal for the next several years. The boat clubs themselves were often in a state of flux, depending on the financial state and general enthusiasm of their members. Most of the original clubs that had been established prior to the Civil War were little more than ramshackle wooden boatsheds, with names like Neptune and Nautilus, Camilla and Chebutco. Many of these had either changed hands over the years or been renamed and rebuilt out of sturdier materials. Vesper was one of the clubs founded after the Civil War in 1865, and it was part of the stalwart group of nine boathouses that became known as Boathouse Row, including Malta, Penn Athletic Club, Crescent, Vesper, University Barge, College, Fairmount, Bachelors' Barge, and Undine. Vesper had distinguished itself with its eight-oared crews, who won both the 1900 and 1904 Olympic Games. They were regarded as one of the strongest competitive clubs on the river.

The clubs also made up an alliance formally called the Schuylkill Navy, a group that touted itself as the first athletic governing body in the United States. It had been formed, in part, to repel a city plan to eliminate public use of the river after the creation and development of the city waterworks. Under this threat, the boathouses had banded together and stood firm against the proposal to knock them down and take over the land surrounding Fairmount Park. It was a real estate battle, but a political struggle as well. In the end, the boat clubs won and held onto their charter, although the city was able to exercise some degree of control in terms of the quality and construction of the buildings, many of which had fallen into various states of decrepitude.

Since the days of Thomas Eakins, many other important changes had taken place in the sport of rowing, both from a technological and a social standpoint. The two forces were not unrelated, for with the refinement of the equipment came a refinement in the rules of the game. In many ways, it could be argued that Jack Kelly came to the river at the right time and the right place, for he was the beneficiary of a few very important decades of development. While other American sports were just getting organized, and the rules of play were still a little primitive, rowing had already dealt with the problematic issues of cheating and commercialism that would beleaguer other sports throughout the nineteenth century and beyond.

The Schuylkill Navy, in fact, had also been formed to try to clean up the sport of rowing, which had fallen into disrepute at the turn of the twentieth century. Its rise and fall from popular grace was largely due to a sudden rise in professional gambling, which threatened to sully the clean image of the oarsman that Thomas Eakins had worked so hard to romanticize on canvas. Had her son been born two decades earlier, in fact, Mary Kelly might have had to consider how she felt about her son making money with a set of oars, instead of a pair of fists. In fact, he just missed the heyday of these professional oarsmen, the "prizefighters" of boating who vied for huge sums of money in staged races around the world.

Some of the more talented professionals were still rowing when Kelly took his first strokes on the Schuylkill, but they were a dying breed, both in the United States and abroad, discredited by crooked gambling practices. The most famous of these occurred at a highly touted matchup between Canadian Edward Hanlan and American champion Charles Courtney, sponsored by the Hops Bitters Company. It is difficult to imagine the enormous appeal that rowing and oarsmen had for the American public at the turn of the twentieth century. Thousands of spectators would often line the banks of the river or lake where the oarsmen were competing, which in this instance was Lake Chautauqua, New York. The two scullers had faced off previously with an inconclusive result. Courtney, a country boy from upstate New York, had learned to row on Cayuga Lake and had been undefeated in amateur competition. Going pro, he later admitted, was a big mistake, but the lure of big money and the encouragement of his supporters outweighed his better judgment. In addition to the winner's purse, there were often side benefits to be gained as a "professional" sculler. Sometimes complete strangers would hand him large amounts of cash after he had won, part of the proceeds from successfully betting on him. And of course it could work the other way around—sometimes the betting men wanted you to lose.

The first time Courtney raced professionally, in 1877 against James Riley, he was served some "bad tea" before his race, which immediately made him so sick that he could not compete. A year later, he rowed against Hanlan, a brilliant five-mile battle in Lachine, Canada, where the lead changed several times as the two scullers vied for position around the various turns in the river. At the finish line, both boats were hemmed in by spectator launches, and Hanlan proved better at maneuvering around them. He won by the small margin of one-and-a-half boat lengths, although some claimed that Courtney had been cheated, or that he had perhaps thrown the race.

The Hops Bitters contest was set up as a rematch, with a prize of $6,000 promised to the winner. Hanlan, who delighted the crowds with his colorful personality, arrived at the regatta with three boats and a small entourage in tow. He was a small but well-proportioned sculling marvel, a dandy complete with dark, wavy hair and a handlebar mustache. He had studied the mechanics of rowing extensively, and had acquired the technical ability and fitness level to quickly change his speed and stroke rating at will, in order to befuddle his opponents. By comparison, Courtney was more of a draft horse—bigger, stronger, and less socially agile. He brought only one boat to the event and kept to himself, despite numerous invitations to parlay with his competitor.

During their previous encounter, Courtney had nevertheless proven himself to be a formidable adversary, the first one capable of keeping pace with Hanlan. Some spectators still contended that Courtney had won the previous contest; accordingly, the winner's purse for the rematch was quite a handsome sum. It was enough, apparently, for someone to saw Courtney's boat in half the night before the race. When he discovered his boat in two pieces, the American sculler insisted on a delay while another shell could be made for him. The referee denied this request and instructed him to row in a borrowed boat. Courtney refused. Hanlan proceeded to row over the course alone, and then demanded the $6,000 prize. The "non-race" was hailed as a fiasco by the press and held up as the ultimate end result of professional gambling and commercialism.

Hops Bitters, a company whose reputation was already in question, ended up sponsoring a race as dubious as its mysterious tonic, a cure-all touted as "The Invalid's Friend and Hope." Even the opportunistic Hanlan was left empty-handed. The check he was handed promptly bounced when he tried to cash it.

There was only one cure, it seemed, for the sport of rowing, and that was to purge it of the professionals and the rampant commercialism that came with them. The question was, how?

~

The French word "amateur," originally derived from the Latin *amator* or lover, was generally defined as "one who engaged in an activity for pleasure, rather than financial benefit." It was a term that would help establish new standards for rowing and other sports as they moved into the twentieth century. Having witnessed the problems of "professional" regattas, where gambling concerns took control and nearly ruined the sport, the Schuylkill Navy, joined by other clubs around the country, decided to set down new rules of proper conduct. While these rules would differ slightly from club to club, they gave birth to the concept of the "amateur" athlete—one who did not accept money for rowing races or seek to earn a living from the sport. It was a dramatic move, a symbolic pruning of the very tree that had first brought American rowing into prominence. Ultimately, the amateur rules would reduce much of the sport's popular appeal, but they would also save it from self-destruction.

The first written definition of the amateur oarsman in the United States read like a legal document:

One who does not enter into an open competition; or for either stake, public or admission money or entrance fee; or compete with or against a professional for any prize; who has never taught, pursued, or assisted in the pursuit of athletic exercises as a means of livelihood; whose membership of any rowing or any other athletic club was not brought about, or does not continue, because of any mutual agreement or understanding, expressed or implied, whereby his becoming or continuing a member of such club would be of any pecuniary benefit to him whatever, direct or indirect; who has never been employed in any occupation involving any use of the oar or paddle; who rows for pleasure or recreation only, and during his leisure hours; who does not abandon or neglect his usual business or occupation for the purpose of training, and who shall otherwise conform to the rules and regulations of this association.

With the amateur rules firmly set in place, Jack Kelly's mother did not have to face the same concern that Charles Courtney's mother had—that her son would turn professional and essentially become a gambler. Of course, Jack wouldn't be able to get rich from rowing either, but that was all right by Ma Kelly. He had a job, laying brick, working with his hands—a much more honest way to make a living.

During his first year at the Vesper Boat Club, Kelly experienced immediate success as a member of a junior eight-oared crew that won the local Schuylkill Navy Regatta. The following year, however, Kelly tried his hand at sculling in a single. Team rowing and single

Jack Kelly Sr. sitting in his car outside of the Vesper Boat Club, circa 1917. © JOHN B. KELLY III

sculling, he would soon discover, presented different sets of challenges and rewards.

The benefit of team rowing, particularly in the popular eight-oared shells, could quickly show a novice like Kelly the proper way to execute a good, basic stroke. In an eight or a four, each rower was assigned to either the port or starboard side, and each held one oar, or "sweep," on that side. Unless you were assigned to the lead seat, or stroke position, your main task was simply to follow the oarsmen in front of you. Proper rhythm and timing were presented by visual example, and an ill-placed stroke had immediate, negative repercussions. One would not only stand out, like a member of a choir singing off-key, but the progress of the entire boat would be impeded. In this way, rowing in a team boat was similar to the technique used in bricklaying to erect a long wall of bricks. Jack's brother Charles, who served as a foreman, would place two skilled masons on either end so that everyone in between them would have to work just as hard and fast, or they would fall behind.

Sculling, where each oarsman held two shorter oars, or sculls, was technically more challenging than sweeps. Generally speaking, it required more finesse and fine motor control. While sculling could be configured for team boats as well, in quadruple and even octuple sculls, it was more common to see singles and doubles. The single sculler had the additional challenge of being a soloist, alone responsible for success or failure. When things went wrong, there was no one else to blame, and when you got tired, there was no one else to sustain you. For these reasons, fewer people chose to compete in the single scull, especially early in their rowing career.

Despite the challenges of the single and the obvious appeal of eights, however, it was the image of the lone sculler that had remained lodged in the back of Kelly's mind, and the more he rowed, the more he was drawn back toward this original boyhood dream. Single sculling, too, offered certain freedoms that team boats could not. When something went wrong in a crew, for example, everyone suffered, and this could become a constant source of irritation and speculation among the team members. If this uncertainty persisted, the quest to identify who wasn't pulling his weight, or who was throwing off the balance of the boat, could ruin a crew by turning it inward against itself.

Kelly quickly experienced this frustration himself during his first away race, a doubles' contest on the Harlem River in New

York. At the start of the race, he and his partner made a memorable debut, capsizing almost immediately. After their boat rolled, pitching them into the water, the two Vesper juniors proceeded to float a half mile downstream, carried along by a swift, spring current. Eventually, the river patrol rescued them, well after they'd had time to get thoroughly soaked and humiliated. Flipping a double scull was not easy, and it created a great deal of embarrassment and frustration. Kelly, of course, felt that his partner had been responsible, and on his return to Philadelphia, he lobbied hard to be allowed to compete in the next junior singles competition, to be held in New York that spring. The Harlem, after all, was the home of his sculling hero, Fred Sheppard, and Jack longed for the chance to impress his old rowing idol.

His next race, however, did not present that opportunity.

The junior sculls event on the Harlem River was a well-organized affair, and even provided stake boats at the starting line. These were moored dories, evenly spaced, which allowed the referee to bring the six competitors more easily into alignment. A volunteer, sitting inside each dory, helped guide the oarsmen backward into the floating starting blocks, and then reached out to hold onto the stern of each racing shell. In this way, the competitors were all brought into line, without the constant jockeying for position, forward or back. Held firmly at the stake boats, they merely needed to adjust to port or starboard to ensure that they were pointed straight ahead. Then, when everyone was set to go, the starter would call out the race commands, the gun was fired, and the boats released.

Normally this system worked splendidly, but when Kelly decided to jump the gun, things quickly went awry. It could have been that the Vesper sculler wasn't used to stake boats and had only competed in "floating start" races where the boats were lined up unfettered. It could have been that Kelly fully intended to leave the line early, and simply did not count on the tenacious grip of his volunteer attendant. In any case, when he prematurely began pulling on his oars, the unfortunate boy holding his scull was dragged right out of his dory and into the Harlem River. With this human anchor attached to his stern, Kelly performed a complete backward somersault, landing neatly in the familiar waters himself.

For everyone who witnessed it, the acrobatic double dunking was a rare moment of unchoreographed comedy. For Kelly, however, it was another embarrassing disaster on the Harlem.

"Haven't you ever raced before?" the starter asked him, begrudgingly helping Jack back into his boat.

"Yes," Kelly admitted, "I'm the one who upset in a double the last time I raced here!"

Fueled by his embarrassment, the Vesper sculler somehow managed to get back into the race and placed third in a field of six. It was a remarkable comeback, when you considered that it took at least a minute to reenter a rolled boat. But that, of course, was not what everyone remembered, and when Kelly returned to Philadelphia, he found his locker at Vesper plastered with photos of diving and swimming champions.

His single sculling career was certainly not off to an auspicious start, unless you factored in the entertainment value of his various races. While Kelly may have possessed the ambition and fitness to be a rowing soloist, he lacked the boat skills that would allow him to demonstrate the power and mental toughness he had developed in other sports. Capsizing and "crabbing" (where a misplaced oar went deep and got pinned below the surface of the water) were all too frequent occurrences during his first several regattas.

During his next race, held in Washington DC, Kelly got himself so wound up at the starting line that he proceeded to catch three starboard crabs in succession, and then found his boat sitting broadside to the rest of the field.

"Go get 'em anyhow, kid!" starter Joe Nagle urged him.

Kelly managed to straighten out his course and began a desperate charge back into the field. It was an impossible task for the average oarsman. But after what seemed like an eternity, he actually began to pass a few boats. This gave him some encouragement, and he decided to make a game out of the race, pretending he was back on his bicycle, passing Ford Model As along the Schuylkill on the way to the boathouse. As he caught each successive boat, he grew more and more excited by the possibility of victory. The extreme effort, however, was beginning to take its toll. Kelly was now well beyond a state of fatigue; he was growing dizzy from lack of oxygen. His legs were beginning to ache as well, and he felt sick to his stomach.

Still, he kept passing boats. There were several entrants in the race, but he couldn't remember how many boats he had already passed. Finally, nearing the finish line, he came within sight of one last sculler. His eyes were going glassy, dancing around in his head, but Kelly sensed that there was no one else to beat. He made his final surge, trying to pass the leader, and came up short by a mere half boat length.

It was another remarkable, come-from-behind effort, and Kelly was exhausted to the point of passing out. To ensure that he did not capsize again, he locked his oars into his lap for a few minutes while he caught his breath. Without the clumsy start, he knew that he could have easily won the race. But second-guessing like this was not a worthwhile enterprise. He started back for the dock, paddling along slowly, still trying to recuperate and put his efforts into perspective. Suddenly, a powerboat full of festive spectators pulled up alongside him. Among the group was Lady Nagle, the well-loved mascot of the Harlem Club.

"Well, you big rummy," she shouted out through a megaphone. "What delayed you? I lost $5 on you!" Kelly smiled despite himself.

Chapter Five

IN ORDER TO TRULY APPRECIATE JACK KELLY'S STRUGGLES IN A single, it helped to know a little bit about both sculling and the evolution of rowing in general. Even to a casual observer, the modern competitive practice of the sport was clearly very different from the utilitarian boating from which it had sprung. Rowboats had become racing shells in a fairly short period, and with the change in technology came an accompanying challenge of learning technique. A person could not simply jump into a single scull and master it without a lengthy course of study. This could take weeks, months, or even years, and the debate about proper form was endless. In short, what had once been a matter of brute force, performed by lumbering ferrymen, now came to be seen as an art form, a science, and for some, even a religion.

The challenge, of course, was part of the appeal. When young Jack Kelly had first witnessed the scullers out on the Schuylkill, what caught his eye were not a bunch of clunky rowboats, but slivers of wood, ten inches wide and twenty-seven feet long, weighing between twenty and forty pounds. With only a few inches of freeboard separating them from the water, these masters of the river must have appeared to Kelly as if they were flying on magic carpets. Their lightweight, narrow craft, however, represented a few critical decades of development, and they required several seasons of

Jack Kelly Sr. rowing on the Schuylkill, wearing the green cap that would become his trademark, circa 1917. © JOHN B. KELLY III

dedicated practice before they revealed their secrets to an apprentice waterman.

Rowing had begun in the United States as it had in most countries, as a means to transport people and cargo. The first boats were dories, gigs, and scows, and they helped move goods across rivers, lakes, and harbors. Most of these watercraft were propelled by four- or six-man crews staggered on long, fixed seats. The hulls were of lapstrake construction, where planks of oak were laid parallel to the boat's keel, overlapped slightly with one another for strength.

Perhaps the best American examples of these oversize, round-bottomed rowboats were called the Whitehalls, named after the Whitehall landing at the Battery in New York Harbor. In fact, some of the first boat races in the United States took place in New York City between these four-oared ferryboats. What must have first been casual duels between boats eventually blossomed into more formal competitions, beginning in the early 1800s. By mid-century, American colleges had also become interested in boat racing, and began to purchase boats for both recreational and racing purposes. The first intercollegiate athletic competition in the United States, held in 1852, took place between the Harvard and Yale crews, who met on Lake Winnipesaukee in New Hampshire "to test the superiority of the oarsmen of the two colleges." Harvard won.

At least a century before boat racing got its start in America, England had been cultivating a similar passion for the sport. The watermen of London, like the gondoliers of Venice, were among the first to gain recognition for their rowing skills, ferrying passengers up and down the Thames. In 1715 an Irish-born actor named Thomas Doggett helped bring attention to the watertaxi men by endowing a local race for apprentices called Doggett's Coat and Badge. The winner of this five-mile competition, from London Bridge to Chelsea, received a cash prize and a long overcoat, in addition to an impressive medallion that said "Liberty." In the century that followed, Oxford and Cambridge Universities, as well as boys' schools like Eton, also took up team rowing, and it was in England that the first major physical changes to the sport occurred.

As boat racing became more popular as a spectator sport, it was natural that attempts would be made to increase the speed of the rowing shells. The first big development was the addition of the iron outrigger, a metal armature that allowed the oarlock pin, or pivot point of the oar, to be extended away from the hull. Prior to riggers, the oarlocks, or thole pins, were simply attached to the gunnels of wide boats, limiting the length of the oars and the beam of the boats themselves. With outriggers, first successfully designed by Harry Clasper in England, the width of hulls could be dramatically reduced, from four feet to only two feet in the case of team boats, and even less in the case of single sculls.

Next, attention fell to reducing the overall weight of the boats and the friction from water along the outer surface of the hull. Both problems were solved by creating shells with light, smooth outer skins, doing away with the heavy lapstrake planking that had served workboats so well. Cedar and mahogany, both resistant to rot and bendable in narrow thicknesses, were perfectly suited to this purpose. The new shells were considerably lighter. By comparison, a lapstrake eight-oared shell used by Oxford for its first race against Cambridge in 1829 weighed in at 600 pounds, while their 1857 boat—with riggers and smooth skin—weighed less than half that much.

The narrower boats were longer, of course, in order to bear the weight of the oarsmen, but they were also extremely sleek and streamlined. On the bottom of the hull there was less wetted surface area, or water friction, that might slow the boat down. On the topsides the gunnels were now swept extremely low, allowing the boats to slice better through any wind. The narrowing of the boats also brought the oarsmen on alternate sides both directly over the keel and in perfect alignment with each other. This eliminated the extra room beside them, which had once allowed for cargo or a passenger. "Barge clubs" soon became boat clubs, and trips along the river were less and less for sightseeing than for fitness and for honing rowing skill—for it took far more concentration and control to maintain one's balance in these narrow racing craft.

Last but not least came the evolution of the sliding seat and the swivel oarlock, both of which came into vogue in the 1870s. The basic idea of the former had existed for quite a while, beginning with oarsmen who greased their leather-seated pants. A moveable seat had the benefit of allowing an oarsman's legs to be employed, and it also extended the overall length of the stroke. Both of these advantages led to increased speed, but there were also some negatives. Creating a seat with wheels that did not jam or fall apart took time to perfect. One of the first working prototypes was built by American oarsman Thomas Farron in 1877, but it was an unruly device and unsuitable for novices. The swivel oarlock, which developed as a natural accompaniment to the moving seat, allowed the longer arching oar to have a greater range and was credited to American Michael Davis.

More than any other innovation, the sliding seat radically changed the way oarsmen rowed and the amount of power they could produce. It also led to numerous debates about "appropriate" rowing technique, most of which focused on the question of when the legs should be used in relation to the back and arms. Trial and error, combined with a study of physics, led to various successful rowing styles. But some countries, like England, were slower to change their ways. Beyond the issue of mechanical merit lay the question of how these new technologies would affect tradition, aesthetics, and sportsmanship. After all, Edward Hanlan had been the first to master the use of the sliding seat, and while the diminutive Canadian demonstrated the benefit of this advance, proving that size was less important than skill, he was not the poster boy for fair play.

All of these technological changes served to transform rowing from a slow-moving recreational activity to a fast-paced sport with real crowd appeal. Six-oared shells and then eights came into vogue as the ultimate team challenge, pioneered by Oxford and Cambridge in the early 1800s, and soon afterward imitated by Harvard and Yale. In England, these bigger boats carried with them a symbolic past, harkening back to the days when the kings and queens of England were borne up and down the Thames in a royal barge. With the demise of the professional scullers at the turn of the twentieth century, team rowing now reigned in the public eye, particularly at colleges and amateur clubs.

Yet the single scull, to which Jack Kelly gravitated, had not lost all of its popularity. True, it was less visually dramatic than the bigger boats, but it did present a boat race as a mano a mano competition, much like a boxing match. The professional scullers of the late nineteenth and early twentieth centuries had helped create this appeal, and despite their moral and financial misdoings, they had secured a permanent spot for the one-man boat in the public eye. Some of the old sculling pros, in fact, now found their way into coaching positions at American universities and colleges. Charles Courtney, the famous sculler who had been defeated by Edward Hanlan, took the helm at Cornell and proved to be an even better coach than he had been a professional oarsman. Hanlan, erratic and whimsical, was considerably less successful at Columbia.

Jack Kelly had not forgotten the image of Fred Sheppard, the hero of his boyhood excursions along the Schuylkill, and during his next trip to the Harlem River, he was surprised to find himself entered in a race alongside his former rowing idol. Sheppard was a middle-aged man now, but he still rowed and occasionally raced for pleasure. Kelly was thrilled to see him again, but also mortified to discover that he was slated to compete against him. It seemed all wrong and he approached Sheppard to tell him so.

"Sir, I feel guilty about racing against you this afternoon. Why, in your prime, I wouldn't belong on the same river as you. If I'm in first and you're second coming down the stretch, I'm going to ease up and let you pass me," he said.

The veteran sculler smiled at Kelly and then shook his head.

"Son, I'm old and you're young. I can't keep up with you young fellows anymore. You go out and win it—if you can!"

Sheppard then suggested that Kelly get off the starting line as fast as possible and hold onto the lead. There was both a challenge and a blessing in the old man's voice and Kelly now realized what he had to do. If he was to become a champion himself, he needed to put his reservations aside and defeat his old idol. Unbeknownst to Sheppard, however, Jack had been sick for several days prior to the competition, and he had not been able to hold down any food. That very morning he'd decided to drink a concoction of raw egg in a glass of sherry, some advice from an old British training manual. Needless to say, the cocktail didn't help. Although Kelly got off the starting line quickly, grabbing the lead as he was told, the rest of the race became a long, painful odyssey. Toward the end, he rowed in a blurred state of consciousness, barely aware of the other boats. But as Jack crossed the finish line and received a loud cheer, he knew that he had finally succeeded in winning. Sheppard congratulated him on the water, shaking his hand. He had shown the younger oarsman what competitors were really meant to do: to push each other forward, not hold one another back. It was a lesson that Kelly would never forget.

—⁓—

Despite the fact that amateur boat races now lacked monetary prizes for the victors, they still drew a large following of devoted fans, particularly among the college-educated. Within the confines of universities and fraternal organizations, rowing offered an ideal means to teach the importance of athleticism, brotherhood, and dedication to a common discipline. In the British public school system of the mid-1800s, rowing, along with rugby and several other "manly" sports, became associated with a Protestant movement known as "muscular Christianity," which sought to revitalize the ranks of young male churchgoers. The movement spread to America after the Civil War and gave rise to organizations like the YMCA. Of course, winning was still important, and side betting continued to be a popular pastime among the spectators on both continents. This informal exchange of money, naturally, had no bearing on the athletes themselves. What they reaped from rowing were its more "internal" benefits—such as physical well-being, mental discipline, and moral fortitude, not to mention fame and glory.

Jack Kelly was no college boy, having barely completed the eighth grade, yet he seemed to grasp the intrinsic rewards of rowing intuitively. It was part of the invisible currency that seemed to pass between serious oarsmen, along with the intense silence in which the sport was conducted. Thomas Eakins had once captured this quality of mind on canvas—the way that an oarsman's eyes were focused forward in order to follow the exact movements of the others in front of him; how he learned to listen for the single

drop of the oars to the water and feel the exhilarating surge of uni-
fied power that came as a reward. Even single scullers, who had no
one to lead them and no one to follow, often became so engrossed
in the constant challenge and thrill of the rowing motion that they
sometimes completely forgot where they were and ran into shore
or even hit bridges.

Bolstered by his success on the Harlem, Jack returned to the
Schuylkill and began to accumulate an impressive string of victories and a local reputation as one of the best oarsmen along Boathouse Row. In 1912 at age twenty-two, he was elected captain of
Vesper, replacing an older man named Frank Muller. He trained
every day after work, and even on Sundays, after attending early
Mass at St. Bridget's. When darkness fell, he found his way back
to the Falls and sat down alone to the plate of dinner that his
mother had left out for him. One night, however, Mary Kelly sat
down with her youngest son and began to express her growing
concerns about his training schedule. What was so special about
rowing, she prodded him, that he had become so obsessive? Why
was it so different from any other sport? And why did he have to
push himself so, day after day, week after week? Other East Falls
boys were already starting their careers or getting married, but he
seemed to be unconcerned about anything but being a fine oarsman. After her youngest son mumbled a few platitudes about how
rowing was a real "he-man" sport that took "guts and determination," Jack finally put down his fork. Briefly forsaking his meal, he
launched into a long, passionate explanation:

"In rowing, you can let up, slacken off, or fall back, at any time.
The decision is entirely yours. No one forces you, the way a fist-
fighter must defend himself, or a halfback must keep going with

a football tucked under his arm, or a hockey player must dodge to keep the puck and shoot. It's your own decision. You have to beat back the lash and hurt yourself with the sculls. The water rushes by, the slide hurts your backside, your hands burn from the oars, your back aches, exhaustion blinds you, your arms and legs are like heavy weights—but there's no encouraging voice beside you, no helping hand. You've got to rely on muscle and heart, on spirit and soul, on will and determination, such as no other sport demands."

Jack looked up at his mother, and there was a moment of silence as he picked up his eating utensils.

"So I guess you can see why I want to be a champion," he added.

His mother's eyes had begun to widen during the long speech, and now they began to twinkle. She was aware now that Jack needed to succeed at this odd preoccupation before he could do anything else in his life.

"Off to bed with you," she told him. "You have a race tomorrow."

Beyond all the high-minded sentiments that Jack Kelly expressed to his mother, there was another, more practical reason why he now felt obliged to excel at rowing. His boyhood friends and acquaintances from East Falls were well aware of his growing athletic prowess, and as keen sportsmen, they took an interest in his career. They began to show up at his local races, not only to root him on but also to place bets on him. Many of the wagers were small initially, but the more Jack won, the larger they became, and the greater the number of fans Kelly attracted. The more dedicated among the East Falls contingent often made a party out of the Schuylkill Navy regattas, piling into rowboats large enough to hold kegs of beer and concertina bands. Eventually, the situation grew out of control.

On one memorable occasion in particular, his Irish fans decided to disembark on Peter's Island in the middle of the Schuylkill, piloting a boat named the *Mayflower II*. The long strip of land, located near the finish line, would provide them a better view of their local hero, who could otherwise only be identified from a distance by the green cap he had begun to wear. Gradually emboldened by their keg of beer, the spirited group began to sing any song with a "Kelly" theme, and when Jack himself rowed by, they let him know, in no uncertain terms, that he needed to win his races that day. Otherwise many of them would be out an entire paycheck. After a few of the East Falls revelers managed to fall into the river, however, a Fairmount park guard arrived and escorted the group of pilgrims back to dry land. They would have to watch the races from shore like everyone else. Fortunately, Kelly was victorious that day.

Jack's usual post-race haunt was the Gunboat, an East Falls diner located at the corner of Midvale and Ridge Avenues. An oddly shaped building with nautical lines, the Gunboat was run by the gregarious Irishman Ed Byrne, and it boasted a clientele of golfers, boxers, and football players, many of whom played professionally or in semi-pro leagues. Occasionally, a local celebrity would even stop by to discuss the sporting news of the day. Kelly himself still played a little football and basketball, in addition to boxing and rowing, and he was fast becoming the talk of the diner, the next local boy to make good as a sports celebrity. The Gunboat boys were also his "spin doctors," not only setting the odds on him when he competed but also justifying his occasional letdowns.

Not everyone in East Falls, however, was a devoted Kelly fan. One weekend, after his daily row, Jack got himself involved in an impromptu argument with a Gunboat regular named Pat McCarthy. McCarthy was an ex-professional fighter who had a penchant for bullying some of the men at the diner. He was not someone to disturb. As Jack sat alone, drinking his daily quart of milk, he couldn't help but listen as McCarthy began one of his typical harangues. Kelly noticed that he always seemed to direct his attacks at less powerful prey, easy targets who would never dare stand up to him.

"You sure know how to pick your opponents, don't you, Pat?" Kelly suddenly shouted out across the diner.

"Suppose I pick on you, Kelly?" McCarthy retorted.

"Fine," Jack replied. He stood up.

The din of voices at the local eatery suddenly fell silent. McCarthy slowly stood up, too, and pushed aside his chair, all the while glowering at Kelly. The small crowd of regulars, sensing a fight, began to prick up their ears. Before things could get started, however, owner Ed Byrne quickly told Jack and Pat that if they were going to fight, they'd have to find another place to do it, for he didn't want his restaurant ruined. Paddy Neilan, one of the regular customers, suggested Dobson's lot just up the street. Since it was the weekend, everyone knew that the lot would be empty and unpoliced, and it was a fitting arena for the impromptu match, a place where Irish sweat and blood had already been spilled.

The small crowd of men from the Gunboat grew as they marched up the block and word of the fight spread throughout the neighborhood. Soon a hundred or so locals were assembled in a makeshift boxing ring. Bets were quickly placed on either side, as Kelly and McCarthy readied themselves, removing their shirts in the summer heat. It was a fight that had been brewing for some time, and it would establish, once and for all, who was king of East Falls. McCarthy was the cocky, ex-pro fighter, but Kelly was the up-and-comer, an all-around athlete. Since they had left the diner, neither man had spoken, but the crowd could sense the growing hostility between the two, building up for the volley of fists.

Without much ado, Kelly charged the more experienced boxer and was met with a crushing blow to his nose. Instantly, it began to bleed. It was a punch that would have stopped many other men, but McCarthy was surprised to find that Kelly seemed unfazed. Those who had done battle with Jack before knew that he possessed an extraordinary ability to withstand pain, never showing an opponent any sign of weakness. He also had relentless stamina from his rowing, and in a fight like this, staying power and resilience paid off. As the long minutes wore on, Kelly's short, explosive body shots to McCarthy's ribs and stomach began to render the older man glassy-eyed and wobbly. Kelly's final combination was a right jab to the heart, a left uppercut to McCarthy's stomach, and a right cross to his head. As McCarthy dropped silently onto the pavement in a lifeless sprawl, the bystanders groaned in communion with the fallen man. It had been a long and difficult fight to watch, lasting over twenty minutes. Both men were now covered in blood. But after several seconds had passed and McCarthy hadn't moved from the ground, a sense of dread began to creep over the small crowd.

"You kilt him, Kelly!" one of the men shouted.

Jack quickly knelt down beside McCarthy and tried to find a pulse. It was very weak and he and a few of the other men began to work on McCarthy, giving him water and massage. Finally, after what seemed an eternity, McCarthy came to and began to look around him.

"You had enough, Kelly?" he asked faintly.

"Yeah," Jack replied, smiling with relief. "Let's call it a draw."

———

When Jack finally arrived back home, bloody and bruised, the first question out of his mother's mouth was not "Are you all right?" but "Who did you pick a fight with now?" When Jack explained that it was Pat McCarthy, the well-known bully, Mary Kelly just nodded, giving her silent consent. Jack knew if he had picked on someone smaller or less worthy, he would have received another blow to the head that day—his mother's southpaw hook, against which there was no defense.

Chapter Six

JACK'S OLDER BROTHER WALTER, WHO HAD MOST FREQUENTLY FELT the sting of his mother's wedding band, had long since left home to seek his fortune. His late-night carousing and lack of steady income had eventually made him less loveable and more of a liability to his parents, and he had drifted south, to the shipyards of Newport News, Virginia. During the Spanish-American War, he served as a machinist's mate on a steamship that transported troops to Mexico, and he also ran a small cantina onboard. It was a successful enough enterprise that after the war, Walter opened another eatery on dry land called the Mecca Café. He was a soft touch to those in need, but the restaurant did exceptionally well for a while, until Walter went bankrupt betting the entire business on a whimsical but spirited run for Congress. He delivered the same impressive speeches to the people of Virginia as he had once done on the corners of East Falls, but in the end he lost the election by one vote.

While he was out of work figuring out his next career move, Walter decided to pay a visit to an old fishing buddy named John Jeter Crutchfield. "Judge" Crutchfield presided over the petty cases at a local police court, without the hindrance of attorneys or a jury. A tall man with a serious demeanor, he doled out quick sentences as he saw fit, often adding a ration of light sarcasm to

Walter Kelly and Jack Kelly Sr. standing together at the beach in Ocean City, New Jersey. Aside from George, Walter may have been the least athletic of the Kelly brothers, but he was an active sports fan nonetheless and touted his younger brother's success at every opportunity.

the proceedings. Most of the petitioners in the courtroom were barely literate, let alone capable of defending themselves, and one by one they approached the bench, only to find themselves at the mercy of a judge with an unflagging wit. As someone who shared an appreciation for humor, Walter soon found himself entertained for hours. He looked around him and noticed that he wasn't the only one watching the show. Apparently "Justice John's Court" was a well-known stopover for those passing through the Norfolk area with nothing better to do. Crutchfield himself loved playing to the crowds. What Walter found in his friend's courtroom, however, was not only an entertaining way to spend an afternoon but also the inspiration for his next career. He was not serious about becoming a judge himself, but he wondered if the courtroom could be brought to a bigger stage.

After several more visits to the courtroom, Walter began to formulate the idea for an act called "The Virginia Judge," based on the scenes and dialogue he witnessed. He scribbled down notes and began to rehearse, acting out the part of both judge and defendant. When he finally thought he had it right, he packed his bags and headed north. He changed his friend's name to Judge John Dudley Brown, but otherwise his jokes and wry charac-ter were barely altered. After a few impromptu performances in saloons and at political rallies in New York, Walter was noticed by an agent and invited to audition at a popular theater called The Green Room.

Vaudeville, like American sports, was another class leveler, a pastime that could be enjoyed by both rich and poor, sitting together in the same theater. "The Virginia Judge" became a series of short skits acted out in monologue, where various poor, uneducated

Southerners were brought to trial and quickly sentenced by a sarcastic judge. Walter acted out all the parts, portraying the dimwitted men and women who were accused of petty crimes and the quick-witted judge who dispensed justice. He was simply reproducing a slice of American life, but Southerners, particularly poor blacks, took it on the chin, all for the benefit of a good laugh. Ironically, only a few decades earlier, the Irish had experienced this same characterization on the stage—as poor, uneducated bumpkins with a vague concept of morality.

Walter's fame as "The Virginia Judge" quickly rose to international proportions, reaching a high point when he was invited to perform at London's Palace Theatre in 1908. Before he left for England, however, he decided to return to East Falls to show off his newfound fame and to try to reconnect with his all-but-forgotten family. He had left the Kelly clan under heavy scrutiny and only kept in touch with P. H. when he occasionally needed money. But now he was a phenomenal success on the stage, and his hope was to be welcomed back to Midvale Avenue as the prodigal son who had at least achieved financial success, if not a more upstanding lifestyle.

When Mary and John Kelly saw their son for the first time in five years, however, they were more than a little taken aback. Walter was dressed in a fancy suit, complete with straw boater, cane, and cigar. His mother smiled quietly while his father simply frowned. "What do you think of your son now?" Walter bellowed, unfazed by the cold reception. No one said a word as he entered the house except Grandfather Costello, who gawked at his grandson's gaudy attire and blurted out:

"Holy Killarney! Stay inside, lad—don't let the priest see ya!"

When the Kellys finally got used to Walter's new clothes and his confident bearing, they all sat down to a special steak dinner and listened as he told the tale of how he had risen in the theater world. Jack, George, Grace, and Elizabeth all beamed at their older brother as he described the auspicious night when the headliner at The Green Room in New York, Marie Dressler, had taken ill and Walter was asked to entertain the crowd. It was then that he had first unveiled "The Virginia Judge" to try to appease the disappointed crowd:

"Order in the court!" he had shouted at the audience, immediately catching their attention. "Dan, get those dogs away from the stove. It smells like a tan yard in here! First case on the docket—Sadie Anderson."

"Yes, sir, that's me."

"Thirty days, that's me."

"Next case—Rufus Johnson. Rufus, you're charged with larceny of two chickens from the premises of Howard Brooks on Briarfield Road. What have you to say for yourself?"

"Wal, Jedge, I never was near Mr. Brooks's house and the Lord may strike me dead if I stole those chickens."

"Rufus, you stand aside for ten minutes, and if the Lord don't strike you, I will give you thirty days."

It was a far cry from Shakespeare, but the Kellys laughed uncontrollably—particularly Ann, Grace, and Jack—until at last their digestion and better judgment were compromised by the charismatic clown. Walter pressed on with his act for most of the evening, until he was certain that he had won over his entire family. He knew he was playing to his toughest audience. Beyond mere acceptance, Walter was hoping that his humor would serve to exonerate some of his past behavior. In the end, even Ma Kelly caved in and proclaimed loudly that another one of her boys had achieved great success, albeit in a rather unorthodox fashion. Only Grandfather Costello, who had lived through the Irish potato famine of 1845–49, still had trouble coming to terms with Walter's occupation, not to mention the rich food at the dinner table. When a thick steak was placed in front of him, the old man looked down at it mystified, until someone finally asked him what was wrong.

"The world's upside down!" he said. "For years I had good teeth and nothing to eat in Ireland. Now here I am with a steak big enough to wrap a child in, and not a doggone tooth left!"

And in between Walter's jokes, Costello kept turning to his grandson and asking him where his tools were.

"Tools?" Walter finally asked him, somewhat annoyed.

"I mean, what other work do you do beside all that gab to be gettin' all that money?"

Walter informed him that he didn't need to do anything else to earn a living, and that he was currently making $400 a week.

"Begorra!" his grandfather exclaimed. "The people can't all be crazy, lad, so get it while the gettin's good!"

Walter told the old man that he would not be staying in East Falls very long, for he was on his way to England to perform at the Palace Theatre. When he heard this bit of news, however, Costello reacted even more strongly and pleaded with his grandson not to go. In his youth, he explained, he had spent many years as a nationalist rebel, fighting against the English landlords in Ireland. By the mid-nineteenth century, the English had taken over much of the Catholic-held land in the country and subdivided the rest into small, untenable plots. This set the stage for the devastating potato famine. In the end, at least a half million Irish souls were lost and thousands more fled to other countries, like Costello. It was a four-year period not easily forgotten and it set a hostile tone for all future relations between England and Ireland. As one of those fortunate enough to survive the tragedy, Costello now testified to the cruelty of the English and admitted that his hatred and distrust of them ran deep. He didn't mention to Walter what he had done in retaliation, but it was enough for him to feel compelled to warn his grandson.

"The mere mention of the name Kelly will destroy any chance of success," he said adamantly. It would immediately label him as an Irishman.

Despite his grandfather's words of caution, Walter decided to press on following his theatrical destiny. A few weeks after reuniting with the Kelly clan, he was boarding the *Lusitania* in New York, bound for Liverpool.

<hr />

Walter's show at the Palace Theatre happened to coincide with the 1908 Olympic Games, which were being held in London that summer. A keen sports fan, he was sitting in the stands a few days after his performance, waiting for the marathoners to arrive. The 26-mile race had been lengthened 285 yards by the British hosts that year because this extra bit allowed the runners to arrive at the Royal Box from their starting point at Windsor Castle. No one questioned the change, for the Brits had developed many of the rules for amateur sports during the nineteenth century, and they were regarded as the undisputed legislators of proper athletic conduct and procedure.

Walter was in a good mood, for his "Virginia Judge" routine had gone over well with the overseas audiences, despite a last-minute panic that they would not understand American slang. A few days prior to his engagement, he had watched a few other London humorists perform on stage and grown concerned that his script needed to be revised to better suit the English tastes. A few minutes into his monologue, however, Walter finally relaxed and fell back into his normal routine. An audience was an audience, and the British crowd loved him just as he was. The following day in the papers, the theater critics raved and his contract at the Palace Theatre was immediately extended for an additional four weeks. Even King Edward VII requested a private performance from the American humorist. All of Walter's pre-show anxiety had been largely unfounded and his grandfather had been completely mistaken about the British sentiment toward the Irish.

Yet only a few days later, as an anonymous American sitting in the Olympic stands, he witnessed the animosity that he had initially been prepared for onstage. The Olympic events in London had gotten off to a bad start between England and the United States, as well as Sweden and Finland. At the opening ceremonies, the British hosts had forgotten to provide flags for these countries. This was taken as a slight rather than an oversight, and when the athletes from each country paraded around the track, the American flag bearer, a gargantuan shot putter named Ralph Rose, refused to lower the Stars and Stripes as he passed by the Royal Box. A hush came over the London-based crowd, which had been applauding at regular intervals, and then silence gave way to booing and cursing. Later, Rose was quoted as stating, "This flag dips to no earthly king," and from that day forward, it never would.

The Anglo-American tension only grew stronger over the next few days, as the Olympic events yielded surprisingly few victories for the British and many for the US athletes. In one running event, the Americans who placed first and second were accused of fouling the British runner and were asked to re-run the race. They refused and were denied their medals. And when an American distance runner named Johnny Hayes unexpectedly won the marathon, matters only grew worse. The Brits began to boo him loudly at the stadium, and when Walter stood up to cheer on his countryman, he was immediately assailed.

"Sit down, you bloody Yank!"

"Sit down yourself," he shouted back. "Where are your Englishmen? They ought to be up in front. Didn't George Washington teach you Brits how to run?"

The incident was all it took for Walter to get warmed up. Later on, while celebrating the US victories at the American Bar at the Cecil Hotel, he casually joked to his two companions that the only events the Brits could win were archery and knitting. A contingent of English fans, seated nearby, was not amused. Suddenly a huge brawl erupted. Unlike his brother Jack, Walter was neither much of a fighter nor an athlete of any sort. He did, however, manage to travel in the right company, for his escorts that evening were none other than two US Olympic boxers, Jimmy Britt and Kid McCoy, along with the shot putter Ralph Rose. The three of them easily protected their sharp-tongued comrade, leaving a trail of surprised opponents in their wake.

When the police finally arrived and began to escort the men to jail, Walter unleashed his verbal skills, talking his way out of a night spent behind bars. Within the hour, the Americans were back at another English pub, arguing with the locals until a second fight broke out. In this manner, the quartet spent their entire evening, getting into a string of brawls, nearly landing in jail, and then letting Walter talk his way out of trouble. It was an odd sort of sporting event that only the Irish could have invented, which involved both quickness of fist and quickness of tongue.

Chapter Seven

THE OLYMPIC ROWING EVENTS THAT YEAR WERE HELD THIRTY miles outside London in the sleepy little village of Henley-on-Thames. In a show of dominance, the British crews swept all of the races, including the eight, the four, the pair, and the single. Henley was also the location of the annual Henley Royal Regatta, the oldest formal rowing competition in the world, founded in 1839, and an event that easily eclipsed the Olympics with its overall prestige and pageantry. Henley and the River Thames were as important to the development of British rowing as the Schuylkill River and Philadelphia were to the American evolution of the sport. And yet the two waterways and the cities that surrounded them were vastly different in very important ways, particularly in regard to their social milieu.

Walter did not witness any rowing races, but if he had, he might have warned his little brother not to cross the Atlantic to try to match oars with the Brits. If they were not amenable to an American runner, they would most certainly not welcome an Irish-American oarsman—particularly one who laid bricks for a living. The reasons were manifold, involving issues of nationalism and class, as well as differences in the development of amateur rules.

Unlike the US regulations, the British amateur rowing rules were less concerned about removing money from the sport than removing class—the working class. Unsurprisingly, the men who authored the first drafts of these exclusionary provisions were well-educated "gentlemen" who wanted to preserve rowing for their own kind. These were doctors, lawyers, clergymen, university dons, and the editors of publications like *The Field* and *Bell's Life*. An amateur, they made clear, could not be someone who either made his living by working around boats or made a living with his hands.

Curiously enough, the amateur rules in England may have been prompted in part by one of the first appearances of American competitors at the Henley Royal Regatta in 1878. The Anglo-American rowing rivalry had been initiated a decade earlier in 1869, when Oxford and Harvard met for the first time in four-oared shells. When Oxford triumphed, the *Times* in London wrote an article betraying both the British dislike of American athletes who trained to win at all costs, with no sense of developing themselves as "socially responsible" beings, but also a long-standing grudge born of having lost the Revolutionary War:

> *The victory was a victory of education and the advantage was all on our side. We live—not in rowing alone—a closer life. The competition is sharper. The lessons of the past are more searching and more exact.*

The *Times* reporter continued:

> *It is terrible to think how many millions of patriots would have gone to bed with aching hearts…to renew in painful dreams the bitter memories of national disgrace, if Harvard had beaten Oxford. The surrender of BURGOYNE or CORNWALLIS, the reluctant recognition of the United States, becomes a trifle in comparison to what our defeat would have been.*

Still, among the general public on both sides of the Atlantic, the event was hailed as a great commercial success, win or lose, for it immediately generated more interest in rowing, particularly in America. A slew of colleges added crew teams to their ranks and it was not long afterward that the first American boats began to show up at Henley for the July 4 weekend regatta. But added to the intense nationalism in British sport was the studied class snobbery that did not bode well for foreigners who came to try their luck against British crews, particularly Americans. If they won, they were often derided as lacking the qualities of a "true amateur" in the British sense of the term—i.e., those of a gentleman—and were generally not invited back. If they lost, it was a victory not only for British rowing superiority but also a superiority of morals and values.

In contrast to many of their foreign opponents, the English were trying to cultivate rowing as more than just a competitive outlet. It was, in a sense, an art form, appreciated by those who understood the value of the rules, the particulars of the venue, and even the style of the movement—all of which contributed to a pleasing aesthetic and an educational experience. In the British orthodox style of rowing, equal emphasis was placed on how a crew rowed (i.e., their form) as on how well they placed among the field. Entire books were written on the subject, with some authors even going so far as to suggest that there was a "musical" influence in rowing that should also be considered.

On the other extreme was the crew that tried to win at all costs, relying on brute force and willpower. This was essentially what American rowing represented to most Englishmen, an unschooled effort of force. Nine years after the Oxford-Harvard affair, the first American crews made their appearance at the Henley Royal Regatta. Columbia College from New York brought a four, along with a group of French-Canadian oarsmen from Monroe, Michigan, known as the Shoe-wae-cae-mettes. Although the Columbia oarsmen acquitted themselves well and won the Visitors' Cup event, "the Shoes" raised many an eyebrow with their odd antics, both on and off the water. Apparently, the French-Canadian transplants were quite fit, although physically quite small, and they created boat speed and a high stroke rating with a series of short, punchy strokes. This chaotic flurry of oarsmanship was an ungainly sight to the refined British crowd. Additionally, when the Canadians took their stroke rating up to an impossibly high mark of fifty strokes per minute, the bowman Joseph Nadeau would utter a high, piercing yell, much like an Indian war cry.

Although "the Shoes" were defeated in the final by a crew from the London Rowing Club, the mere fact that this group of Canuck hillbillies could muscle their way through the heats was disturbing. To the Brits, it was aesthetically offensive to see a crew "bull" their way down the Henley course, as the French Canadians managed to do; in the final race, the yodeling Joseph Nadeau even collapsed in the boat from his extreme efforts. Win or lose, boat racing was supposed to exhibit a level of technical self-mastery that made it beautiful to behold. Needless to say, the Canadians were not invited back the next year when they presented their application to the Henley Stewards, the conservative group that oversaw all the foreign entries including singles. In fact, shortly after "the Shoes'" first and last appearance at the regatta, a group of British oarsmen quickly assembled and wrote down amateur rules for rowing. In addition to having most of the same provisions as the American rules, written six years earlier in 1872, the English guidelines also stated that an amateur could not be "a mechanic, an artisan, or a laborer." Furthermore, any foreign entries to Henley would now have to be signed by a notary public, certifying that none of the members of the crew was engaged in these "common" professions.

The ostensible reason for this exclusion, put forth by the Metropolitan Rowing Association (MRA), later called the Amateur Rowing Association (ARA), was that someone who worked with his hands all day would have an unfair advantage over those who did not. By logic, the extra physical "training" a laborer received on the job would make him stronger than his peers. A mason, for example, who worked with heavy stone all day would undoubtedly develop incredibly strong hands, not to mention his arms and back. And how could a businessman, doctor, barrister, or any academically trained man compete against that?

Not everyone in British rowing agreed with this rule or the reasoning behind it, most notably a London-based group known as the NARA (the National Amateur Rowing Association). London, like Philadelphia, had its own group of blue-collar athletes, many of whom could express the opposing argument that a laborer was often so physically exhausted by his daily trade, that he generally had neither the time nor the energy to train after work, particularly when it might deprive him of pay. Furthermore, not all "tradesmen" were engaged in manual labor that benefited their physical well-being. A bus driver, for example, led a sedentary life.

Nevertheless, in the end this set of amateur rules largely prevailed, particularly at places like Henley, which went on to become part of the British high social calendar (along with Wimbledon and Royal Ascot). Amateur sport in late-nineteenth-century England was seen as something to be indulged in only by those with adequate leisure time for the purpose of building character rather than advancing fame or fortune. These exclusionary provisions served as a barrier, effectively separating the upper and lower classes. Some were less subtle about their dislike for the lower classes, like Caspar Whitney, a well-known writer on sporting themes, who exclaimed: "To allow a mixing of professional and amateur is as senseless and impractical as the negro fraternizing with the refined and cultured members of the civilized world."

Other sports, like football and rugby, were considered more suitable for the working class, where they could grapple with one another. Rowing, however, was slowly commandeered for a higher purpose, along with sports like tennis and polo. At Henley, which had originally been a local regatta open to all comers, the working-class watermen were now relegated to the sidelines, tasked with setting up the booms and poles that delineated the course, removing the swans, and perhaps, if they were lucky enough to win the Doggett's Coat and Badge race, enjoying the privilege of ferrying the royal party about in their barge. But they certainly wouldn't be seen rowing against the gentlemen.

Joseph Dempsey, Jack Kelly's first coach, had taken a Vesper crew to Henley in 1905 and matched them against the prestigious Leander Club. Vesper had won the St. Louis Olympics the previous year, with Dempsey rowing in the 7 seat, but it was considered an incomplete victory without a British crew in attendance. The ordeal and expense of sending a crew abroad, of course, was no light burden, particularly for amateurs who needed other sources of income to support their athletic endeavors. More than anything else, it was this prohibitive expense that would prevent England, France, and America from meeting each other with greater frequency. The Philadelphians, however, were bent on matching their might against England's best boat the following year, and they proceeded to raise the necessary funds to send a crew overseas.

When Leander got word that Vesper was coming to challenge them, they began to assemble an all-star crew, drawing members from three different colleges. This was not unusual for English clubs or universities, who typically culled the best oarsmen from various feeder programs or colleges. The American club rowing system was different, however, and believed in the solidarity developed by drawing boat membership from within their immediate ranks. Each system had its own merits and shortcomings, with issues of both club loyalty and rowing technique being the two main causes for concern. A mixed crew might contain superior individual oarsman, for example, but a lack of uniformity due to stylistic differences and insufficient time practicing together as a team. On the other hand, the smaller circle of talent within its closed ranks might limit a club team like Vesper.

At Henley, both crews quickly proved their superiority by advancing through to the two-boat final. After recovering from a bad crab off the starting line, the Americans regained their composure and pulled up even with the British, only to lose in the final stretch by a margin of two seconds, or three quarters of a boat length. Cecil Willis, the Leander coach, graciously praised his American rivals, proclaiming that they were "the finest and fastest crew from the United States to enter an English race." Equally gracious, Coach Dempsey commented that the race had been "a struggle which carried with it almost as much honor and glory for the loser as it did for the winner."

Despite these exchanges of praise, however, the outing soured when the British later discovered that the members of the Vesper eight had been issued post-race "travel money." Evidently, the club funds that had been raised for the Henley trip were improperly dispensed to each boat member, handed out after the race to spend as they saw fit. The British viewed this act as a flagrant violation of the amateur rules, which clearly stated that oarsmen should not draw money from their sport. To the Henley Stewards, the Vesper

Vesper Boat Club vs. Leander, finish line at Henley, 1905. It was after this race that Vesper was accused by the Henley Stewards of "paying" their athletes to row and forbidden from entering subsequent regattas.
© BILL MILLER, FRIENDS OF ROWING HISTORY

men appeared to be no more than hired hands. And so, in the end, Dempsey and his crew were not only defeated but also officially discredited at Henley and banned from entering the English regatta again. It didn't help matters that the Philadelphia oarsmen had carried on in a "loud and raucous manner" in the local pubs.

Nor did it help that American crews had a prior history of ill-wrought victories at Henley. Ten years before this, in 1895, Charles Courtney had brought a Cornell crew overseas to compete in the Grand Challenge Cup event. In a heat against local favorite Leander, the umpire called out, "Are you ready?" Although several members of the English crew replied, "No," their voices weren't heard above a strong wind. The starting commands were given, and the Americans rowed away. Initially, a few members of the Leander boat began to pull on their oars, but soon stopped when they realized that the rest of the crew wasn't ready. The Cornell boat continued to row down the course alone, instead of stopping to see what was wrong with their competitor. To the English crowd, this was a serious breach in sportsmanship, and the incident was not easily forgotten.

Despite the exclusivity of the event, or perhaps because of it, Henley continued to hold a nostalgic appeal in the eyes of the entire rowing world. It was embellished with ceremony, costume, and ritual, and it harkened back to the days of chivalry, when contestants competed not only for prizes but also for honor and strength of character. The narrow corridor of water known as Henley Reach, cordoned off by booms and poles, looked a lot like a watery jousting field, where the combatants rode on boats instead of horses, and held oars instead of long lances. They rode with each other, of course, rather than against, and instead of trying to unseat each other physically, they would try to do so much more subtly—"out-rowing" one another with skillful force. Win or lose, to be accepted at Henley meant having run down the watery gauntlet, past the spectators and the Stewards' Enclosure, and been deemed a worthy crew.

Dempsey and some of his old Vesper crewmates began to fill Kelly's head with tales about the English regatta, and to hold out the Diamond Challenge Sculls prize for singles as an award no less desirable than the Holy Grail. Neither Dempsey nor Jack Kelly's brother Walter, however, bothered to mention that a trip to England might have unfortunate consequences, having less to do with his Irish or American lineage than the fact that he worked with his hands. For as a journeyman bricklayer, the Vesper oarsman was unlikely to be considered a true amateur in the eyes of the Henley Stewards. The omission of this simple caveat would have profound consequences on Kelly's life.

Chapter Eight

DEVELOPING TRUE EXCELLENCE IN ROWING, PARTICULARLY SCULL-ing, was a long process that required both tenacity and technique. It could not be rushed, and in this regard it was as much like learning to play a musical instrument as it was a purely physical endeavor. After several years of practice, Kelly had learned how to harness his great size and strength, and not let these assets get in his way. He no longer capsized at the beginning of races, although he still had some trouble turning his boat around a stake. These finer aspects of boat handling, in fact, were subtleties that required many years of study and the eye of a good coach. Like any art form, this part of the learning process involved the acquisition of a sense of style, a distinct way of moving through the water that fused a solid understanding of rowing technique with the particular physical attributes that an individual had to offer.

In 1914, at six feet two inches, Jack Kelly was a virtual giant among the Irish immigrants in his neighborhood. Height could be an asset to an oarsman, for it allowed one to lever the oars through the water with more obvious mechanical advantage. In a scull, Kelly's long torso swung back and forth like a pendulum, and his power seemed to originate from the smooth acceleration of his hips and shoulders. As in a golf or baseball swing, however, there was much more to executing a good rowing stroke than met the

Jack Kelly Sr. wearing Vesper Boat Club shirt. © JOHN B. KELLY III

eye. The physics of rowing, in fact, were very different from these other activities, since both the oarsman and his boat moved during the course of the rowing motion, while the oars, which visually appeared to trace a giant arc, actually traveled only a few feet through the water. This was because the more one pressed against water, the more resistant it became. The ideal way to apply one's power wasn't to swing at the water or clobber it with the oars, but to use it as a steady surface to lever the boat forward.

In this respect, rowing had more in common with swimming. Athletes in both of these pursuits needed to gain a feel for water, to work with it rather than against it. Unlike a swimmer, however, who lay immersed in water, an oarsman sat on top of it, in a tippy, narrow "canoe." The perpetual imbalance of a rowing shell gave rise to the last set of technical challenges. Most of them revolved around the fickleness of water, which could be affected by temperature, wind, and tide, in turn altering the demands of the rowing stroke. The effect of shifting water conditions on the hull and the oars could be significant and even require re-rigging a boat and oars, or changing their dimensions. This required the eye of a good coach, or someone who understood the mechanics of rowing.

The old professional British watermen had been the first real masters of boatmanship. One could easily imagine how the Thames ferrymen, for example, dealing with constant tide shifts, varying currents, and different weather conditions, had gained this sort of firsthand experience over time by virtue of their daily trade. It was a sailor's knowledge, but with a set of oars. Instead of learning when to pull in the sheet, one learned when it was prudent to shorten or lengthen one's strokes, or how best to row into a headwind or with a tailwind. There was no better teacher than the water itself, of course, but as with any trade, some of the tricks could be passed on from father to son, or friend to friend, to quicken the learning process.

When rowing became a sport, a century or so later, this teaching role was taken up by the coach, who was either someone who possessed this firsthand experience himself, or someone who espoused a theory based on a study of physics or engineering. Ironically, the old professional scullers, the same ones who had been banned from the sport, taught many of the best amateur oarsmen of the early twentieth century. The reason was simple. An amateur coach by and large had not experienced the sport to the same degree as the professional waterman. In both England and America, however, this dirty little secret was often kept under wraps, for any amateur who openly acknowledged his connection with a professional was held guilty by association.

—⁓—

To gain as much experience as possible on the water, Kelly continued to row and race in both team boats and the single, often competing in several events in one day. This full competition schedule was partly responsible for the development of his unique and unorthodox racing strategy, which was different from most of his competitors. In most cases, particularly in dual racing, it was an advantage to take the lead early and hold on to it for the duration of the race. Particularly in rowing, where oarsmen faced backward, the sculler who lead the race early on had the advantage of seeing his opponent and managing his own efforts accordingly. If the trailing sculler attempted to surge forward, closing the gap, the leader could execute a countermove.

This cat-and-mouse game could go on indefinitely, the leader rowing just hard enough to stay out of the visual range of his opponent. Generally, the longer the opponent remained behind, the greater the chances were that he would stay there for the duration. This was the opposite of sports like running and horseracing. In these, hanging back could afford the best view of the field, because the competitors all faced forward. In rowing, falling behind meant losing your sense of connection to the rest of the field. Most team boats, of course, had the benefit of forward-facing coxswains, who could describe the boat's position during the course of a race. But in singles, a trailing sculler had to turn his head around to view the field, often disrupting the balance of his boat and sometimes even the rhythm of his stroke.

Like everyone else, Kelly enjoyed getting off the starting line first. He wasn't a small, quick oarsman, but he made use of another ability that more than made up for this deficit. Over the course of a number of races, he had noticed that each starter had his own particular nervous tic, which would usually telegraph the exact moment they would fire the gun. Some men pulled at their coats or squinted their eyes, while others moved one corner of their mouths slightly. Kelly catalogued each of these movements, making a science of it, and then took full advantage of this knowledge whenever he raced. Just before the gun went off, he would shoot forward and gain a half-boat length on the rest of the competitors.

It was impossible to say whether he developed this technique on his own, or borrowed it from one of the old professionals who still plied the Schuylkill River. It was certainly a "trick" that paid dividends. Psychologically, a fast start drew "first blood," and often served to throw Kelly's opponents off balance. Even though it might yield only a one-stroke difference, this was still an advantage that had to be accounted for at some point in the race. Most of Kelly's better opponents would try to make up the lost water right away, rowing much harder than they had originally planned. This is exactly what he wanted, for it set them up for the second part of his strategy.

Once the flurry of the first twenty strokes was over, Kelly would lengthen and relax into an easier cadence, a shifting of gears commonly known as "the settle." He still drew his oars strongly and steadily through the water, but now took his time coming forward to the next stroke. This syncopated slowness allowed his boat to keep gliding smoothly forward as his body moved in the opposite direction, readying for the next catch. It was a style of rowing that created less check in the boat, and also conserved his efforts for the main body of the race, which was an important consideration for someone who might need to compete several times in one day. The slower pace, of course, allowed Kelly's more eager opponents to wrest the lead from him, and convince themselves that once they had passed him, the race was virtually won. It was a false sense of confidence, however, for soon they found themselves holding off an opponent who refused to fade away.

Once he was passed, Kelly then firmed up his strokes just enough to maintain visual contact with the field in front of him, glancing over his shoulder to keep an eye on the back of their boats. Kelly seldom tried to pass the leaders early on through the first five hundred meters, but he stayed close enough to let them know he was still there. He was, in a psychological sense, hanging on their coattails, conserving his energy for the final part of the race. His long strokes helped in this regard, for compared to his competitors, he took fewer to cover the same amount of water. Furthermore, as the race progressed to the halfway point, his continued presence just behind the leader eventually became annoying and stressful, and what had begun as an advantáge (i.e., occupying the lead) eventually became more and more of a burden. Under these conditions, by a thousand meters the lead sculler had usually began to pattern his strokes on the trailing oarsman, or even worse, to row a little higher in order to maintain the lead.

This tendency was the beginning of the end for the leader, who would soon find himself overextended and struggling at 1,500 meters, while Kelly would only be expending about 80 percent of his maximum effort, biding his time and waiting to make his move. Then, coming into the final two minutes of the race, he would put on an enormous surge. Even if an opponent suspected that it might be coming, Kelly's powerful and furious sprint was utterly devastating. Few oarsmen had enough energy to hold back this effort, particularly at such a late point in the race, for they had wasted it earlier just trying to keep ahead.

As he began to win more and more races, however, Kelly's reputation for jumping the start soon stood out in people's minds, not the way he rowed the rest of a race. Most of his competitors were so incensed by Kelly's ability to steal the lead that they largely ignored the fact that these first few strokes were fairly irrelevant to his overall race strategy. Jumping the gun was really just a game for Jack, something to try to get away with because it was fun, and because it tweaked the noses of everyone else on the line. Not everyone, of course, shared his Irish sense of humor, particularly the starters themselves, who became wary of Kelly's antics.

At the beginning of one competition held in Boston, an ex-Harvard oarsman named Elliot Saltonstall cautioned the Vesper oarsman before the race that he was well aware of his questionable tactics.

"No funny stuff today," he warned Kelly.

"Yes sir," said Jack, feigning obedience.

Saltonstall then proceeded to line up the five singles, and when the bows were all even, he loudly bellowed out the starting commands. After a brief pause, he fired the gun. All the while, his eyes were trained on the muscular sculler from Vesper, the favorite to win, wearing the striped maroon and grey tank top. Saltonstall had fully expected him to jump off the line, despite his pre-race warning. Much to his surprise, however, when the gun went off and the other boats flew forward, the Philadelphian did not move. Kelly continued to sit upright, poised to go, as if he had never heard the gun.

"What's the matter?" Saltonstall called out.

"Is it all right for me to go now, mister?" Kelly asked.

Before the ex-Harvard oarsman could figure out what to say, Kelly broke into a wide grin and rowed off quickly to catch the rest of the field. Despite his late start, he eventually passed the struggling group and won the race easily by a margin of more than two boat lengths. The performance did little to diminish his growing notoriety, but it did silence Mr. Saltonstall for the day, as well as other locals who thought they had Kelly pegged. By giving everyone else a big lead in the race, Jack let it be known that jumping the start was not the key ingredient to his success, but merely part of his character. Beyond the challenge of boat racing, he took an equal delight in throwing people off guard whenever he got the chance. It was a trait cultivated by an Irish sensibility, of having been raised in a house full of smart alecks. On dry land as well as on the water, Jack found it difficult not to fall into this prankish behavior, as he did with a reporter he met on the way up to Boston for the 1914 National Championships.

Coincidentally, the sportswriter who was covering the event sat down next to Jack when he boarded the train in New York City. When the news stringer discovered that the young man sitting next to him was actually an oarsman himself and rowed in Philadelphia, he could not believe his luck and he began to pepper him with questions about Jack Kelly.

"That fellow is breaking all the records, isn't he?" the reporter asked.

"I believe he is a bit overrated," Kelly said, with a straight face.

"How do you figure?"

"Well, I train with him every night and he never beats me."

At this remark, the reporter fell silent and figured that he was simply in the presence of a jealous rival. Oddly enough, he had never bothered to ask Kelly his name and quickly dismissed him as a person of little consequence.

Early the next morning, Kelly was milling about in front of the Union Boat Club, dressed in his street clothes, when the same reporter showed up. He was anxious to secure an exclusive interview with Mr. Kelly as soon as possible, before anyone else showed up, and he asked Jack if he could help out. Instead of revealing himself, Kelly kept a straight face and told the man that he would be happy to fetch Kelly from the locker room, for he was just heading inside the boathouse to change as well. The reporter was grateful. After Jack entered the building, he took his time drawing out the hoax as long as possible. By the time he emerged from the boathouse, wearing his maroon and grey Vesper shirt, a bevy of cameramen and other reporters had gathered, and they immediately surrounded him. The reporter was confused.

As he began to field questions from the lively group, Kelly looked over at his traveling companion from New York, and as their eyes met, he lifted his chin and smiled. When the New York sportswriter finally realized what had happened, he shook his head, momentarily embarrassed, and then laughed out loud. Kelly had made a fool out of him, but he had deserved it.

"One on me, Jack!" he called out.

In a way, Jack Kelly was a little like his country—confident and strong, and a little precocious. He had now won fifty-five races in his eight years of competitive rowing, an enormous accomplishment for someone still in his mid-twenties. From 1914 to 1916, Kelly ran up an unprecedented thirteen straight victories, and now when reporters asked him who he thought would come in first for a certain race, he would often reply, "Don't you mean who will come in second? Because I will be first, of course!" The press loved Jack Kelly's confidence, for he had the aura of a champion and a physical presence to match it. No one in this country seemed able to beat him, although there were two Canadian scullers, Bob Dibble and Tom Rooney, who still gave him trouble.

Anticipating his success at the 1916 National Championships that summer, one of the Philadelphia newspapers, *The North American*, ran a two-page spread on Kelly, complete with a chart of his entire racing career, a short Kelly "fact sheet," and an elaborate photo layout, showing the photogenic twenty-six-year-old standing with two oars, sitting in his boat, and staring dreamily off into the distance. The corresponding handwritten captions read, "Kelly, the brawny athlete on the slip of the Vesper Club"; "Kelly, wearing his famous green cap"; and "Kelly, who has brought rowing fame to Philadelphia." All of the photos were embellished with elegant, embroidered margins, and the last one was particularly striking, a close-up of Kelly's handsome profile from the shoulders up. With his faraway gaze, long Roman nose, and mouth that seemed to curl up at the corners in a knowing half-smile, he looked more like a movie star than an athlete.

In the body of the article, the East Falls native was referred to as "one of the finest scullers in the history of the sport." It went on to describe how "the young giant, who stands six feet, two inches and weighs 172 lbs" was going to win the 1916 National Sculling Championships in Duluth, Michigan, an honor which had been held for the past three years by Canadian champion Bob Dibble. Dibble was even larger than Kelly, standing six feet three inches tall and weighing nearly two hundred pounds. He had beaten Kelly on three different occasions, albeit once on a technicality. He was an older man and a former wrestler, and he reveled in the combativeness of a close one-on-one race. In this regard he seemed to hold a slight psychological edge over Jack Kelly, but with each race he seemed to be losing a little ground. From a practical standpoint, Dibble was also better at turning his boat around a stake, a seemingly simple maneuver that had given Kelly trouble in their previous encounters. However, this year at the Nationals, the competitors would row over a straight two-thousand-meter course, with no turn in the middle. Many sportswriters concluded that this fact, combined with the gradual improvement of Kelly's race times, meant certain victory for the American.

As race day drew near, there was suddenly another reason why Kelly was almost assured of victory. Apparently, Bob Dibble had recently enlisted in the Canadian Army and he would not be allowed to attend the Nationals. Kelly was far from pleased by the news. He had been preparing for his annual reckoning with the Canadian champion, and without him the competition would be practically meaningless. He was so moved by Dibble's patriotism that he sat down and composed a letter to his adversary:

I learn from the newspapers that it will be impossible for you to take part in the races of the National Regatta, to be held in Duluth in August. I need not tell you that this information is a source of keen disappointment. I looked forward to our race with much anxiety, and with the hope that I have so far improved as to be able to win from you the title of national champion sculler, which you have so honorably and willingly defended.

Your loyalty to king and country has made it impossible for you to appear at the starting line, and I am sure that you, too, feel a keen disappointment. If you are compelled to forfeit the title thru allegiance to your country and loyalty to its cause, I commend you for your action.

These were very formal words for the boy from East Falls, and they expressed a different side of his character, a noble sentiment that seemed to run beyond his humble upbringing and eighth-grade education. Dibble appreciated Kelly's letter and suggested that the two of them meet the following September for a series of dual races on the Schuylkill. Then they could establish, once and for all, who was ultimately the better sculler. Sadly, the proposed skirmishes would never happen. Suddenly America was joining the war effort as well, after dragging its heels for three years. All of its eligible young men, particularly athletes like Kelly, were being called into various branches of the armed service.

When Jack ultimately lost the Nationals to another Canadian adversary, Tom Rooney, his mother mailed him a telegram with a poem of sorts:

How many times did Caesar flunk?
How many times was Nelson sunk?
You're not beaten until you stay beaten.

The message was appropriate in more ways than one, for Mary Kelly's youngest son was about to head off to a larger battlefield.

Jack thought he might like flying, and first tried to enlist in the Lafayette Escadrille, a small group of volunteer American pilots who flew with the French Air Force under the auspices of the US Ambulance Corps. Entry into the Escadrille, however, required a $1,000 initiation fee, and Kelly didn't have the money. Soon afterward, he tried to enlist in the American Air Force, but he failed to pass the equilibrium test. Flying, of course, was a natural fit for an oarsman, and single sculling, in particular, was a lot like piloting a small plane. But it was not to be, and Jack ended up in the US Ambulance Corps as a medic with a bunch of ex-football players from the University of Pennsylvania and Lafayette College, all of whom were trained at a base hospital at Penn.

Walter Kelly, like P. H., was too old to fight, but promised to do his part by entertaining the troops overseas. George, who had already joined Walter on the vaudeville circuit and had even begun to write his own plays, was reluctantly conscripted into service as well. Even the Kelly women, most notably young Grace, joined a women's support group, started by Bessie Dobson, the daughter of one of the infamous carpet mill owners. They met once a week in a place called "The White House" to knit socks and scarves and gather other provisions for the soldiers getting ready to ship out overseas. It was the beginning of a friendship between the two families that Ma Kelly would have never predicted, but the war had a way of bringing unlikely people together.

—◆—

Like most young Americans, Jack Kelly had not spent much time thinking about how the war might affect his life. The growing conflict in Europe had been generally viewed as an affair that had little to do with the United States. But when innocent American lives were lost on board the *Lusitania* the previous spring, public sentiment began to shift. The impact of innocent people drowning was a powerful one. One Army enlistment poster showed an unidentified woman sinking into an eerie green sea, eyes closed, holding a baby in her arms. Images like these were necessary to elicit the sympathy of an American public who had been casually observing the war. If Jack Kelly had seen the poster, he might have been particularly moved, for the winter before he shipped out to France, he lost his youngest sister, Grace.

The two of them were skating together at Gustine Lake, located just below East Falls. Perhaps from brother Walter's influence, the twenty-two-year-old Grace fancied herself an aspiring actress, but she also tried to keep up with her athletic brother whenever the opportunity presented itself. Jack always pushed himself around the perimeter of the pond at a furious pace, trying to make the outing into a training session. Keeping up with him was exhausting work for anyone, and on this particular day, when Jack was nearly done, he told his little sister she should sit down and watch him while he did his final laps around the lake. Like any kid sister, however, Grace rushed after him instead, and in the middle of a sprint, she collapsed. Jack took her to the hospital as fast as he could manage, but later that day she died of heart failure.

The family, particularly Mary Kelly, was devastated by the loss of their youngest child.

"The sun will never shine quite the same for me again," she announced after the funeral. Jack was feeling guilty enough already and his mother's words echoed loudly in his ears. Like many family tragedies, however, Grace's death ultimately drew mother and son closer and provided a moment of family communion. Mary Kelly already knew how it felt to lose a child, her firstborn, and she now reminded Jack that he had been named after another, earlier John. It was an Irish custom to do this, a symbolic way to replace the dead child in name if not in spirit. But who, they both wondered, would bear the name of young Grace?

PART TWO

On Schuylkill River, June 2, 1935. © TEMPLE UNIVERSITY LIBRARIES, URBAN
ARCHIVES, PHILADELPHIA, PA

Chapter Nine

SAILING OVER TO FRANCE ON THE USS *LEVIATHAN*, KELLY WAS immediately recruited to fight in a boxing match. The *Leviathan* was the largest troop ship afloat in 1917, transporting twelve thousand soldiers packed in like sardines. The men slept in bunks spaced eighteen inches apart, and walked along corridors less than two feet wide. The accommodations were not much more spacious than a submarine, and in the ten days it took to cross the Atlantic, the soldiers needed some form of diversion to release the growing anxiety created by not only the cramped quarters but also the lurking danger of German U-boats. A ship's boxing match was just the thing. It relieved stress and, in an odd sort of way, it got the soldiers ready for the reality of war.

Unsurprisingly, many of the American Expeditionary Forces were college athletes of note, and along with them came a curious array of coaches brought overseas in a unique campaign organized by the YMCA. The coaches were enlisted not only to help train the new recruits but also to organize sporting events for the men while they were overseas. There were baseball coaches from Yale and Brown, football coaches from Dartmouth and Columbia, track coaches from Bowdoin and Colgate.

Bert Bell, one of Kelly's newfound friends from Camp Merritt, had helped arrange the boxing championship. Prior to his enlistment, Bell had been a quarterback for the University of Pennsylvania, and during basic training he had quickly identified Jack as a gifted athlete. He had also discovered his prowess in the ring. An incorrigible gambler, Bell had convinced the *Leviathan*'s athletic director to make the boxing tournament include a cash prize of $50. The ex-quarterback, of course, had no intention of fighting himself, but he knew that Kelly would probably enter if money were involved. Both of them, it seemed, were hopelessly in debt, due to a shared weakness for shooting craps. Back at the training base, they'd lost a bundle rolling bad dice. The boxing match offered an instant means of redemption.

It wasn't the first time that Bell and Kelly had teamed up to recoup their gambling losses. At Camp Merritt, they had once wandered into a local gym and seen a sign that promised $50 to anyone who could beat the local wrestler, a flamboyant character named "Cowboy Jones." Sensing an opportunity for financial gain, Bert and Jack had run back to the barracks and convinced a wresting pal of theirs to take on the pro. Mike Dorias was fresh out of college and somewhat naïve, but he also had an excellent reputation for winning matches. The only problem was that he frowned on professional wrestlers, who often resorted to underhanded tricks. Furthermore, Dorias didn't care to wrestle for money, because it might jeopardize his amateur status. Knowing all of this, Kelly and Bell slightly altered the details of the situation. They told Mike that they'd just met a real loudmouth who'd insulted them in conversation. They wondered if he could "take care of him" as a favor, by going up against him in the ring. It was a matter of honor, they explained, neglecting to tell Mike about the $50 prize. The naïve Dorias agreed to wrestle and easily won the match. Later, Jack and Bert collected the money.

Onboard the *Leviathan*, however, Kelly would have to do all the fighting. He'd lost most of the $350 he'd brought with him on craps, and he was hoping this match would supplement the $30 a month he would receive during his military service. As luck would have it, there was only one other skilled boxer onboard the ship, a Californian who outweighed him by ten pounds. As the championship progressed, both of these men easily worked their way through the preliminary rounds before they faced off against each other in the final bout. The Californian was a strong and able boxer, but in the second round Kelly knocked him out. Word of his victory spread quickly among the men and then spread to shore when the boat came into port.

When Kelly had been in France only a few days stationed in Brest, he was cleaning the company latrines one morning when two soldiers came in lamenting the recent news that some "god-damned pill roller" had won the ship's boxing championship. A "pill-roller" was army slang for anyone in the Medical Corps, a derogatory term that registered their lesser status in the military world. Ambulance corpsmen were generally college boys, who volunteered as a way of participating in the war without putting themselves directly in harm's way. Being an ambulance corpsman, however, was not an easy job or even a particularly safe one. In addition to working around the clock, the medics often endangered their own lives when they hauled injured soldiers off the battlefield. Many famous Americans would emerge from the ambulance service, including the writers Ernest Hemingway and John Dos Passos, both injured in the line of duty. Others, like Harry Crosby, would return psychologically scarred. Still, soldiers referred to them as "pill-rollers," and the medics didn't appreciate the term.

It was humbling enough to come all the way across the Atlantic, only to find himself cleaning toilets. But to stand there and suffer the abuse of two jealous soldiers proved too much for the twenty-eight-year-old from East Falls. Without a word of warning, Kelly set down his broom and slugged one of the men on the jaw, neatly dropping him to the bathroom floor. Then he turned to the other man and identified himself as the "pill-roller" they had just been talking about. The second man wanted nothing to do with Kelly. He was left untouched with the promise that when his friend came to, he would tell him that Jack Kelly was now "champion of the latrines."

Kelly quickly went from mopping up bathrooms to cleaning up the wounded on the battlefields. The field medicine he learned and practiced was often quick and primitive by necessity, focused on preventing blood loss and shock. Injured soldiers would then be transported to the main dressing station, where the gas victims were separated from others. Tetanus antitoxin was quickly administered to everyone to stem the possibility of infection. Wounds were redressed when necessary and tourniquets were examined, and when absolutely necessary, blood vessels were lanced open and dead tissue removed, to reduce the spread of infection. It was exhausting work, and when Kelly received transfer orders to move farther away from the front lines, he was relieved to get a break from the nonstop activity.

Along with the transfer orders, Kelly also received the letter from his mother expressing her growing concern about George, his next older brother. The aspiring playwright was serving as a noncommissioned officer, and she hadn't heard from him in quite a while. Ma Kelly never worried much about Jack, but George was more a literary than a soldiering type. She sent off a similar letter to Walter as well, expressing these anxious sentiments:

"I haven't heard from George in weeks," the letter ran. "He has been exceptionally good about keeping me posted, but lately there has been no word on him. He's the frail member of the family, and with winter approaching, I'm concerned. George is a cold soul, not strong enough for that life in the trenches. Of course, I don't worry about Jack being cold. I know if there is one blanket in France, he will have it."

Not long after his mother's letter arrived, Jack found himself so busily engaged as a boxer that he nearly forgot about the missive. His upset victory over the enormous French brawler had led to several other bouts, and Jack's commanding officer now promised special favors if Kelly successfully worked his way toward the AEF Championships. In between fights, he continued to clear the battlefields. Ambulance work was completely engrossing, and one day when Jack stopped in at another company's mess hall, he realized that he hadn't had a meal in twenty-four hours. He sat down alone and began to attack a huge pile of food, when he suddenly noticed that two other soldiers, sitting nearby, were observing him. Nodding toward Kelly, one of them turned to his friend and said, "Just in case he meets Maggie."

Kelly dropped his fork and stared directly at them.

"What did you say?" he asked.

The soldier repeated the comment. Kelly was a sergeant now and outranked the man who had spoken.

"Where the hell did you hear that?" he demanded.

"Oh, we have a kid in our company. He's in the field hospital now, and he's always saying that, Sarge."

Jack Kelly Sr. and brother George Kelly in France, 1918. © JOHN B. KELLY III

"What's his name?" Kelly asked.

"Same as yours, 'Kelly,'" he replied. And instantly, Jack knew he had found his brother.

George had a cold and was feeling miserable. Military life simply did not suit him. What he really wanted to be doing was writing plays back home, where he had begun to establish himself as a noted thespian. Jack promised that he would try to get his brother transferred to his outfit to look after him. Maybe he could even get him discharged somehow. Meanwhile, the two brothers talked at great length and remarked on the coincidence of their chance encounter, following so quickly on the heels of their mother's letter. She did have an uncanny knack for knowing things, without needing to possess all the prerequisite facts. Mary Kelly's prayers, too, seemed to carry some import, for George and Jack had been brought together that day only because of an infamous Kelly family tale, the "just in case I meet Maggie" story.

❧

Mary Kelly was sitting up at home one night, keeping George company after a late dinner, when some corn bread suddenly arrived at the door. It was sent over by her cousin, Maggie Costello.

"Wouldn't you know," Mary Kelly complained, "that Maggie Costello would send over this Johnny-cake after dinner was over." Annoyed, she continued her harangue. "It's always like the Costellos to be late and here's this lovely cake and our dinner is over and we can't enjoy it."

George, who had just come home himself, was sitting down to eat and observed his mother buttering and nibbling bits of the corn bread as she spoke derisively about her cousin. "Why, Mrs.

Kelly," he said, "for one who seems so upset by the late arrival of the Johnny-cake, you seem equally able to enjoy it!"

His mother stopped eating for a moment and stared at him, blank-faced, with a few crumbs of corn bread stuck to the corners of her mouth.

"George," she said indignantly, "this is only in case I meet Maggie."

George laughed out loud at the comment and remembered it forever after, repeating the story over and over again. The punch line became an oft-repeated quip within the Kelly family circle, but neither George nor Jack could have guessed that it would ultimately bring them together on the battlefields of France.

By now Jack's commanding officer was so happy with his victories that he promised to help Jack in any way he could, even lending assistance in securing an early discharge for his brother George. Although neither man knew it at the time, the war was nearly over. But Jack Kelly was not quite done fighting. At the AEF Championships, he took apart ten more opponents and was described as "a terror" by Arthur Daley of the *New York Times*. Among those in the know, the AEF Championships were slated to be the debut of a rising star named Gene Tunney, but Kelly was making them into his own private showcase. Fortunately for all the bookies, Kelly broke his ankle during his semifinal match. He took his injury well, however, and later teased Tunney, the eventual champ, that he was lucky he got off the hook so easily. For Kelly, the boxing had merely been a way to keep in shape for rowing, get George out of the war, and generally try to stay out of trouble. He had done well for himself and for others, he thought, boxing his way to the top, rescuing many wounded off the battlefield, and advancing to the rank of sergeant.

But now he had to return home and face his most formidable opponent—his mother.

Just before he left for the war, Ma Kelly had taken her youngest son aside and given him a few choice bits of advice. The words, however, came out more like a veiled threat. She informed Jack that she knew all about the terrible acts of needless violence that occurred during wartime, and if he indulged in these atrocities, he would never be allowed back on her doorstep. Not altogether surprised by the lack of sympathy in his mother's voice, Jack assured her that this would never happen, that he would never indulge in the spoils of war. When he returned to East Falls, he promised, she would find him the same person who had left. She would be proud of him. Now, only a little more than a year later, Kelly was finally going home. He had kept his word to mother and to country, and he was ready to resume his old life again. Yet like so many men who had gone off to war, he would return to a changed landscape, full of shifting alliances.

Chapter Ten

STANDING ON A BEACH IN OCEAN CITY, NEW JERSEY, A FEW months after the war had ended, a young boxer named Jack Dempsey set eyes on a beachgoer he had never seen before. What caught his trained eye was the man's impressive physique, not hidden by his full-body bathing suit. Automatically, he began to take his measure in the same way he would size up an opponent. He reckoned he was in his mid-twenties, and he had broader shoulders than Dempsey himself but a smaller waist. His legs were very long and well muscled, and accounted for much of his great height. His arms were also exceptionally long, giving him an outstanding reach. "Thoroughbred" was the term that came to mind. Dempsey, who had fought his way up from a bar room brawler to become one of the finest heavyweight contenders in the country, had seen his share of well-trained athletes, but he was completely awed by the sight of this man. He began to ask around about him, until finally a mutual friend introduced him to Jack Kelly.

The two men hit it off immediately and began to discuss their training regimens and backgrounds. Both had been born into large families of uncertain means, and both had worked their way up from virtually nothing. Athletics had been the main focus of their lives, and each dreamed about becoming a world champion some day—Kelly with his oars and Dempsey with his fists. After

A mock fight at the beach, Ocean City, New Jersey, Labor Day, 1913. Before he learned how to row, Kelly trained as a boxer, and his skills as a pugilist came in handy on more than one occasion. © JOHN B. KELLY III

they chatted for a while, strolling along the beach, Dempsey casually asked Kelly whether he knew anything about boxing.

"Sure," Kelly replied, "enough to protect myself against some of these champions fighting today."

Dempsey stared at him, a bit taken aback. He was a hard-headed, explosive boxer who fought with such unbridled ferocity that he often took his opponents apart in one round. Kelly was much the opposite in temperament—cool and confident. His remark came out like a left jab, sharp and quick, and it instantly put his companion on edge. Dempsey couldn't decide whether Kelly was joking.

Kelly, however, was quite serious. After all, if he hadn't broken his ankle toward the end of the war, he would probably have beaten Tunney for the AEF Heavyweight Championship, and who knows where that victory could have taken him? Back in France, Kelly and Tunney had faced similar opponents in other fights, and in many cases Jack had disposed of the same people with more apparent ease. Dempsey was eager for this inside information, as he was about to make his debut as the US heavyweight champ, and ultimately he would have to face Tunney in the ring. But neither Dempsey nor Tunney would ever face Jack Kelly, or know how they would have fared against him. As Jack finally admitted to his dark-haired companion, his competitive boxing days were over. He would never have the opportunity, as Dempsey soon did, to step into the ring and vie for the first million-dollar purse in sports history.

Kelly certainly could have used a few extra dollars. He had walked away from the war with nothing to show for it except for a change in military rank. That, unfortunately, didn't mean much back in East Falls, where life had gone on without him. While he had been stationed in France, his father had died of a heart attack, and Jack's position at P. H.'s construction company had been given away to his brother Charles. Down on his luck, Jack thought about a story his Grandfather Costello once told him, about the first days after his service in the American Civil War. Finally released from the four-year ordeal, his grandfather was on his way home, crossing the bridge from Baltimore to Carrollton, when he reached in his pocket and discovered his last penny. Instead of lamenting his poverty, however, he threw the penny into the local river for good luck. Some 620,000 people had died in the Civil War, which pitted not only North against South but also Irishman against Irishman, many of whom had just come to the United States. Costello counted his blessings; he was lucky to be alive.

By comparison, the war that Jack Kelly had just returned from had taken only 57,000 American lives, and the majority of these soldiers had fallen victim not to bullets, gas, or bombs, but to the 1918 flu epidemic. Many died after they returned from the war, catching the disease in closely packed army bases, like the one Kelly returned to at Camp Merritt. There he bumped into a fellow soldier to whom he owed sixty francs from an old card game. After he paid off the debt, Kelly found himself with a single franc to his name. Remembering his grandfather's story, he tossed the French coin away.

Sensing their brother's state of affairs, Walter and George pooled their resources and lent Jack $7,000, enough capital to start his own construction business. Both had become well established in thespian circles and were beginning to reap the financial rewards. Jack was grateful for the loan and quickly assembled a work crew from East Falls. Soon his red and white KELLY FOR BRICKWORK signs began to appear at sites around the city, from libraries to railroad stations. There was more than enough work for him to get by while he learned the managerial challenges of negotiating his own contracts. Ma Kelly helped him in this task by asking him important questions about each job before he took it. Was it well financed? What were the labor conditions? Could he get the building materials?

"It isn't that I know more than you," she told him. "I don't know as much. But I'm not ignorant about it either. If I don't do anything more than ask questions, that helps. Because when you tell me just how you stand, you tell yourself, too."

It was typical Ma Kelly advice, tinged with an edge of maternal authority. The budding success of his business venture, however, was not quite enough to satisfy him. Something was missing from his life, and Jack knew what it was as soon as he found his way back to the Schuylkill River and wrapped his hands around a pair of oars.

———

The war, ironically, had provided rest periods for Jack Kelly that he had not been able to afford in his earlier life. The hot summers in Philadelphia, in particular, had always been a difficult time for him. After a long day of laying brick, rowing on the Schuylkill was a backbreaking enterprise that left him tired and stale, and often he would lose too much weight and become depleted. But the war, with its periods of intense activity followed by ceasefires, not only allowed Kelly's body to get stronger but also provided him the opportunity to recuperate. Equally important, his time away from home had made him realize how much he missed rowing and needed it in his life. Every time he remembered what it was like to row, his body felt an intense longing, and he mentally reaffirmed his goal to become the best oarsman in the world. Even though he could not find his way to water or a boat, Jack found himself rehearsing future races in his mind—an odd, obsessive sort of exercise that would much later be termed "visualization" by coaches and sports psychologists, and used by high-caliber athletes to sharpen their minds before competitions.

In addition to boxing, basketball had also helped keep Kelly in shape during the war. Coached by George Zahn of Princeton, Jack's team managed to win twenty-five games straight on the way to a victorious AEF Championship. So when he returned home from overseas, Kelly found himself in the best physical condition of his life. As he got back in a scull and regained his sense of balance, he quickly realized that he was actually stronger and faster than ever, and he began to revisit his goal of becoming the world champion. He was only twenty-nine, after all, a time when most men just begin to reach their physical peak. Patrick Henry, however, was less than pleased when he discovered that Jack was entertaining the notion of training hard again.

"If you want to be successful in business, you'll have to give up rowing," P. H. nagged. While his older brother hadn't lent him any money for his new company, he had "loaned" him a few pieces of heavy machinery. And he was never, it seemed, short on giving advice.

Jack tried to explain to P. H. that if he didn't fulfill his boyhood dream, he would bring this same lack of determination forward into any future business venture. Psychologically, it would ruin his chance of success in life. Furthermore, as an aside, he told his older sibling that any obstacle that he might encounter in the career world would certainly pale in comparison to what he had already endured in rowing, not to mention the war. Patrick Henry, who had been neither an athlete nor a soldier, could not appreciate these sentiments, however, and the disagreement marked the beginning of a long-standing rift between the brothers. It didn't help things either when Jack reputedly began to "borrow" some of his older brother's gear without asking permission. Many of the construction businesses shared a communal lot for their machinery, and each company painted their equipment a specific color, to label it as their own. While he was first getting established and lacked certain resources, Jack reputedly had one of his workers sneak into the lot at night and repaint whatever he needed.

Mary Kelly was less judgmental about the whole matter of balancing sports and career, but she, too, had grown a little concerned. After all, when was Jack going to get on with his life? Even for an Irish boy, he was getting a rather late start out of the nest. He still lived at home and she was still preparing his meals late at night, after he returned from his long rowing sessions. Instead of badgering him, however, she decided to apply the same Socratic method to her son and his rowing plans as she did to his bricklaying business, asking him if his goals were realistic. How could he work and train and not get stale? And how could he become the champion of the world? The Olympics, after all, hadn't been held in nearly eight years.

"Thoughts are things," she said finally, "but they won't be things if you just think about them. You must put forth whatever effort or intelligence is required to bring them into being."

Kelly took this as a blessing rather than a reprimand. In the back of his mind, he was certain that rowing was going to take him somewhere, toward an unseen destiny. And so, every afternoon after completing a full day of work at Kelly Brickworks, Jack made his way down to the Vesper Boat Club and renewed his boyhood dream in the muddy waters of the Schuylkill, rowing until darkness fell. A nice, long swim might have offered him more respite, instead of the punishing workouts that he now subjected himself to in his efforts to regain his racing form. Behind the hard work, however, lay a daily baptism that somehow replenished Kelly's spirit and moved him closer to the greatness he sensed in himself but had not yet been able to prove to the world.

He did not pursue his dream single-handedly. Frank Muller, whom Kelly had once replaced as Vesper captain, had developed into a fine coach. Muller had been experimenting with some different ideas about rowing technique and training, and focused his efforts on developing proficiency in small boats. Realizing that he had a champion on his hands, Muller insisted that Kelly commit himself to sculling and forbid him to row in eights and fours. Not only did the finer motion of a scull require this specialization, but a single itself was much like a suit of clothing, and needed to be worn every day to ensure a good fit.

Stroke after stroke, race after race, Kelly began to find his balance and rhythm again. Under Muller's watchful eye, he not only left a trail of defeated scullers in his wake, but he also began to set a string of local records. In the 1919 season, Kelly even dispensed with his old Canadian rivals, Bob Dibble and Tom Rooney, and went on to win the National Championships that summer. His undefeated season began to attract attention from the press, who resumed their interest in the outstanding Philadelphia oarsman. Billy Muldoon, a well-respected athletic trainer, was quoted as saying that he had never seen a better-conditioned athlete in his entire life. Adam Peet, a well-known rowing authority from New York, claimed that Kelly was the best sculler he had seen in his forty years of competition. Muller himself was more to the point when he was asked for his overall assessment.

"How fast is Kelly?" one reporter inquired.

Muller shrugged. "To tell you the truth, I don't know, but it's a length and a half faster than anyone else."

The prize that Jack began to set his heart on was the miniature pair of silver oars known as the Diamond Challenge Sculls. Kelly had dreamed about winning the Diamonds even before the war, back when he had heard the stories about Henley from his old coach, Joe Dempsey. He was attracted by the ritual and pageantry, and then, of course, there were the prizes themselves, exhibiting some of the same attention to detail that marked the running of the regatta itself. The winner of the Diamond Challenge Sculls actually received two prizes: the six-inch set of crossed oars, crafted out of frosted silver and fillet gold and bound at the center by a wreath of green enamel set with rubies and brilliants; and a silver-gilt "pineapple" cup, an impressive chalice that could be kept for life. The silver sculls had to be returned each year, but the victor did get his name engraved on a permanent plaque, which for an oarsman was the closest thing to immortality.

Kelly had been reluctant to enter Henley previously. As a journeyman bricklayer and a general laborer before the war, he had heard about the English amateur rules. But the Great War and the aid of the Americans had reportedly eased these exclusionary restrictions. In 1919, in fact, Henley had been run as a "Peace Regatta," and professionals and amateurs were allowed to compete against one another, as well as several squads from Allied countries still stationed in England. Additionally, Kelly now ran his own bricklaying company, which was certainly a step up from being a journeyman bricklayer. And so, hoping that he might now be allowed to compete at Henley, Kelly discussed the situation with his friend Russell Johnson, who was secretary of the National Amateur Association of Oarsmen (NAAO). As it turned out, Russell was on his way over to England to purchase some Airedales, his favorite dog breed, and he promised to discuss the matter with the Henley Stewards.

Meanwhile, another interesting rowing competition had emerged. Apparently, the Olympic Games were going to be held again, after a long hiatus brought on by the war. They would be held in Antwerp, Belgium, in late August, and more importantly, the United States was finally thinking about sending along a contingent of oarsmen to compete: a four, an eight, a pair, and a single sculler. In 1912, when the Games had been held in Stockholm, the United States had not funded any rowing teams, so this announcement was big news for anyone who pulled an oar. As Kelly mulled over the Olympic news, he received a call from the *New York Times*. Apparently, there was some speculation about whether Jack would choose the Olympic Games or the Henley Royal Regatta, since both were being held that summer. Based on a rumor that Kelly would prefer the former, another American sculler, Dr. Paul Withington, had already sent in his Henley entry form. But Kelly assured the *New York Times* reporter that he would much prefer the British regatta, and if he got into Henley, he would probably not attend the Olympic Games, since the events were too close together to allow for proper training.

"I would rather row in the Diamond Sculls than the Olympics," Kelly told the reporter, "but before I can row in the English race, the approval of the American and English rowing authorities is necessary."

When he was questioned further about this, he went on to explain: "It is by no means certain that the English authorities will accept me." He cited the old Vesper crew of 1905 that had rowed on the Thames and "violated so many rules that they resolved that they would never permit a Vesper oarsman to row there again."

"Of course," he added, "it is foolish that any such reason as that should bar me, but it is possible."

The note of caution quickly proved unnecessary when Russell Johnson returned from England to report that he had managed to speak with most of the Henley Stewards, and they assured him that Jack's entry would be favorably received. Kelly was overjoyed with the news and immediately sent out his formal application, approved by the members of the NAAO. He also began his preparations for the trip. He purchased a new single scull and had it crated up, and then booked passage on the SS *Philadelphia*. Competing at Henley was the chance he had been waiting for, to test his skills against the English amateur scullers who were considered among the best in the world. Like his brother Walter, he would be finally able to prove to himself and everyone else that his years of sacrifice and training had not been in vain.

However, not everyone was impressed with Jack's Henley quest.

"If you had given up rowing, you would have $100,000 by now," P. H. chided his younger brother. It was now a year since Kelly Brickworks had been started, and while it wasn't a complete failure, it wasn't exactly thriving either. "Ma always said you were stubborn," he continued. "Stubbornness can blind a man to everything else, and only occasionally does it pay off."

Jack's jaw tightened. He was tired of his brother's lack of faith in him.

"I don't think you really know how important winning the Diamond Sculls is to me," he retorted. "It's the greatest of all rowing events, and I simply must win. The war took a year out of my life,

Pat. Time is flying. I won't get another chance like this. I know if I win the Diamonds nothing will be too big an obstacle for me to hurdle later."

Patrick Henry looked at his brother and realized it was no use continuing to argue.

"You win, Jack," he said, lowering his head. "Good luck," he added. But the words came out more like a curse than a blessing.

Chapter Eleven

Three days prior to his departure for Henley, Jack received an urgent telegram, sent to his house by Russell Johnson, who had received it first. Mary Kelly was standing nearby when Jack fetched the mail, and she watched her son's face turn ashen as he read the note. He kept reading the words over and over, until finally his tears began to fall on the little piece of paper. Then he crumpled up the telegram and let it fall to the floor, using the back of his hand to hide his face.

"What is it?" she asked, guessing someone had died.

For a long while Jack could not answer. Then he told her: "The Henley Stewards have rejected my entry to the Diamond Sculls. They're sending a letter to explain why." The exact text of the note was even shorter:

The entry of J. B. Kelly to Diamond Sculls not accepted. Letter follows. Advise Kelly.

Mary Kelly came over and placed her hand on Jack's shoulder. She knew what his father would have said right now.

"I don't understand it," Jack blurted out, his sadness giving way to shock. "Why would they have told Russell Johnson I could compete?"

His mother, who had never been comfortable expressing her affection, began to rub her son's shoulder. "I know you have had your heart set on winning the Diamond Sculls, son. And I know how hard you have prayed for it all these years. But it isn't going to do any good to fret and stir and ask good God why he has said no. There is some reason, and perhaps some day you will find the answer—whatever is, is best."

He recognized his father's words and tried desperately to take them to heart. As the next few days passed, however, and no further letter of explanation arrived, Kelly began to sink deeper into depression. It was not a place he liked to dwell. Even though he'd been aware that rejection was possible, and had even mentioned it in passing to the *New York Times* reporter, he wasn't prepared for this result. Emotionally, he'd already committed himself to the big race, in the same way he committed himself to a big fight. The letdown was simply too overwhelming.

There were two possible reasons for the Henley rejection that would be brought forward and debated for years to come. One was the issue of Jack Kelly's amateur standing, as it was interpreted by the Henley rules of rowing. The other was the question about the Vesper Boat Club's past infraction in 1905. Since no clarification was ever received by Kelly, he could only speculate as to the proper weight given to each condition.

On at least a few different fronts, Jack Kelly certainly did not fit the mold of the British amateur or "gentleman oarsman" of his day. Certainly, if you were to examine his application through the eyes of the Henley Stewards, it was clear that Kelly's background was

"The Stewards of the Kelly Clan." Back Row (left to right): Charles, George, Patrick Henry, and John Brendan. Front Row (left to right): John Henry and Walter. © JOHN B. KELLY, III

one that could arouse caution at the very least. His overall resume lacked some important elements. In terms of education, he had not finished high school, let alone attended an Ivy League college. He had worked in the trades and then gone directly into business, taking a few night school classes in engineering along the way. Not only that, but he had worked with his hands, first performing some general construction and then laying brick.

Technically, if Kelly had worked through his bricklayer's apprenticeship but not continued as a full-time laborer, he might still have been considered an amateur by the 1897 British ARA standards. But the Henley regulations were more stringent. In any case, he was truly working class, a tradesman by any measure, despite the fact that he didn't haul around his own bricks anymore. More importantly, although it was likely never discussed, Kelly had technically broken another portion of the amateur rules. Although he had not, to anyone's knowledge, received money for his rowing competitions, he had occasionally won bets from his boxing matches. It was a harmless thing, perhaps, but it was there nonetheless, and if anyone had ever cared to make a serious inquiry, they would have discovered this technical flaw in his amateur resume.

The Vesper question, of course, revolved around the 1905 trip to Henley, in which the members of Joseph Dempsey's boisterous eight had been given traveling money in order to tour Europe after the race. Truth be told, very few foreigners, particularly Americans, had ever gone to Henley and come away feeling completely welcome. Most were never invited back, like E. H. Ten Eyck, a single sculler from Wachusetts Rowing Club, who won the Diamonds in 1897 and was subsequently looked upon with great disfavor. Part of the problem was that a small cadre of influential British oarsmen always felt that Henley should be a closed affair, restricted not just to amateurs but to British amateurs alone. After all, only national applicants could be screened with any real authority, and only these oarsmen truly understood what the event was all about. Foreigners, on the other hand, were always a mixed blessing. While they did make the event into a world-class competition, lending it more international prestige, they were troublesome for various reasons.

First, and most obvious, the hometown Henley crowd wasn't thrilled when outsiders beat their local and national favorites and took the coveted prizes out of the country. Jack Kelly had been quoted in the Philadelphia papers as saying that he was going to "try to lift the Diamond Sculls from England," as if winning were an act of thievery. Some thought it was. Americans, for the most part, didn't come to Henley to socialize, and they often kept to themselves, following a strict training regime. The British press and the local fans didn't care for this sort of behavior; it was considered standoffish and ungracious at best, and "professional" at worst. Eventually, the unwritten understanding at Henley was that a few foreigners were fine, to add some color and interest, but they shouldn't be allowed to walk away with all the prizes. After all, the English had by and large invented rowing, and it was disheartening to be beaten at their own game, just as it would be for an American baseball team, for example, to lose to the Japanese.

Screening the amateur credentials of foreign entries was always problematic. When E. H. Ten Eyck had come overseas with his father, for example, suspicions were immediately aroused. The father had been a well-known professional in his day, and despite the fact that his son was only seventeen at the time and could hardly have amassed any sort of record, amateur or otherwise, his father's background worked against him. A true amateur did not receive coaching from a professional, even if it was his own father. It didn't help matters when the two Americans were spotted dining with some old British pros during their trip.

Although Jack Kelly's amateur standing had been vouched for by the NAAO, he had all the earmarks of a pro to the Brits, even if they couldn't quite prove it. His posted times on the Schuylkill were incredibly fast, close to world record pace, and he clearly took his rowing far too seriously. Ironically, to the Americans, Kelly's devotion to his craft was judged exactly in the reverse, as an example of what a dedicated amateur should be. And so, in the end, the controversy reflected as much a difference in culture as in rules.

News of Kelly's rejection spread quickly in Philadelphia, and it soon became a subject of great interest in the newspapers. Many noteworthy local oarsmen were solicited for their opinion, and all of them stated emphatically that Kelly was a "clean amateur" and had never accepted money in the sport. Most of them considered the Henley rejection a complete surprise and something that could only be viewed as a personal affront, or perhaps a mistake. They soundly dismissed the Vesper infraction, now fifteen years old, of having any relevance. Nevertheless, the mysterious decision had been made, and no letter of explanation would ever follow. Even the Henley minutes, taken by the Stewards at that time, listed both reasons as being discussed, with no definitive conclusion.

In the meantime, Jack Kelly made up his own mind.

"The old rule obviously hasn't changed," he told his mother. It was now a few weeks after the telegram had arrived, and the two of them were sitting at home.

"What rule?" she asked.

"They won't let a man who has worked with his hands row against their gentlemen."

"And why not?" Mary Kelly asked, her voice rising.

"They claim that a fellow who works with his muscles has an unfair advantage over an aristocrat."

He knew exactly how these words would affect his mother, and he watched as the fury began to gather behind her eyes. It was just the sort of thing that she expected to hear about the English. And if there was one thing the mother and son shared, it was the challenge of a good fight. Kelly sat back now, having shared his burden, and proceeded to feed on his mother's rage. In the end, because of the silence from overseas, he decided that he could only take the telegram one way, incorrectly or not. No matter how you looked at it, he had been deemed "unacceptable" in the eyes of the Stewards. It was a personal slight and nothing less.

To some degree, the widespread broadcasting of Kelly's rejection had taken the matter out of his hands and brought it into a larger public forum. If Jack had been a little uncertain at first about how to handle the bad news, the press clearly pointed the way, and his mother pushed him in the same direction. Now every retelling of the story simply confirmed the injustice. The words dug deeper and deeper under Kelly's skin, like a persistent splinter that now became a wound. The pain set in motion not only the old Anglo-American hostility, but for Kelly the more ancient

Irish wound that had been passed down to him from two generations. Every curse that his mother and grandfather had ever uttered against the English now surfaced in his mind, bolstering and blinding him in equal measure. And in the midst of it all, one thought became clear, forged in the fires of Kelly's anger and embarrassment. He made a vow to himself that he would never forget this day, and he would have his vengeance, even if it took him a lifetime.

Chapter Twelve

WHILE THE DOOR TO HENLEY HAD BEEN SLAMMED IN KELLY'S FACE, another door was still open. The Olympics may not have held the prestige of the Henley Royal Regatta, but they also lacked the class prejudice. They would be held that year in Belgium, a small country that had made an enormous contribution to the war effort. Kelly made hasty preparations. Before he could represent the United States, he first had to qualify at the Olympic rowing trials, which were being held on Lake Quinsigamond in Massachusetts on July 23 and 24. While his focus was still on the single scull, Kelly decided to add another challenge to his Olympic quest. In a move that most oarsmen would consider unusual and overly ambitious, he decided to try out for the double scull as well.

The choice was peculiar for a few reasons. The obvious one was that few oarsmen would ever attempt to row two events at such a high-level competition. After all, it was exhausting enough to row a single scull two thousand meters against some of the best competitors in the world, but to double up and try to advance through the heats in another event was entirely unprecedented. Swimmers, certainly, competed in more than one event, but most of their races were only twenty-five to one hundred meters long, relatively short distances that allowed their bodies to recuperate between heats. Physiologically, a two-thousand-meter rowing race was a very different experience, more akin to running the mile in track and field.

To add the double scull event, with its accompanying heats, meant rowing at this grueling length several times. And Kelly was no longer a young man, but a thirty-year-old. His older body might very well be able to push harder than most, but it could not recover as quickly from sustained, intense activity.

And then there was Kelly's choice for rowing partner, Paul Costello.

Paul was his first cousin, a nephew of the infamous ("just in case I meet") Maggie Costello. He was a dark-haired, dour-faced young man, with sloping eyebrows that made him look like he was always wincing. Unlike Kelly, Costello wasn't always comfortable in the public eye, and most of the photographs taken of him were less than flattering. He had one of those sad, serious faces that had probably always made him look old, despite the fact that he was actually two years younger than Jack. From afar, he seemed to possess the constant dissatisfied aspect of Eeyore, the unlucky donkey from Winnie-the-Pooh. In reality he was an amiable man with a generous heart, but his modesty prevented him from playing to the crowds as his cousin did. When reporters asked Costello how he would do during a race, or how he had done afterward, his standard response was, "I let my oars do the talking."

Physically, Kelly and Costello might as well have been Abbott and Costello, as their sizes and body types were radically different. Kelly was statuesque and lean, with extremely long limbs, and Costello was six inches shorter and weighed about fifteen pounds less. This mismatch was only accentuated when the two cousins got into a boat together. Seated behind Jack in the bow of

Paul Costello in his single scull. Largely overshadowed by his older, more successful cousin, Costello was an excellent oarsman in his own right.
COURTESY OF THOMAS E. WEIL

their double scull, Paul looked like an ungainly dwarf, although he actually had a remarkable physique, built up not only from rowing but also years of gymnastics training. In modern rowing nomenclature, he was a lightweight rower, while Kelly was a true heavyweight. At the time, however, no such weight distinctions were in place, and lightweights and heavyweights raced against each other, or together.

Being a lightweight was not always a disadvantage. In fact, at least in smaller boats like singles, history had often proven that an oarsman's strength-to-weight ratio was more important than pure mass. Edward Hanlan, the famous Canadian professional, had been very small but well proportioned. A British study in the early 1900s had also proven that the best oarsmen, in fact, were generally not the biggest men on the squad. After all, more mass demanded more effort, which was one reason why Kelly himself always dropped his weight down to 175 pounds when he was in his peak racing form.

Nevertheless, in a double it was important to have two oarsmen who could "blend" their strokes together, and Kelly and Costello were severely challenged in this respect. Kelly's reach was simply too long for his cousin, who could not extend as far forward to the top of the stroke, or "the catch," where the oars were lowered into the water. Subsequently, at the conclusion of the stroke, Costello's blades always emerged before his cousin's. Even to an untrained eye, the sight was aesthetically displeasing. Reporters and rowing experts alike picked up on this immediately and concluded that the Vesper boat "lacked harmony," despite an undeniable level of fitness.

But this external lack of unity was only half of the picture. Despite his shyness in the public eye, Paul Costello seemed to have no problem verbalizing on the water. A persistent worrywart, Paul would badger his older cousin during their practices and races, often second-guessing him or openly criticizing Jack's predilection for an easy pace. In response, Kelly would fire a witty retort over his shoulder or totally ignore his cousin. While it was generally considered verboten to talk in a team boat, let alone argue, the constant verbal banter between the two cousins seemed to develop naturally. They carried on like a comedy team, Paul playing the straight man, Kelly the jester. From Jack's perspective, Costello might be a little annoying at times, but he was fun to have around, like a kid brother. He offered company and comic relief for Kelly, who had spent many lonely miles out alone on the river. Most important, Costello was remarkably strong, and Jack knew that he could always count on him to pull his hardest when the two of them raced.

Costello, in fact, was extremely underrated. The previous summer he had posted a better time than Jack in the 1919 National Championships, albeit in a different category. Jack had won the elite singles with a time of 7:51, and Paul had won the senior singles, a "less competitive" event, in 7:38. Fortunately for Kelly, then, his cousin would not be rowing against him in the Olympic Trials, but with him in the double. Instead, Jack would get to row largely unchallenged, against a field of men he had easily beaten before. And just as well, for as Paul and Jack arrived in Worcester and began to practice on Lake Quinsigamond, Kelly could not locate his single scull. It was supposed to have arrived by private car, driven up from Philadelphia, but it was nowhere to be found. Finally, instead of worrying about what had happened to his boat, Jack took to the water another way, swimming in the lake to keep his muscles loose. The swimming, he discovered, took his mind off the races and helped him keep cool in the summer heat.

It also made him remember the last time he'd gone swimming.

———

Two weeks before the Olympic trials, Kelly had been faced with a more daunting challenge in the single, an old score to settle with his nemesis, Bob Dibble. Dibble, of course, was the Canadian sculler who had beaten him on three occasions before the war. He, too, was planning to represent his country in the Olympics, and as a tune-up, he decided to drive down to Philadelphia and row against Kelly in the People's Regatta. It was July 4, the same weekend that Kelly would have been racing at Henley if his entry had not been denied.

Like Kelly, Dibble had come out of the war with a few minor injuries but nothing serious enough to prevent him from putting Kelly back in his place. He had attained the rank of lieutenant, compared to Kelly's lesser standing as sergeant, and at six feet three inches, 195 pounds, the Canadian champion was physically bigger as well. Following the war, however, Kelly had beaten Dibble for the first time at the 1919 Nationals. Dibble was not pleased with the loss and had spent the past winter training very hard. The July 4 race was publicized as a preview of the American and Canadian Olympic hopefuls, but all the insiders in rowing knew that the singles pairing was really a grudge match between Kelly and Dibble. Thousands of spectators thronged to the banks of the Schuylkill, and many side bets were riding on the race.

When the gun went off, Dibble muscled his way out to a slight lead and began to increase it through the first few minutes of the race. Kelly was unsurprised by the move, for Dibble always rowed a strong first half and liked to assert his dominance early on. Kelly had actually been training himself on the Schuylkill against a local double scull in preparation for this match, and he was fully prepared to relinquish the lead. As the two oarsmen passed under the Strawberry Mansion Bridge, however, Kelly was taken aback when he looked over his shoulder and saw Dibble executing a mid-race sprint. This was an odd move, so early in the race.

"Goodbye, John!" Dibble called out, repeating the same taunt he had used in a prior race, two years earlier. Now the big Canadian was a full three lengths ahead, enjoying a huge lead over his American rival.

Kelly, however, stuck to his own plan, keeping his rhythmic strokes long and steady. As good as Bob Dibble might be, Jack had to believe that he couldn't maintain this early burst of speed, which required a much greater expenditure of oxygen. Slowly at first, then stroke by stroke, Kelly began to draw himself closer, narrowing the gap between his boat and Dibble's. Three lengths was an enormous margin to be made up, but he resisted the impulse to start sprinting as Dibble wanted. Sprinting took a lot of energy, and it also compromised the steady run of a boat between strokes. He fully realized now that Dibble's race strategy had set him up to do exactly this, to chase after the Canadian without regard for his own pace. It was difficult to hold back, but somehow he managed, and finally, with only a quarter mile to go, his boat drew even with Dibble's. It had been extremely hard work to catch up to him, especially in the 100-degree heat, but now the real battle began. Locked together, vying for the lead, the two scullers traded strokes with each other. Dibble, it seemed, was not going to let Kelly pass him this time, and as the two boats sped toward the finish line together, the cars following the race along the shore began to blow their horns with growing excitement. The boat race had become a fierce battle, and sooner or later one man would have to break.

Dibble's pride was on the line. He had brought many fans down with him from Canada, promising them a good race in which he would emerge as victor. Money, of course, was part of the motivation to win. But Kelly couldn't afford to lose either. He knew that his East Falls contingent from the Gunboat had probably staked their most precious family heirlooms on the race. Despite the heat, neither man would back down. Kelly's eyes began to sting from the sweat, dripping down from his furrowed eyebrows, and the unavoidable pain began to seep into his muscles. Soon, he knew, the pain would become intolerable, but he fought against it by counting off each stroke and focusing on the fact that Dibble had to be suffering equally. The real trick was not to show the pain. Now, in fact, was the time to strike harder, and so he forced himself to take a "power ten" and empty himself of his final reserves.

To Kelly's surprise, the ten hard strokes took him clear of Dibble by an entire boat length. The Canadian seemed unable to respond. His earlier move had indeed proven too costly. As the two scullers crossed the line, separated by a two-second distance, they immediately slumped over their oars. Kelly had won again in a brilliant battle, but the effort and the heat had severely drained both men. As they sat in their boats, drifting in the light current, several minutes passed before they could even lift their heads and acknowledge one another. It was their custom to shake hands after each race, however, so finally Kelly and Dibble slowly began to maneuver their sculls in toward one another, like two tired boxers falling together in a clinch. It was then, as they drew closer, overlapping oars, that Kelly looked over at Dibble and noticed he didn't look right—his face was very pale, a ghostly hue of greenish-white.

Before Jack could comment on this, his Canadian rival graciously extended his hand. Kelly reached out to meet it, but before they could make contact, Dibble's expression suddenly fell lifeless and he collapsed. His huge body pitched sideways into the Schuylkill, and automatically Kelly swung into the water after him. As he did, however, the iron rigger from Dibble's boat caught him in the solar plexus and completely knocked the wind out of him. While Jack was struggling to regain his breath, he looked down below the surface of the water and saw Dibble's body beginning to descend. He quickly dove under and grabbed one of his wrists, pinning it to the top of the overturned boat. Then he wrestled the Canadian's head out of the water and somehow managed to hold him aloft until a rescue launch arrived.

~~~

Kelly mulled over Dibble's defeat as he swam in the cool waters of Lake Quinsigamond, waiting for his boat to arrive. In the end, the Olympic Trials at Worcester would prove uneventful, as Kelly and Costello breezed through the finals and Jack won easily in his single. But as Kelly began to turn his attention toward Belgium, he thought about his old rival, Bob Dibble, and their dramatic encounter just two weeks earlier. Heat exhaustion and the effort to hold back Kelly had done him in. Dibble had spent the entire afternoon recovering from the incident at a local hospital, but it took him even longer to reconcile the loss. In the end he would decide not to go to the Olympics. He had discovered, the hard way, that when you picked a fight with Kelly, the consequences were often severe.

Chapter Thirteen

THE MODERN OLYMPIC GAMES HAD BEEN HELD ONLY FIVE TIMES previously, and they were still struggling to develop a critical momentum. The games had originally been revived in 1896, as a way to bring European countries together in a spirit of peace and athletic camaraderie. But the War had broken many nations apart and left others in economic and political disarray. Germany, Austria, Bulgaria, Turkey, and Hungary were not even sent invitations to the post-war event, and the newly formed Soviet Union decided not to attend (and would not do so until 1952). It had been eight years since the Olympics had last been held, and although the Swedes had organized them splendidly in 1912, prior events had not been as successful. Now, after a catastrophic war that had left most of Europe in tatters, their future seemed even more uncertain.

Pierre de Coubertin, a French aristocrat born in 1863, had been the main instigator of the modern games renaissance. A passionate idealist and educator, he had taken three years to secure funding and garner widespread interest in the games, originally a Greek celebration begun around 700 B.C. The original Olympics had ended around A.D. 393, when the Christians condemned them as a pagan practice. Coubertin was less concerned with these pagan roots than he was with the "lack of vitality" that he noticed among his French countrymen. The French, he felt, lacked the necessary physical prowess to defend themselves, and so he had undertaken a quest to inspire greater physical well-being.

His travels eventually took him to England, where he became enthralled by the studied cultivation of sport and art, muscle and mind, which had taken root in the British public schools during the eighteenth century. Sport, it seemed, had become an integral part of every English boy's education, if one were to believe popular books like *Tom Brown's School Days*—a virtual treatise on the benefits of soccer, rugby, and rowing that Coubertin read with zeal. In addition to what he found in schools, the Frenchman also discovered that various national "Olympic" games already existed in England, providing the seeds for his greater vision of such an event.

He flattered the British and courted several European contacts in an effort to organize the first International Olympic Committee in 1894. It was quite an accomplishment for the idealistic Frenchman, for earlier efforts to regenerate the Olympics had all failed. Coubertin, it seemed, possessed the right amount of persistence, prestige, and political savvy to finally make the complex political alliances work. An eloquent speaker, he made one of his first appeals to the French organization Union des Sports Athlétiques in Paris, on November 25, 1892, by saying:

"Let us export our oarsmen, our runners, our fencers into other lands. That is the true Free Trade of the future; and the day it is introduced into Europe, the cause of Peace will have received a new and strong ally."

These noble sentiments, of course, had not prevented the Great War, nor protected the French from the German army. Berlin, ironically, had been the scheduled site for the cancelled 1916 Games. The French, who had held a very disorganized second Olympics in

1900, were even less prepared to do so in 1920. The United States was also ruled out as a viable location, too far away to attract a full international contingent. Finally Belgium, which had suffered greatly during the war, was awarded the honor of hosting the ceremonies. It was a mixed blessing, since the war had ravaged the tiny European nation, making funding and materials for the games difficult to acquire.

Construction of the Olympic site had not even been completed when a record 2,600 athletes arrived in Antwerp. The stadium was unfinished, and adequate housing was impossible to find. Many were herded into cramped quarters and asked to sleep on folding cots. Some of the American athletes complained about the poor accommodations and threatened to leave if improvements weren't immediately made. Many, including Kelly, found it difficult to sleep, for his roof leaked when it rained, and loud music played late into the night from a nearby cabaret. Coach Frank Muller was concerned about this and started scouting about for other lodgings. Kelly himself was more interested in the condition of the rowing venue, which was set about five miles northwest of Brussels on the Grand Willebroek Canal.

Despite its promising name, the Grand Canal was not very picturesque. In fact, as the popular British sporting magazine *The Field* described it, Willebroek was anything but grand. It had a rough, unpaved road on its right bank, bounded by an "odoriferous ditch." Its left bank featured a "continuous line of factories," several of which discharged streams of hot water from their condensers right into the murky waterway. In short, the canal was not up to British standards "from an artistic or picnic point of view." On the other hand, as the writer from *The Field* acknowledged, "from a purely business point of view of boat racing, it was as good and fair a test of the merits of competition as is possible to imagine . . . there was never for one single instant the slightest advantage at either station." In the world of rowing, this was truly a rare occurrence. As a man-made waterway, the canal had a fairly uniform depth of fifteen to twenty feet, and no current to affect a difference in the lanes. Accordingly, even though it failed to gain high marks for aesthetics, the Grand Canal was at least remarkably fair.

As soon as Jack Kelly learned that the Henley champion, Jack Beresford Jr., would be competing in his event, he hoped that he would be put in a different heat bracket than the winner of the Diamond Sculls. If his wish came true, there was a small but not impossible chance that both oarsmen might progress through their various heats and face each other in the final. He prayed for this arrangement every morning and every night, and he was overjoyed when Frank Muller announced one afternoon that Beresford would indeed be competing in the other bracket. Kelly was still smarting from his Henley rejection, but now the opportunity for redemption was at hand. His father's words began to echo in his ears: "Whatever is, is best." Now all he could do was to bide his time well—eating, resting, and training—and patiently wait for the larger plan to unfold. On this front, Coach Muller had brought along some other good news. He'd recently met some oarsmen from the US Naval Academy, and after hearing about Jack's inability to get a good night's sleep, they'd invited him to share their quarters.

Like many Irish Catholics, Kelly had been brought up to believe in divine justice and the power of prayer, combined with a dash of pagan superstition. Whenever he left his house for a race or

Jack Kelley Sr. wearing his Olympic racing shirt, 1920. Kelly would have preferred to participate in the Henley Royal Regatta, which was more prestigious at the time. © JOHN B. KELLY III

a long journey, his mother would make the sign of the cross on his back, a precautionary measure for her son's safe return. Whenever he raced, Frank Muller would symbolically "baptize" him in river water, a purification ritual pre-dating the modern Christian practice. Kelly's relationship to God, in fact, was very Old Testament in nature, a deal-making style of petitioning his deity that offered self-sacrifice and physical purity in exchange for divine intervention. He hadn't taken a drop of alcohol during the entire decade of his rowing career, despite constant invitations from friends. And Kelly had certainly made other, larger sacrifices to arrive at this moment in his life, putting off a career and a marriage.

In his mind, however, any hardships he had endured were only a part of God's master plan—to put him through "the crucible of life" and test to make sure that he was fit to be a champion. Now he was ready. Nothing would be sweeter than to face down the English champ, to beat the man who had taken away the prize that he had set his sights on for so long. Kelly put all of his longing into a single prayer and promised God that if he would just set him up against Beresford, he wouldn't make another request for a long time. It would be up to Jack to fulfill his own destiny.

Curiously enough, the opponent whom Kelly had set his heart against was more similar to him than he could have ever imagined. Jack Beresford Jr., in fact, shared a lot more with Kelly than an identical first name. Although "Beresford" indeed sounded English, the Diamond Sculls champion was actually the grandson of a Polish immigrant, his father a furniture maker who had dropped his family name of Wiszniewski. Rumor had it that he had made his fortune selling wooden munitions boxes during the war. He was also regarded as "a good oar." Jack Jr. was born in 1899 and had been lucky enough to attend the Bedford School, where he got his first taste of rowing. He was good enough to eventually be elected "Captain of Boats," and stroked the first eight. Like Jack Kelly, who was the former stroke of the Vesper junior crew, Beresford was also a keen sportsman and on his way to becoming an outstanding rugby player when the war intervened.

At age sixteen, he lied about his age and tried to join the British army, only to be called back home by his father. After a year had passed and he was of legal age, he promptly reenlisted. Like Kelly, he was ultimately deployed in Northern France. While this may not have seemed so unusual, the fact that both men sustained leg injuries during the war that focused their attentions on rowing was certainly a unique coincidence. Kelly had been involved in a truck accident while driving ambulances; Beresford had been shot and wounded in the lower shin bone. Kelly had to give up boxing because of his bad ankle, one of the many sports he had considered pursuing; Beresford had to give up his dream of becoming a national team rugby player.

Beresford's father, Julius, had begun rowing in London at the Kensington Rowing Club and later for the Thames Rowing Club, and had quickly become obsessed with the sport. When he wasn't in a boat, he was often seen walking along the tideway, studying other oarsmen. His passion eventually earned him an Olympic silver medal as a member of the 1912 British coxed four. But it took a war wound for his son to spend any serious time in a scull and to take any interest in his father's furniture manufacturing business. During his convalescence after the war, Beresford Jr. began rowing dories along the Cornish coast and liked it well enough to progress into lighter craft. A natural athlete with an overzealous father, Beresford quickly began to ascend the ranks. First he won the Wingfield Sculls, which served as the national sculling championships in England, and then he confirmed his superiority at Henley by winning the Diamonds. If his ascent in rowing seemed unnaturally fast, it was only a taste of things to come. Jack Beresford Jr. was on his way to becoming one of the most decorated oarsmen England would ever produce.

With his high, Slavic cheekbones and neatly parted blond hair, Beresford Jr. cut a dashing figure in a boat. He weighed only eleven stone, or 154 pounds, but he had a powerful upper body, an enormous reach, and the tenacity of a terrier. At age twenty-one, his only apparent deficit was that he didn't yet have the competitive seasoning of his American rival. What he did possess was the optimism of youth and a natural feel for rowing. By comparison, Jack Kelly's rise to prominence had been more gradual and hard won. He was now thirty-one years old and had been in boats for over eleven years. Still, even if "the Iron Man" from Philadelphia was in phenomenal shape, it certainly would take longer for his older body to recuperate between races than it would for a twenty-one-year-old. And since he had taken on the additional challenge of competing in the Olympic double sculls, many thought that Kelly had spread himself far too thin.

Just to get through the heats and face the blond-haired British champion, in fact, Kelly would have to defeat another outstanding sculler, Clarence Hadfield D'Arcy. Hadfield D'Arcy was a New Zealander who had won the singles event at Henley the year before in 1919, when the race had been called the Peace Regatta. That year, an exception had been made to allow professionals to compete against amateurs, and the New Zealander had beaten all comers. In his own heat, Beresford would have his hands full as well, against a Swiss sculler named Max Schmid who had won the European Championships. There were ten single scullers in all, representing Great Britain, New Zealand, Switzerland, Sweden, Denmark, Czechoslovakia, Holland, Italy, Belgium, and the United States.

There were also four other rowing events, including coxed pairs, coxed fours, double sculls, and coxed eights. The US Naval Academy was representing the eight, and a four from Pennsylvania Barge Club was also competing. The American crews, however, were not yet held in very high esteem, for they had never crossed the Atlantic to compete in any of the European Championships, nor attended the Olympics in Sweden. The story in Stockholm was that the US oarsmen were given no funding by the AAU and were told that they would have to pay their own way. Most of them couldn't afford the expense, and so they had stayed at home while other American athletes carried the day.

In the first heat, held on Friday, Jack Beresford beat Max Schmid by one boat length, with a fast time of 7:45.0. Trailing both of them was Gustav Zinke, the Czech entrant. All but the British were surprised by Schmid's early dismissal at the hands of the twenty-one-year-old from Thames Rowing Club. Unfortunately for Schmid, the event was run Henley-style, where only the top sculler in each of the four heats would move forward to the next race. The second heat yielded slower times, and the winner, Fritz Eijken of Holland, crossed the line in 7:50.0, well ahead of the oarsmen from Italy and Belgium.

Jack Beresford, 1927. Although Beresford could affect the air of an English gentleman, he was a fierce competitor on the water. © JOHN BERESFORD COLLECTION, COLD ASTON, GLOUCESTERSHIRE, ENGLAND

In his first race, Kelly was paired up against the Nordic champion, Nils Ljunglöf of Sweden. It should have been an easy outing. Not far into the race, however, a vine got stuck underneath Kelly's shell and he immediately began to slow down. By 500 meters, the vine had still not dislodged itself, and Kelly faded back, now two boat lengths behind. He had to act quickly, or his dreams of Olympic glory were going to come to an abrupt end. Normally, when an object got pinned under a shell, there was only one way to dislodge it. The sculler had to come to a dead stop and then back up his boat in the reverse direction. In the middle of a race, however, this was not a viable option, and so in a panic Kelly started "chopping" at the vine with his oar. Miraculously, it broke free. He surged forward, quickly catching the Swede, and won his heat with the fastest time of the day, 7:44.2.

Finally, in the last heat of the day, Hadfield D'Arcy won his match with a very slow time of 8:05.0. It was good enough, however, for him to finish a length and a half ahead of his opponent from Denmark, Theodor Eyrich.

Not long after his traumatic heat in the single, at 3:15 p.m., Kelly had to jump straight into the double scull with his cousin Paul Costello. Their semifinal heat was scheduled to go off at 4:05 p.m., which left them only about fifteen minutes of preparation for their race against Bastian Veth and Koos de Hass of Holland. Costello's nerves, as usual, were a total mess, but the two Vesper comrades still won easily in 7:16, eight seconds ahead of their competitors. As it turned out, there were only six double sculls entered in the Olympics that year, and Great Britain had not even entered a boat. This was due less to a lack of interest in rowing than the devastation of the war. Any European athlete, in fact, fortunate enough to attend the Olympics in Antwerp was also lucky just to be alive.

In the semifinals the next day, Beresford breezed through his race against Fritz Eijken, winning by three lengths and posting the exact same time as the day before, 7:45. Following this heat, Kelly handled Hadfield in his usual fashion—hanging back about half a length behind the New Zealander until the final quarter. Then he picked up the pace and "rowed the heart out of him," as he described it later to some eager reporters. Many British sportsmen who were in Antwerp had bet heavily on Hadfield, and they were noticeably disgruntled by the loss. When the two scullers finished their race, however, Hadfield called out gamely to his American opponent:

"You sculled quite well. You are too bloody fit for me!"

Kelly smiled and waved, admiring the man's candor. Hadfield was a fine sculler all right, but he was clearly not in top form. And if there was one thing that Jack had learned in all of his years of rowing, it was that you had to be fit. You could scull as beautifully as you liked, just as you could box with great artifice, but ultimately it was not about aesthetics. It was easy to forget this about rowing and get caught up in all the technical jargon, the merits of rigging, or the "style" of a crew. But in the end it all boiled down to a battle of wills, and if your opponent could take everything that you had and still keep coming, you were in big trouble. The New Zealander had rowed with nearly perfect form, but Kelly had simply broken him.

Immediately after the race, reporters were abuzz with the news of the Olympic sculling final: The United States would meet England in a sensational matchup. Jack Kelly, the sculler who had been denied admittance to the Henley Royal Regatta, would meet Jack Beresford Jr., the man who had won the event.

Chapter Fourteen

BEFORE KELLY PULLED AWAY FROM THE DOCK TO ROW DOWN TO the starting line, Coach Frank Muller dipped his hand into the murky waters of the Grand Canal and splashed the water over him for good luck. Both of them knew that none of Kelly's prior 125 victories meant anything right now. His fate relied on the outcome of this one race. Paul Costello paced along the dock, a bundle of nerves. He knew it, too. Thousands of spectators, who had gathered along both banks of the Grand Canal, began to sense the growing tension in the air. Over the past few days the press had made it virtually impossible for anyone not to know something about Jack Kelly and his personal history. The *New York Times* gave Kelly a slight edge, but everyone else was undecided. The King and the Queen of Belgium sat in the Royal Box, along with the US Ambassador Brand Whitlock, King George V of England, and other foreign dignitaries.

At the starting line, as Kelly maneuvered his boat into position, a string was drawn tightly across the canal, a Henley technique to ensure that the bows of the two boats would be even. As Beresford swung in alongside him on his left, the starter began to call the oarsmen to attention, explaining the French commands and the flag protocol. Kelly began to utter a silent prayer to himself, which was cut short by a loud salute from the US Navy crew. The members of the eight, who had graciously provided him with food and lodging all week, were keyed up to row a closely contested final of their own later that afternoon against a British crew from Leander. They were also present to collect on a bet.

When both boats were nearly ready, Beresford looked over at Kelly and nodded. Jack returned the silent acknowledgement by lowering the brim of his green cap. Countless days of anger and frustration were welling up within him, creating a surplus of adrenaline, but he knew he needed to stay calm. This was particularly difficult to do with his feet strapped into fixed wooden clogs, preventing him from shifting around from foot to foot, like a runner or a ball player letting off pre-race jitters. Instead he had to sit perfectly still, like a rowing statue in mid-stroke—oars buried and arms extended, legs half bent and ready to explode. Kelly trained his eyes on the Belgian starter, Victor de Bisschop, whom he had studied at some length during the preliminary heats. The man wasn't using a pistol but a striped flag that said *Arbitre,* or "official." He would raise it aloft with the French phrase "*Êtes-vous prêt?*" ("Are you ready?") and then drop it with the word "*Partez!*" ("Go!"). Everyone, of course, either listened to the starter's voice or looked at the flag, but Kelly did neither. Instead, he focused on the man's prominent Adam's apple, which he knew would jiggle just prior to the second command. When he saw the jiggle, Kelly flew off the line—a few critical strokes ahead of Beresford.

The Middies from the US Navy were stunned, for they had studied both men in the preliminaries and calculated that Beresford would be a little quicker off the starting line. Based on this research, they had bet Kelly a champagne dinner that he would be trailing the Englishman after the first ten strokes. They hadn't factored in Kelly's surprise tactical maneuver. Beresford, too, was caught off guard and quickly countered by taking several strong strokes at a very high cadence. Eventually, with a great deal of exertion, the younger sculler edged his way out in front.

It must have felt good initially to take the lead, just as it had for many of Kelly's opponents. Slowly, however, as the race progressed, Beresford sensed that something was not quite right. Although he had gained a half-boat-length margin, he couldn't seem to increase this or "break contact" from Kelly. It was almost as if there was an invisible rope connecting his boat and the American's. When he raised his stroke rating at the five-hundred-meter mark, Kelly took it up as well and stayed right with him. When Beresford surged again, at one thousand meters, Kelly again matched this effort and continued to maintain his exact, annoying position just abreast of Beresford's stern.

It was clear now to the British sculler that the American preferred to sit back and wait to make his move. It was too late to do anything about this or to consider changing tactics. He had to stay in the lead. Beresford had come through the halfway mark with a time of 3:42, ten seconds faster than anyone in the heats. Even when you factored in the slight tail wind pushing the two boats down the course, this was a blistering pace that would be difficult to maintain. Kelly sensed it, and occasionally began to look over his left shoulder at Beresford, gauging his physical condition. The race had become an intense game of cat and mouse, but with the American constantly bearing down on the Brit, it was becoming more and more apparent that Kelly was the predator and Beresford the prey.

By 1,500 meters, Beresford had finally begun to show some signs of weariness. His strokes became choppier and his breathing more labored. Still, Kelly waited to make his move. If he went too early and the Englishman found a second wind, the younger sculler might be able to hold him off, thwarting Jack's patient, row-from-behind strategy. Kelly was waiting longer than he ever had before, but he was also competing against one of his strongest opponents. Doubts began to creep into his mind, when suddenly an odd image emerged. It was a vision of his mother, sitting on her porch on Midvale Avenue in her favorite rocking chair. She said nothing, but smiled and rocked in silence, waiting to greet the victor of the race.

Suddenly, Beresford veered over into Kelly's lane. The umpire barked out a loud warning to the leader. Before stringent rules about lanes had been enforced, this was once a tactic used by the old professional scullers. It threw "wash" at the trailing sculler and made it difficult to row through the turbulence of the lead boat's wake. In this case, however, Beresford was simply tired. Kelly sensed it. He also knew that if he surged now, straight ahead, and managed to touch oars with the Brit, Beresford would be disqualified and the race would be handed to Kelly on a technicality. But this was not the way that he wanted to win.

As Beresford was still adjusting his course, Kelly decided to make his move. It was a sudden, almost violent display of power. In a rapid flurry of strokes, Kelly actually rowed around his opponent, making it look like he was impatient to get by. It was none too soon, actually, for there were only a hundred meters left to row. Now it was Kelly's race to win or lose. A single boat length ahead, he kept a watchful eye behind him, still worried that the Brit might have something yet left in him. Every bone and muscle in Kelly's body ached from the effort to pass Beresford and hold the lead, but with each stroke he reminded himself that his opponent had to be enduring equal pain.

"Harder, Kelly, harder!" he goaded himself.

As the two boats sped toward the finish line, fifty thousand excited fans began to yell and clap and create a loud roar. Kelly's last-minute surge had brought everyone on both sides of the canal to their feet. There were naval officers in their dress whites and families with small children, floating along the banks in pleasure boats. Beresford was pale now and Kelly was numb, but somehow both men crossed the line a mere second apart. Kelly, the underdog, had won, but the British sculler hadn't buckled either. The crowd continued to applaud wildly for both oarsmen as they came to rest. The dramatically close contest would go down in the Olympic chronicles as one of the best singles matches ever witnessed. Kelly's time was 7:35.0—a world record.

Kelly looked down at his chest, still heaving for air, and suddenly saw the American flag embroidered on his white shirt. He stared at it for a while, almost mystified. The reality of his circumstances hadn't yet settled in. Part of him was still in the filtered state of mind that he and Beresford had entered, blind to everything but each other. Who were all those strange people, standing on the shore? He blinked, and slowly began to remember who and where he was, but for a brief moment he had become a boy again—as if, in finally completing his childhood dream, the years had melted away. He began to recover his composure as the two boats were called over toward the Royal Box. Beresford, too, had been silent for a long while, perhaps replaying the race over and over in his mind.

"Nice race," Kelly finally called out.

Beresford nodded. "Great race yourself. Well sculled."

It was a brief exchange between the two scullers, but right now it was all that they could manage. Kelly's normal post-race ritual was to scull up alongside his opponent, overlapping his oars on the other man's boat in order to reach over and shake hands. This was certainly the gentlemanly thing to do, but he sensed hesitancy in Beresford's voice. Was it rudeness or simply respect? For Kelly the race had been so emotionally charged that he was still looking for a reason to dislike his British-born opponent. Only later, on dry land, would the two become friends.

As Beresford and Kelly waited patiently in their boats, Hadfield D'Arcy rowed out to join them. He would be awarded third place for posting the best time among the semifinalists. As the flags from each country were raised on separate poles, the melody of "The Star-Spangled Banner" began to fill the air. The New Zealand flag stopped first, then the British flag, and finally the Stars and Stripes. It reached the top of the highest pole with the closing notes of the national anthem. Kelly lifted his chin up to try to hold back the tears. He felt the gooseflesh rise all over his body as the music gave way to the roar of the crowd. He still could not believe where he was and what had just happened. King Albert looked especially pleased with the results and invited Kelly over to his rowing club, the Royal Club Nautique du Gand. He wanted to show him around and present him with the club colors. But first, Kelly had another appointment with his cousin Paul Costello.

As he put his boat away and tried to ready himself for his next race, Kelly suddenly did not feel well. He was lightheaded and a sharp pain had begun to develop in the pit of his stomach. The pain grew so intense that he had to lie down for a few minutes while Costello grew more and more concerned. Finally Paul fetched a trainer from the Navy crew, despite Kelly's assurances that he was all right and that he had rowed conservatively in the single to save some energy for their race. Jack admitted that he hadn't eaten anything that morning, for fear of getting cramped up. Perhaps it was just a case of nerves, the trainer suggested, the psychological exhaustion of unburdening himself of the Henley curse.

Costello didn't feel very well, either. During Jack's duel with Beresford, he had run along the canal for the entire mile and a quarter, instead of resting before his race. The thrill of watching his cousin win had been worth it, however, and looking down at Jack now, writhing in pain, Paul suggested that maybe they should just drop out of the doubles final.

"We got what we came over here for," he said.

"Don't talk crazy," Kelly replied. "This is the Olympic Games. Nobody quits here. I got my championship, and now we are going to get you a medal. Come on!"

"But do you feel well enough to row?"

"I'm fine now," Jack said. "The pains are gone. Don't worry anymore. This one's in the bag."

By the time Costello and Kelly had paddled up to the starting line for their double sculls final, they seemed to have fallen back into their usual good humor. Jack attributed his stomach ailment to nerves and informed his cousin that the pressure was gone. He would be just fine. They would have a nice little paddle down the Grand Canal, and then Paul and he could pick up their gold medals at the Royal Box. As Kelly prattled on with his pre-race banter, Costello grew more quiet and grumbled to himself. He wondered whether he liked his cousin better when he had been indisposed. Kelly was now in a state of total euphoria and seemed totally unconcerned about their race. But from Jack's perspective, racing in any team boat was a breeze compared to rowing in a single. This was especially true when you had Paul Costello in the bow, a bulldog of a man who always seemed to pull harder than his partners. Kelly never told him this directly, but their boat went fast mainly because of Paul. Jack's primary job, in fact, was to regulate his cousin's enthusiasm during the race by holding down the stroke rating as long as he could.

Because of unequal pairings during the heats, it would be a three-boat final, with the Italians and the French matched up against Paul and Jack. The Frenchmen had won the European Championships that year, and they had been given a "row over" in their heat, with no opponent to face them. Because of this, they were extremely well rested and ready to show what they could do. In their own heat against a boat from Norway, however, Paul and Jack had posted a time that was ten seconds faster than anyone. The way Kelly saw it, he and Paul could afford to sit back and relax for a little while, while France and Italy simply wore themselves out. Then, just as he had in his single, he would bring up the pace and row right through them.

But as the boats went off the starting line and settled into their chosen race cadence, it was soon clear that Costello was not comfortable with Kelly's strategy. After five hundred meters, Paul looked over his shoulder and saw that they were down by nearly two lengths. He began to panic. He studied the muscles on his cousin's back and calculated that Jack was not rowing very hard.

"Come on," he said. "Let's go!"

"Quarter mile horses," Jack replied, referring to the two other boats, battling for the lead.

Costello was silent for a little while longer.

"You'll wait too long!" he finally shouted.

"Patience is a virtue," Kelly shot back. He knew that he was probably driving his cousin crazy, and he took some amount of pleasure in it. As they rowed past the thousand-meter mark halfway through the race, they were still trailing the leaders. Costello was getting more and more agitated.

"Don't you want to win this one?" he blurted out.

Kelly smiled. "All right, Mr. Costello, let's go!"

Suddenly the US boat began to lift out of the water, surging ahead, as Kelly unleashed the stroke rating. It was the moment Costello had been waiting for all along, and he threw his full effort behind the oars. In a mere twenty-five strokes, Paul and Jack were even with the Italians and the French, who had battled themselves into a state of fatigue. They continued to move away easily and when they were finally ahead by a comfortable margin, Kelly looked over his shoulder and said to his cousin, "Now, Mr. Costello, there's your boat race. Win it. I want to bow to the King again as we go by."

"We haven't won yet," Costello yelled back. Just then a plane flew overhead, its engines whining loudly.

"Wouldn't it be terrible if that plane dropped down and knocked two champions out of the boat?" Jack prodded his cousin.

"What do you mean, two champions?" Costello hollered. "I haven't won anything yet!"

They continued to bicker all the way down the Grand Canal, well out of earshot of the other boats. After the race had ended, Paul received his first gold medal and his own invitation to attend

King Albert's post-race party. A few hours later, as the King had promised, a car came around to collect the two oarsmen and drove them to the Royal Club Nautique du Gand. As the two cousins entered the club, they passed down an aisle lined by young girls who threw flowers at them as they walked by. Jack turned to Paul and said, "If only the boys in the Falls could see us now, they would be tipping their hats."

King Albert, who was an enthusiastic oarsman himself, began talking animatedly to Kelly, expressing his admiration, when Jack suddenly remembered that he had promised to call his mother. Excusing himself from the King, he ran to find a telephone to report the good news. As it turned out, however, Mary Kelly had already received word from a Philadelphia reporter with the *Evening Bulletin* who had relayed the message through a cable service to Midvale Avenue.

"It's just as I suspected and vindicates Jack," Mary Kelly said to the reporter. "I was confident that Jack would win the title, and what makes it more noteworthy is the fact that he beat J. Beresford Jr., winner of the Diamond Sculls race. You know Jack's entry was refused for that race.

"And you might add," the Irish matriarch continued, taking advantage of the publicity to deliver a small lecture, "that now he has won nearly all the rowing honors possible, it is about time he cut down on athletics and attended strictly to business. There are more important things than pulling a boat on the Schuylkill River!"

While Mary Kelly was holding court among the local Philadelphia reporters, her son was in the company of King Albert, who graciously plied him with a celebratory drink. It was the first alcohol that Jack had swallowed in quite some time, but he felt it impolite to refuse. The champagne, unsurprisingly, went straight to his head, after a long period of abstinence and the rigors of the day. Soon everything and everyone seemed wonderful to Jack Kelly. It was like Christmas come early. He looked around for Paul to congratulate him again, but his cousin had been commandeered by a group of fun-loving Italians, who had made Costello an honorary teammate for the evening. Jack smiled, for he had actually planted this idea in their heads by suggesting to them earlier that his cousin possessed Italian blood. With Paul successfully kidnapped, Kelly celebrated the second half of the evening with his friends from the navy crew, who owed him a champagne dinner. The Middies were in good spirits, too, for they had won their final against the crew from Leander, in a race even more dramatic than Kelly's. They had come from behind to win by only six feet.

After a long evening spent visiting various nightclubs in Antwerp, Jack finally lay down in his cot, only to find himself kept awake by the four seat of the navy eight, a Southerner named Edward "Country" Moore. Moore, who had drunk more than his share of champagne that evening, worked himself into a state of insomnia by wondering out loud, again and again, "What would've happened if I had caught a crab?" At first, Kelly laughed and tried to calm Moore down by reminding him that the race had already been rowed, and he hadn't caught a crab. But when Moore kept repeating his self-doubt, Jack began to silently wonder to himself, "What would have happened if I had caught a crab?" As the walls spun around them and their thoughts turned inward, neither oarsman ever found a satisfactory answer, or a way to get to sleep that night.

Chapter Fifteen

THE OLYMPIC AWARDS CEREMONY WAS HELD THE FOLLOWING afternoon in a stadium that had finally been completed at the conclusion of the Games. It was only half full of spectators, however, for many of the local townspeople were still living in post-war poverty and could scarcely afford the high price of admission. When it was Kelly's turn to receive his two gold medals, King Albert turned to his sons and said, "Regard this man well. I rowed, and I know how difficult it is for a man to win the Olympic singles, but to win both single and double in the same afternoon is a feat that may never happen again." His words were, in fact, prophetic. He then turned to Jack and told him that he would commission a special award for his outstanding accomplishments and have it sent to his residence in East Falls. After King Albert finished praising him, Kelly was surrounded by a host of Italian and French counts, who plied him with endless congratulations. He normally didn't mind getting attention for his athletic feats, but he was unused to being embraced and kissed by a battalion of noblemen, and he finally broke free.

"You'd never get away with that sort of thing back in East Falls," he told Paul Costello, who was standing nearby enjoying every minute of Jack's discomfort. Having just spent the entire evening with an affectionate group of Italians, Paul had little sympathy for his cousin.

Both of them were now anxious to return home and resume their normal lives. Along with several other US Olympic athletes, they made their way to Liverpool to board the British steamship *Carmania*, bound for New York City. As Olympic gold medalists, they were treated to first-class quarters, but when they discovered that some other American athletes were restricted to third class, they complained loudly until the special arrangement was annulled. Everyone would travel first class, together. A larger conflict soon developed when the *Carmania* stopped over in Ireland in order to pick up more passengers, and Pat Ryan, the US Olympic hammer thrower, took it upon himself to invite all the Irishmen up to the first-class lounges. Despite strong protests from the British deck stewards, the 270-pound hammer thrower persisted, and soon tensions were running high between British and Irish passengers.

Hostility came easily between the two groups, which were engaged in the long-standing Anglo-Irish War. Ireland was pushing for the right to govern itself, and England was dragging its heels. Part of the delay in granting the "Home Rule" privilege was caused by World War I, when both countries agreed to put the decision on hold. No one, however, had expected the war to last more than a year, and when it did, a group of Irish rebels secretly contacted the Germans to get support as they plotted a revolt. This joint effort, the Easter Uprising of 1916, was a failed attempt to attain freedom that made England and Ireland even more wary of one another. Now four years later, Ireland was still occupied by the Black and Tans, the British police force.

Onboard the *Carmania*, whenever a group of Brits sang "God Save the King," Pat Ryan and his newfound comrades would

strike up a chorus of "Wrap the Green Flag Around Me, Boys."
It was an ironic choice of song, for while most people ascribed
it to the Easter Uprising, it was actually written in Chicago in
1865 and sung by the many Irish immigrants who fought in the
American Civil War. Odder still, Queenstown, the port they had
just stopped in, had once been the main departure point for most
of the Irish immigrants who had left for the United States. Paul
Costello and Jack Kelly were returning home from the same port
that their ancestors had once left, fleeing British tyranny and the
poverty that came with it.

When the boat full of Olympians finally landed in New York,
Paul and Jack were met by a small delegation from East Falls,
including Father John Kelly, the pastor of St. Bridget's, and Bessie Dobson Altemus, the daughter of James Dobson. Altemus had
befriended Jack's sister Grace before the war, and she now took
an interest in his activities. After a brief round of congratulations,
the two oarsmen were escorted to a special train, waiting to take
them straight to Philadelphia. In Nova Scotia, they'd gotten word
of a celebration planned for them back in their hometown, but
they had no idea what lay ahead. When they disembarked in Philadelphia early the next morning, it seemed like the whole city had
turned out to greet them. The mayor and his cabinet were waiting
on the station platform, along with the policemen's and firemen's
marching bands. Beyond them was a massive crowd of 100,000
fans, held back by a squadron of mounted police.

As Kelly scanned the huge crowd, he suddenly noticed a sea of
green. Thousands of people were wearing the same type of green cap

that he had worn in all of his races. The sight was overwhelming. It was as powerful a tribute as when he had watched the American flag rise in Belgium, sitting in his boat in front of the Royal Box. These were his own people, and even more than the King of Belgium, they knew the value of his accomplishments. More important to them than the rowing was the fact that Kelly was a local boy, born and raised in East Falls. He had trained on their river, the Schuylkill River. He was Irish in a town that was heavily populated by the sons and daughters of Erin, and he worked with his hands, laying brick in their city. And this man, a common man, had now risen to Olympic glory. As Kelly looked out and waved at the crowd, he realized that it was their glory, too. For with the green caps and the American flags, they had all become Jack Kelly for a day.

He and Paul were escorted to an open car, along with Kelly's mother and a few other members of his family. They were then driven up Broad Street and through a network of streets that ended in East Falls, where every house was decorated for the occasion with homemade flags proclaiming the victory. The Vesper Boat Club sported a banner that said, WELCOME HOME, OLYMPIC CHAMPIONS. Kelly's emotions rose and fell more rapidly as he drew nearer to home. He was being treated like a foreign dignitary, or a king returning to his home country. He laughed out loud, suddenly remembering what he had done with his own green hat at the conclusion of the Games. Triumphant in his defeat of the English champion, he had packaged it up and sent it to King George V. Inside the cap he'd placed a single brick and a note that read, "Compliments from a bricklayer."

It was only the beginning of a long day of celebrations, ending with a banquet that evening at the Fairmount Inn, where Jack had first taken up boxing as a boy. Many of his close friends from East Falls were there to greet him, as well as Mayor J. Hampton Moore and several other speakers who rose to recap the Olympic achievements of the local athletes in attendance. Jack was seated between two female swimmers, Irene Guest and Eleanor Uhl, both from the Meadowbrook Club of Philadelphia. There were several other Olympians on hand from the US boxing and fencing teams, as well as two members of the Pennsylvania Barge Club four that had placed second in the Games.

The mayor congratulated everyone for their fine efforts over-seas. The greatest praise, however, was reserved for Jack Kelly, who was compared to the baseball player Babe Ruth, the race horse Man O'War, and the tennis player Bill Tilden. As he listened to the various tributes and endless toasts, watching film reels of himself winning on the Grand Canal, Jack suddenly noticed an envelope sitting in front of him. He opened it and found a poem, written by his older sister Ann. She hadn't come to the banquet that evening because she was afraid of becoming overly emotional and ruining everything for him. Instead, she sent this message:

> *Little Brother, years have sped*
> *Since I combed your woodenhead,*
> *Washed your ears and cleaned your shoes*
> *And doctored every scratch and bruise.*

> *For you I buttered loaves of bread*
> *And dragged you screaming, up to bed,*
> *Brought many drinks, told stories too,*
> *When I should have lammed you black and blue*

You were your Mother's pride and joy
I'll say you were a pretty boy,
With your snubby nose and toes turned in
And the bark was always off your shin.

With your fingers sore and your feet all wet
I wonder why we called you "Pet,"
But looking back across the years,
Filled with their sadness, joy and tears,
Now seeing you so strong and tall
Well, really, it was worth it all.

After reading the poem, Jack turned his head upward, as he had done on the Grand Canal when they played "The Star-Spangled Banner," trying to hold back the tears.

There was another woman absent from the banquet that night who had also taken special note of Kelly's return. Her name was Margaret Majer, and she was the daughter of a German Protestant family who lived in the nearby village of Strawberry Mansion. Jack had first met her a few years before the war at a local pool where he attended swim meets. He had been instantly drawn to the blonde athlete, who was a competitive swimmer and gave lessons at the German cultural center pool. Margaret knew who Jack was, or had certainly heard of him, and she was aware that other girls had failed to impress him. But Majer had no shortage of admirers herself, and when Jack boldly introduced himself and asked for a date the following Saturday, she informed him that she was busy. Later, when she mentioned the exchange to her girlfriends, they told her that she was crazy to turn him away, since Jack Kelly seldom asked anyone out.

Jack was then twenty-four, ten years older than Margaret, and it was the beginning of a long, drawn-out courtship that would last a decade. The main obstacle in Jack's life had been his rowing, an obsession that left little room for anything else. After the war, he had made a few halfhearted overtures toward Margaret, but soon his Olympic training had taken precedence over his romantic pursuits. Margaret had several ambitions of her own. At Temple University she received a degree in physical education and then began working at the Women's Medical College of Philadelphia, one of the first all-female medical schools. In 1919 her wholesome good looks had landed her on the cover of *The Country Gentleman*, a national magazine that touted itself as "The Oldest Agricultural Journal in the World."

In the Norman Rockwell-style illustration, Margaret was crouched down on one knee, confidently strapping on a pair of snowshoes. She was bundled up in a leather flight jacket and wore a long plaid skirt that draped over her knees. Her hair spilled out from the sides of a woolen hat and rolled forward and down like a golden wave. She was beautiful and stylish and wholesome in the same breath, with rosy cheeks and thin, plucked eyebrows, her gaze swept forward, determined and focused, as she reached down to fix her boots to the snowshoes. She was a modern American woman, both in dress and in character. Shortly before Kelly had left for the Olympics, Margaret had coolly informed her preoccupied suitor that she could not, and would not, compete for attention with his boat. The two fought briefly and then parted ways.

But now he had returned home, triumphant, to a letter that began:

"Dear Jack. I was happy to see your ambition to win the Olympic Championship come true…"

There was more to the note, but it was brief and perfunctory. To Jack it read more like a coach's congratulations than a love letter, and he was about to dismiss it as nothing but a polite formality when his mother intervened.

"Can't you see that she is opening up the door to you again? Now you trot right over and see her!"

Jack shook his head. "After our last battle, I don't think she would want to see me, Ma."

Mary Kelly laughed. "She wants to see you again, or she wouldn't have written the letter."

Mother and son went back and forth about it for a while, until Jack finally relented and asked Margaret for a date. She accepted the invitation, but it would be another four years of up-and-down courtship before the two were finally married. The years in between were a game of romantic hide-and-seek, a pursuit no less relentless than Kelly's rowing quest, but one in which he employed less straightforward tactics.

Jack's main strategy was to skulk about Margaret's neighborhood, appearing at places where he thought she might be. A more direct approach, he reasoned, might lead to rejection. To his dismay, however, the Olympic champ often found Margaret in the company of other young men, an unforeseen obstacle that sent him back to Midvale Avenue in retreat. When his competitive instincts were fully aroused, Jack finally decided that the best way to get Margaret was to incite "the green-eyed monster." He tracked down the best-looking girl he could find and began to show up with her at local dances and ice cream parlors. He made sure that Margaret saw him, but carefully avoided eye contact. Eventually, the strategy seemed to work, and she and Jack began to date more frequently. Margaret was either jealous, or she was simply taking pity on him.

Chapter Sixteen

As he had promised the two women in his life, Jack buckled down to business for the next several months. His life on the river hadn't entirely ceased, however, and neither had his popularity with the press. If anything, his record-setting Olympic crusade had kept him in the public eye, and he was frequently sought after for various benefits and photo shoots. One of the more notable of these included Kelly, his old boxing pal Jack Dempsey, and the racehorse Man O'War. They were all champions in their respective sporting fields. The jittery racehorse, owned by a son-in-law of James Dobson named Samuel Riddle, suddenly panicked when he arrived at the scene, nearly injuring himself. Dempsey stood nearby, smiling uneasily, with a fedora in his left hand and his other fist half closed, as if he were ready to sock the thoroughbred. Kelly alone seemed comfortable at rest, standing with his hands clasped behind his back and his weight shifted casually onto his left hip. It was an "aw-shucks" pose that projected an easy self-confidence, but there also was a quiet intensity about him, a self-awareness that seemed to attract good fortune. Virtually everyone who would meet Jack Kelly would mention it, that somewhere behind the brilliant aquamarine eyes lay an enormous store of charisma.

Accolades for Kelly's gold medal victory kept rolling in, paying him dividends that would last for years. Six months after the

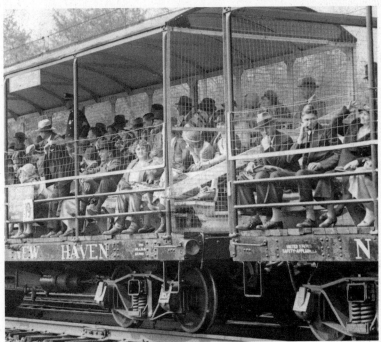

Spectator train, 1932. Kelly and the professional boxer Jack Dempsey
on their way to greet fans (in the first row, on the right). The two Jacks
originally met on the beach in Ocean City, New Jersey, shortly before both
became world champions at their respective sports, and remained friends.
© TEMPLE UNIVERSITY LIBRARIES, URBAN ARCHIVES, PHILADELPHIA, PA

Olympic Games, the King of Belgium's special gift finally arrived
as promised, an elegant trophy of an Olympic athlete holding a lau-
rel wreath. It was neatly inscribed, CONGRATULATIONS FROM KING
ALBERT OF BELGIUM. Not to be outdone by royalty, the Schuylkill
Navy raised $2,500 to create an award called the Philadelphia Gold
Challenge Cup. The prize was presented to Kelly as its first recipi-
ent, and it would be given annually to the world's fastest amateur

sculler, as determined by the US national championships or by Olympic competition.

Along with the championship status came numerous challenges, many of which were announced in the local newspapers. They ran the gamut from the oddly curious to the totally absurd, and most of them would go unanswered. Among the more noteworthy prospects, Kelly challenged the English professional, Ernest Barry, to a match race in Philadelphia. Barry had recently regained his long-standing title as the world's fastest professional on the day before Kelly had become the Olympic champion. Barry never made it overseas. In another challenge that failed to materialize, Jack Beresford invited Kelly to England for the 1921 Henley Royal Regatta. "Lord Beresford," as Kelly had once referred to him in jest, claimed that the 1920 rejection had been a mistake and he was offering an olive branch. Yet despite an evolving friendship between the two scullers, a rematch would never occur. Kelly had everything to lose and Beresford everything to gain. In still another, more bizarre pairing, Kelly mentioned that he and Ethel Bleibtrey, the remarkable Olympic swimmer who had won five gold medals in Antwerp, might try to row a double scull together. Few of these athletic "curtain calls" ever amounted to much, and it seemed that Kelly was now more interested in publicity than actual physical performance.

The reality was that Jack had finished competing in the single, not only because of the enormous time and effort it took to maintain his championship form but also because of the stress of holding onto his mental edge. For those who have never competed on an elite level, this cumulative fatigue might be hard to imagine, but the long hours that Kelly had spent alone in a scull gradually looked less and less attractive. Even when he wasn't sitting in his boat, in the days and weeks leading up to the Olympics, he was always thinking about the race and what it would take to win. Margaret Majer had realized this about Jack when they met before Antwerp, and she had refused to see him until he gave up his racing career.

The time was right for Kelly to step aside and let others achieve their rowing dreams. Paul Costello and Jack Beresford Jr. were both still young, and they would continue to improve with age. Kelly was now thirty-one years old, and he realized that it would be more and more difficult for him to both defend his title and attend to the demands of his career and his family. Jack graciously lent Paul his single and offered to coach him to win the Nationals that summer. Years later, Costello would confide to a close friend and Vesper colleague that he might have beaten his cousin, given the chance. But his claim would never be put to the test.

And no one would ever really know why Costello was asked to leave the Vesper Boat Club shortly after he lost the Nationals that year. Some said that he had been caught partying on the third floor with a bunch of buddies from East Falls; others said that it involved a woman. According to Gus Constance, a Kelly confidant and a fellow Vesper oarsman, the club's demographics at the time were divided between the "genteel" group of Philadelphians and the "toughs" from East Falls, which included Jack Kelly and Paul Costello. Needless to say, some of the high-spirited ways of the Irish brotherhood were frowned upon, and the overall safety of the boat club was brought into question. Other buildings had burned down after evening revelries, and some of them were little more than tinderboxes. In the end, Costello was kicked out as an example of unacceptable "bad behavior," of what would not be tolerated by the membership committee.

It was a move that would cost the Vesper Boat Club dearly.

Immediately after he heard the news, Kelly withdrew his own membership and persuaded several other East Falls oarsmen to resign along with him. As a collective they represented some of the best talent on the river, and the close-knit Boathouse Row community waited anxiously to see what would happen next. The renegade oarsmen talked briefly about forming a club of their own in East Falls, but eventually they decided to join forces with Penn AC. The Penn Athletic Club, as it was more formally known, was originally a downtown social and athletic venue, but it had recently taken over the West Philadelphia Rowing Club located on Boathouse Row. Part of the takeover agreement was that the physical plant would be fully renovated by the new owners. But with Kelly, Costello, and the ex-Vesper group onboard, not only would the run-down boathouse be restored, but the rowing program itself would experience a major upgrade.

Along with the talented group of East Falls oarsmen, Kelly negotiated the return of Coach Frank Muller, who had briefly taken a job at Harvard only to find himself navigating the turbulent waters of university politics. When the Harvard crews he was handed did not immediately succeed, Muller was faced with the unpleasant duty of explaining his losses to disgruntled alumni. Within a few months of Muller's return to Philadelphia, however, his Penn AC boats began to dominate the local regattas. Kelly was elected chairman of the revamped club and saw to its physical resources (compliments of Kelly Brickworks). He also became the oarsman who frequently led the Penn AC crews into battle. While he had retired from single sculling, he stroked a number of the team boats, including doubles, fours, quads, and eights. Unsurprisingly, all of his crews were victorious, save one. But it was in defeat that Kelly often shone the brightest.

It was the beginning of the spring racing season in 1923, and Jack was asked to stroke a Penn AC four that was planning to enter a few local races. Willingly, Kelly obliged. But after spending some time in the boat, he realized that he and his teammates were out of shape. He didn't realize how badly out of condition his crew really was until they were badly beaten at the American Henley Regatta that May by a team from the Pennsylvania Barge Club. It wasn't losing the race that bothered Kelly the most, however, but the way in which Pennsylvania Barge handled their victory. Instead of waiting at the finish line to exchange a few post-race pleasantries, the Penn Barge four, including two former Olympians, began to row directly back to their own dock. When Kelly and his crew had recovered themselves, they caught up with the victors and deliberately pulled up alongside them. Joe Sloak, the stroke of the other crew, was a cocky oarsman whom Kelly disliked.

"Well, Joe," Kelly said, "I can see you don't know how to win a boat race, so keep your crew training until July 4, at the People's Regatta, and I'll show you how it is done."

Sloak nodded, smirking. He assured Kelly that his crew would welcome a rematch anytime. He was obviously quite pleased to have beaten Kelly's Penn AC boat by such a big margin of "open water." This was a term given to the space between two crews at the finish line, when one had broken free of the other and there was no more overlap, or "contact." While it was fine to win by a length or two of open water, extending the margin beyond this distance was generally considered bad form in the rowing world, like continuing to hit an opponent in a boxing match when he had already fallen down. (At Henley, winning margins beyond two lengths of open water were simply recorded with the term "easily," so as not to reinforce the severity of defeat.) Kelly himself had always eased off on his opponents when he'd gained a separation of a length and a half. Sloak and his teammates, however, didn't share this same etiquette.

To beat the great Jack Kelly was to gain immediate prestige. This was especially true among the growing contingent of Kelly detractors, those in the Philadelphia rowing community who weren't overly impressed by his Olympic accolades or his façade of moral righteousness. Who was Kelly, after all, to leave Vesper in ruins and take over Penn AC? Who was Kelly to dictate who rowed in which boat, or to "steal" talent from other clubs? Curiously enough, most of the people who raised these questions didn't come from the upper ranks of Philadelphia's social elite, among whom Kelly did not yet register. Instead, they were members of his own working class, who had begun to realize that Jack had now risen above them on all fronts—athletically, socially, and financially. This was something that wasn't tolerated well in the Irish community. It was like winning in life by a margin of open water.

A month later, the two crews met again, but this time Penn AC was better prepared. Kelly had subjected his crew to a grueling month of training, in which they covered six miles of water every weeknight and twelve miles on Saturdays and Sundays. The word on the river was that Pennsylvania Barge was putting in identical mileage, as this was a grudge match and another chance to beat the great Jack Kelly. This time, however, the script ran differently. It was an old one for Kelly, but it never failed to surprise others. Sloak exploded off the line and took his crew to a slight advantage over Penn AC. Since the boats were straight fours, unmanned by a coxswain, it was even more crucial not to fall too far behind, out of visual range of the other crew's bowman. Kelly bided his time coming through the first mile, however, setting a rhythm that he thought his boat could handle. The Penn Barge boat was still a few seats up, and pushing hard trying to gain even more distance.

As the two boats emerged from underneath the Strawberry Mansion Bridge, hundreds of fans began to scream at them from the shore. Substantial bets had been placed on both Penn AC and Penn Barge, both of which possessed a dedicated local following. By now Penn Barge had moved up to about a half-boat-length lead and showed no signs of tiring. With half the race now over, Kelly suddenly realized that he would not be able to wait any longer to make a move, as he normally did in his single scull. The push had to come earlier, and it would be long and painful, just as it had been during his race with Bob Dibble. The real question was whether his Penn AC crew would go with him, and how Sloak's boat would respond.

As Kelly gradually took up the stroke rating and the power, his boat slowly surged forward, closing the gap between themselves and Penn Barge. Sloak noticed the move and responded, urging his crew to try to maintain the lead. Coming into the final quarter mile, however, the boats had drawn even. The tips of their oars were only four feet apart, and the men in both crews could hear each other breathing. They were beyond being able to vocalize real words, but occasionally a hostile groan would be loosed, hurled at the other boat on the back of an exhalation. Stroke after stroke, the two crews traded the lead, driving forward when the oars were levered in the water and relying on glide between strokes to maintain speed. Rowing was the art of balancing finesse and raw power, of harnessing often barbaric emotions by keeping your mind in your own boat.

Kelly forced himself to look forward, not at the other crew, but his vision suddenly began to blur. His head was throbbing, his legs ached, and with each stroke he silently called out one of his competitor's names, cursing them in his mind. He had never rowed this hard in his life. Every race, it seemed to him, boiled down to the moment when either you cracked or the other crew did. But something else happened when a race stayed this close, making the situation a little different. Like ancient Roman boxers who were tethered together by a rope, two equally matched crews could mentally "clinch" and refuse to let go of one another. This phenomenon made victory an uncertain proposition. But now it was time for the final sprint. Both Sloak and Kelly brought the stroke rating up to forty beats a minute, and Kelly found himself closing his eyes at the end of every stroke just to make it through to the next one.

Finally a gun went off and all the oarsmen slumped forward, practically falling over their oars. As Kelly glanced over, he saw that his crew had won by three feet, a nominal margin in crew racing, but a victory nevertheless. For several minutes, none of the men in either boat could move, and they floated in silence beside one another. When he had finally recuperated enough to speak, Kelly called over to the other boat,

"Well rowed, boys. Now let that be a lesson to you!"

Chapter Seventeen

A FEW MONTHS LATER, KELLY WAS LESS VERBALLY ADEPT AS HE stumbled through a marriage proposal to Margaret in which she had to finish every other sentence he began. Wooing her had proven even more difficult than vanquishing Pennsylvania Barge, or any other rowing adversary. The Olympic athlete, it seemed, was not yet an Olympic lover. This was unsurprising, for the focus of Kelly's life thus far had primarily been on himself and on fulfilling his athletic quest. But as it did with many men's lives, marriage would signal a shift toward helping others, both within Kelly's own family and the larger Philadelphia community around him.

In January 1924, the Kelly-Majer wedding was held at St. Bridget's in East Falls, and Margaret was five minutes late. Jack's friends took full advantage of her tardiness to feed his growing anxiety over the long-anticipated event. Paul Costello, his best man, suggested with a straight face that the bride would probably not show up. Paul had suffered at Kelly's hands on more than one occasion, and now he was finally getting his revenge. When Margaret finally did arrive, Kelly found himself both relieved and then worried about something else: Now the marriage was actually going to take place. He was more nervous than he'd been before any of his races, and his childhood friends unsuccessfully tried to calm him down. Finally Paddy Neilan, one of his old pals from the Gunboat

Jack Kelly Sr. and Margaret Majer on their wedding day, January 30, 1924. © TEMPLE UNIVERSITY LIBRARIES, URBAN ARCHIVES, PHILADELPHIA, PA

Diner, suggested a last-minute exit strategy. When Margaret began to walk down the aisle, he would yell "fire" as loudly as he could. The churchgoers would immediately stampede out, and in the confusion Jack could make a quick escape.

It was a good enough plan, but it was lacking in certain details, such as where Kelly could go into hiding. But if some of Jack's neighborhood pals were worried about losing him to matrimonial bliss, they were soon reassured. After the wedding, Jack and Margaret took a brief honeymoon in Bermuda and then settled into an apartment at the site of the old Gunboat Diner. The landmark restaurant had been torn down only a few years earlier, and its passing was a symbolic harbinger of Kelly's new life. He began to settle into his bricklaying business with more discipline, and promised to hang up his oars for the time being. Thompson-Starret, the same company that he had once worked for as a telegraph boy, now commissioned him to build a twenty-four-unit office building.

For a few months that winter, Jack Kelly appeared to be settling in to the responsibilities of married life. Then one day that spring he came home and informed Margaret that they were going on a second honeymoon of sorts. The truth was that he and Paul Costello were going to row a double in the Olympic Games in Paris. But Margaret could come along, Jack explained. Paul's original plan to row the single had recently fallen through when he was defeated by W.E. Garrett Gilmore, another fine Philadelphia sculler, at the Olympic trials. To salvage the loss, he had impulsively asked Kelly to jump into a double scull with him, and they had won the race easily.

The way that Jack told the story to Margaret, it seemed like the Olympic plan was something of a lark, but actually he and Paul had been planning to row together for months. Margaret, of course, was less than pleased. She raised a feeble protest, asking Jack what would happen to the brickworks while he was away in Paris. But Jack had anticipated this question and assured her that his foreman could easily look after things. Besides, it was only a two-week trip, and when they returned, he promised that he would finally settle down for good and start a family. Kelly, it seemed, had not been quite ready to give up rowing after all.

On the way over to Paris that June, however, Kelly received a minor shock from Dr. Graeme Hammond, head of the Olympic medical team. Hammond had been doing some routine physical examinations on the SS *America*, after treating several athletes for symptoms ranging from infected toenails to tonsillitis. All told, twenty-two athletes found themselves in the ship's infirmary, a small epidemic of minor injuries and illnesses. Either the ship's crossing was giving birth to a spate of bad luck, or the doctor was overly cautious. Kelly was inclined to think the latter, for after his routine checkup, he was informed that he suffered from a "weak heart," probably from overtraining. Hammond told him that it was probably all right for him to row in Paris, but afterward he should retire from competition.

A few days later, a noted Philadelphia physician named Dr. Judson Daland rendered a second opinion, proclaiming Kelly the most perfectly built athlete he had ever seen. Yes, he did have an enlarged heart, but that was typical for an oarsman. His body required more oxygen and therefore a higher volume of blood. Daland not only put Kelly's fears to rest but also promised him that when they returned home to Philadelphia, he was going to commission R. Tait MacKenzie of the University of Pennsylvania to have Kelly's physique rendered in bronze. Jack was entertained, if nothing else, by all the fuss that was being made over him. The "bad heart" story even made it back to the Philadelphia newspapers, and when he arrived in Paris, telegrams started appearing, pleading with him not to compete.

When Paul and Jack showed up at the Olympic Village, they were surprised to discover that there were no accommodations for them, as many of the athletes in other sports had arrived earlier and had already begun to compete. Eventually, they were moved to an old cavalry barracks, with a porch overlooking a busy street. As they were unpacking, Paul and Jack heard a loud whistle go off that sounded like a fire alarm. Then they heard shouting. Jack ran out onto the balcony and saw an elderly woman shouting for help. She was on a second-floor balcony, just across the street, and the first floor of her house was on fire.

Kelly quickly vaulted over his second-story railing, hung from his long arms, and dropped to the ground. Then he ran across the street to find out exactly what was happening. Several people were shouting in French, but no one seemed to be doing much. A few bystanders tried to explain things to Kelly, but he couldn't quite understand. He had forgotten what little French he had learned during the war. No matter, he thought, the situation was clear enough, and he hadn't forgotten his rescue training from the US Ambulance Corps.

Kelly flew up the stairs and quickly lifted the old woman into his arms. On the way down the stairwell, he held his breath as he moved through thick clouds of black smoke. By the time he reached the street, the Frenchwoman had fainted in his arms, but she was safe. As he was transferring her to another person's care, a local man who spoke English finally explained to Kelly why everyone around him had been reluctant to help. Apparently, some high-voltage wires had become crossed with ordinary house lines and over 2,000 volts of electricity were now streaming into the houses. Until the tension line was taken out, the fires would continue. Not only that, but the lethal current had made the entire area into an electrified booby trap. This is what the French locals had been trying to explain to Kelly before he dashed into the house.

His ignorance had inadvertently turned him into a hero, but even after Jack understood the true danger of the situation, he still felt compelled to help. He ran back into the burning house and tore a sheet from one of the beds. The loud whistling noise was still moaning through the air, a sickening sound created by an electrical transformer. He rolled the sheet into a makeshift rope and slung one end of it over the high-tension wire. With a giant heave, he brought it down. Kelly was operating on pure adrenaline now. A young Frenchwoman ran up to him and started dragging him by the hand to another house where his help was needed. When they reached the residence, the woman pointed. There, just inside an iron gate, a man lay on the ground, either unconscious or dead. As Kelly began to approach the gate, an American Army officer who was a member of the US equestrian team rushed forward to stop him.

"Don't go in there!" he shouted. "Everything between the trolley tracks and that iron fence is charged with enough electricity to kill you."

For the first time, Kelly hesitated and felt his adrenaline slowly give way to fear. Yet there was the young woman, and now two others, standing beside him pleading for help. He ran through the open gate to the house, being careful not to brush the gate on the way past. He got to the man and flipped him over. Then he saw a ghastly sight. Underneath the body were eight of the man's fingers, lying in a small pile. Apparently he had tried to grab the high-voltage wire with his bare hands, instead of using a sheet as Kelly had done. The current had severed his fingers and knocked him out. As Kelly looked at the man's fingers and then his own hands, he immediately felt sick and weakened. A host of fearful thoughts invaded his mind. What if he had been this man, dead or crippled, all for trying to be a hero? Jack's body suddenly began to shake uncontrollably, and he broke into a cold sweat.

Then he noticed that the man wasn't dead, for his breath still rose and fell at regular intervals. But could he lift him up and carry him out? Kelly wasn't sure anymore. His knees had begun to shake, and he felt weaker by the moment. Luckily, just then, he felt some-one else by his side. It was Bill Hapgood from the US rowing team. The two of them picked up the Frenchman and carried him safely out of the yard, well past the electrified fence. Then Jack immediately had to sit down and rest before he passed out. He could do no more. He had been extremely lucky and foolish at the same time, but his ambulance corps training had taken over. He remembered now how many men had acted bravely during the war, often those who simply fell into a heroic role as a matter of pure circumstance. Like being an athlete, courage was not simply a matter of natural talent, but of losing yourself in the moment and doing what needed to be done. And then, of course, there was the matter of luck, and of being in the right place at the right time.

In the days that followed the bizarre incident, there was talk among the press of Jack and Bill being decorated by the French government with the Legion of Valor, but the moment soon passed as everyone was swept back into the excitement of the Olympic Games. Jack and Paul sailed easily through their heats and won the double sculls final again. But W.E. Garrett Gilmore, the US single sculler from Bachelor's Barge Club, was upset by Jack Beresford Jr., who came back to win after placing second to the American in the heats. By winning an Olympic gold medal in the single, Kelly informed Beresford, he would now be awarded the Philadelphia Gold Challenge Cup, the honor that had begun with Jack's victory in 1920. Any hard feelings between the two old rivals were long forgotten, and they could celebrate their victories together. Their friendship would deepen and last until death.

For many World War I veterans, however, the Paris Olympics would provide a mixed homecoming. The memory of the battlefield still ran strongly through their veins, like the perfume that rose from the factories on the lower Seine and wafted through the air along the rowing venue. The Games were being hosted in Paris partly to honor Pierre de Coubertin, who was retiring from the International Olympic Committee. But ironically, for some veterans the city was a painful reminder of the very thing that Coubertin had hoped the Olympics would alleviate.

PART THREE

Kelly Sr. swinging daughter Grace at the beach at Ocean City, 1935.

Chapter Eighteen

GEORGE KELLY CERTAINLY HAD NEVER LIKED THE WAR, AND WITH Jack's help he had been honorably discharged from the Army less than a year after he had arrived in France. He had hated nearly everything about military service: the discipline, the bad food, the lack of privacy. He didn't care for the company of most soldiers, who were rough and crass and lacking in the social graces. What he longed to do was to write plays. Before the war, he had followed his brother Walter onto the stage, barnstorming across America in small- to medium-size productions where he had begun to establish himself as both an actor and a budding playwright. His first one-act play, *Finder's Keepers,* had met with some success before the war, and he longed to write more. When he bumped into brother Jack in France, in fact, he had been compiling notes for a bigger play called *The Show Off.*

Like his younger brother, George was a strikingly handsome man. Over six feet tall, he had jet black hair slicked straight back and parted down the middle. His dark brown eyes were soulful and introspective, his chin less chiseled, his lips less severe. In manner and bearing, he was also very different from Jack, more gentle and fussy about small things, like the proper way to make tea (loose tea leaves and never a tea bag). Unlike his athletic brother, he had no wish to return to East Falls. Ultimately, New York City was his destination. And so, like any good actor, he refined his voice, removing any trace of street-tough Philadelphia from it, and proceeded to wash clean his personal background as well. In the remade version of George Kelly's childhood, he never worked at Dobson's Mill as a laborer; he was always a draftsman. He didn't drop out of school; he had a private tutor. In this manner, he selectively modified the details of his life to make it seem like he was a member of the upper middle class, even borrowing rituals straight from the British, like afternoon tea.

And finally, George Kelly was a smashing success. On August 23, 1924, his first big play made its debut in New York, and the entire Kelly clan—including Jack, Margaret, Walter, Ann, and Elizabeth—took the train from Philadelphia to Penn Station. Even seventy-two-year-old Mary Kelly, "the Dowager," accompanied them. As they approached the theater, Jack grabbed his mother's elbow and strong-armed her over to the other side of the street. When she began to protest, he spun her around to face the marquee. In big bold letters it read, THE SHOW OFF BY GEORGE KELLY.

"Go ahead and hurt me, Mary Kelly," Jack whispered in her ear, "but you'll be sorry when my name is in lights." Mary Kelly quickly rubbed the tears from her eyes and erased any tone of emotion in her voice as she informed Jack that she was ready to enter the theater.

As the Kellys sat and watched, they saw much of themselves in George's play. The cast received six curtain calls, and the show was a huge success, hailed by critic Heywood Braun as "the best comedy which has yet been written by an American." The inspiration for his work came mostly from his childhood memories of East Falls, where his quirky neighbors were transferred easily onto the pages of his plays. Many of his characters were easily identifiable to anyone who had ever lived in the Falls, a fact that also made his residence there untenable. George's plays were often about middle-class families and the delicate balance of power that existed between husband and wife. *Craig's Wife*, his next offering, was a character study about an obsessively neat woman who drives her husband crazy with her compulsive behavior. The satire would win him a Pulitzer Prize, launching the next Kelly son into the limelight.

In 1926, two years after George's big debut, Mary Kelly took to her bed and could not rise. She was seventy-four, and she was simply worn out. She had raised ten children, and she had been the mainstay of the family for over fifty years. She had been the exchequer, the cook, and the disciplinarian; also the poet, the philosopher, and the empress dowager. She had ruled with a strong hand and tried to rein in her children whenever they had gone astray. The results, for the most part, were impressive. Patrick Henry was a successful contractor, as was Charles. Walter was an internationally acclaimed actor, George a soon-to-be famous playwright. And Jack was a three-time gold medal victor in the Olympic Games. As her eyes traveled from one child to the next, she had every reason to be proud; she showed no fear of passing into the next life.

"Don't cry over me, do you hear?" she told the bedside gathering. "God made his plan perfect. Don't let anyone try to break it, or he will break them!"

Even on her deathbed, she was issuing orders. Jack had earlier fetched Father Bonner at his mother's request, and he sat with Mary now, holding her hand. Of the children, only Walter had not approached his mother's side and stood off in a corner of the room still wearing his overcoat.

"Don't you want to come over here and stand next to your mother?" Father Bonner inquired.

"No, Father," he said, "this is close enough. I'm too well acquainted with that left hand."

It might have been a line from one of brother George's plays. Without Mary, however, the Kellys were now a family in search of a second act.

Ever since Jack Kelly was a boy growing up in The Falls, he had developed an attachment to a piece of open land that sat on the corner of Henry and Coulter Avenues. It was an old orchard where he occasionally played, climbing the fruit trees to pick apples and pears. Now, with his own plans for a family under way, he purchased the lot and had a fellow oarsman-turned-architect design an elegant three-story residence. It was built of red brick, compliments of the Kelly Brickworks, and it was completed in five months, just in time to house Margaret's first child.

An Irish custom dictated the naming of a child after a deceased relative, with the superstitious hope that the newborn baby would inherit some of the qualities of the person who had died. At baby Margaret's christening, Jack's mother had expressed her disappointment that the child had not been named Grace, after her last daughter who had passed away much too early. This was Jack's youngest sister, who had died of exhaustion after skating with him at Gustine Lake. Now that Ma Kelly had passed away, Jack vowed that their next girl would be named Grace to honor her wish. But it would take a few more years to fulfill this promise. A boy would come first, saddled with another destiny.

John B. Kelly Jr. was born on May 24, 1927. He had blond hair and blue eyes, reflecting his mother's side of the family. After his christening, Jack Sr. was drinking champagne with some friends when he suddenly remembered another vow that he had made several years earlier. It had been after his rejection from Henley, when he had been so angry that he had sworn to get even by raising a son who would become an even greater oarsman than himself. This son would carry his name and he would win the Diamond Challenge Sculls, finally forcing the Henley Stewards to put the name J. B. Kelly on the trophy. Thus, both of them would triumph, the son in deed and the father symbolically. Looking at his baby boy and toasting his good health, Kelly remembered his pledge and the fiery emotions behind it. They were still there, smoldering inside him. And now they began to glow again.

At their residence at 3901 Henry Avenue, the next generation of Kellys would be brought up in a world that was very different from their parents'. There would be no lectures about the family finances being tough, and the children would never be asked to give up their education to help keep the creditors at bay. By the time the last of the four Kelly children was born, in fact, James Dobson and his brother had already died and their carpet and plush mill had rapidly fallen into ruins. Henry Avenue, perched high up above the Schuylkill, had originally been the location of the East Falls ruling elite, including the Dobsons who owned "Bella Vista," while the working-class Irish families were clustered nearer the river. But now Jack Kelly had ascended to higher ground, geographically if not socially.

CHAPTER EIGHTEEN

The fifteen-room residence was a small mansion, with a U-shaped driveway that helped usher in the constant flow of guests, contractors, and servants. These last included an assemblage of maids, a cook, and Godfrey Ford, a diminutive black chauffeur (nicknamed "Fordie") who drove the family downhill to St. Bridget's every Sunday morning, where the Kellys were given generous attention for their weekly patronage. There was a tennis court in the backyard that was flooded in the winter to create an ice skating rink for the children, and in the summer, a KELLY FOR BRICKWORK truck would arrive and install a huge metal bin that served as a makeshift swimming pool, put to good use when the family wasn't sojourning at their summer residence in Ocean City, New Jersey. At Christmastime, the large finished cellar became a winter wonderland, complete with a giant train set that circulated around the entire room. And yet, despite all of the newfound trappings of wealth, the children were drilled with the old-school values that had served both of their parents so well.

Margaret, the new "Ma Kelly," might have omitted the constant moralizing and cutting wit that marked Mary Kelly's reign, but she was not short on family discipline. She insisted on good manners at all times, and any infractions would incur a tithe on the children's weekly allowance. "Peggy" or "Baba," the eldest sibling, was cut from the same cloth as her father—handsome, athletic, and eventually quite tall. Before her height began to attract the attention of young men, she was a charismatic pixie who instantly succeeded at almost anything she tried, and she was prone to fearless displays of fun. Jack Jr., or "Kell," was the sole boy, and he quickly modeled his behavior after his famous father. At the dinner table one evening, a guest asked the four-year-old Kell what he wanted to be when he got older:

The Kelly family at Ocean City, circa 1935. Grace, Margaret, Lizanne,
Jack, Kelly, and Peggy (from left to right). © TEMPLE UNIVERSITY LIBRARIES,
URBAN ARCHIVES, PHILADELPHIA, PA

"I want to be a bricklayer and a rower, just like my dad!" came the reply.

For a while, the next Kelly child, Grace, enjoyed being the baby in the family, but this would be short-lived with the arrival of Elizabeth Ann, or "Lizanne." Soon the girl named after her father's deceased sister would fall into the challenging role of middle child, without a satisfactory means to win her father's affection. It was hard to compete with her sisters, Lizanne and Peggy, both of whom were more physically gifted. Along with young Kell, they easily took to the extroverted, athletic lifestyle that was held up as a model by both of their parents, focusing on swimming as their main competitive outlet. Prone to colds and sinus infections, Grace lacked the same enthusiasm for sports. She did, however, seem to be spirited enough. Once, when Kell allowed Peggy into his "boys-only" clubhouse in their backyard but excluded Grace, she tracked down Kell and socked him right in the eye.

Chapter Nineteen

THREE WEEKS AFTER THE SECOND GRACE KELLY WAS BORN ON November 12, 1929, the US stock market crashed. Jack's brother, P. H., was one of the less fortunate ones. He had built himself a big house like Jack and filled it with children. Now the first millionaire of the Kelly clan found himself struggling to make ends meet. It must have been particularly painful to watch his business collapse while his younger brother's brickworks not only survived but also slowly grew more prosperous. Patrick Henry had been the eldest, the Esau of the Kelly clan, while in some ways Jack played the role of Jacob, the usurper. On the surface of things, it hardly seemed fair. After all, P. H. had labored hard for years while he watched young Jack the dreamer playing around endlessly in boats. Fate, however, had distributed favors on its own terms.

Jack stood by, largely unable to help his brother, for the two of them were both in the construction business and often competed for the same jobs. There was also the matter of Irish pride. Many of Kelly's closest friends in East Falls simply could not bear to ask him for help, even when they desperately needed it. Paul Costello, Kelly's first cousin and former rowing partner, quickly fell from being one of the top-ranked Ford auto salesmen in the state to just another faceless man, standing in the bread lines. Unable to make the payments on his first house, he took to selling apples on street

"P. H. Kelly Family & Home—Conrad & Midvale, 1918." A successful contractor, P. H. was the first of the Kelly brothers to experience great wealth. © EAST FALLS HISTORICAL SOCIETY, PHILADELPHIA, PA

corners and eventually suffered foreclosure. Only a year before this in 1928, Costello had gone to Amsterdam and returned home with his third Olympic gold medal, breaking the world record in a double scull with his neighbor Charley McIlvaine. Now he was practically destitute.

Kelly helped those he could, either finding them jobs or sending them to the river, encouraging them to continue rowing to keep their spirits up. He even set out food tables at the Penn AC boathouse, making it a popular destination for many who suddenly found themselves unemployed. Ironically, the Depression proved to be a boon for the Philadelphia rowing community, at least at Penn AC, where the part-time oarsmen who had once been day laborers now found themselves with plenty of free time for training. The results were nothing less than astonishing. The summer following Wall Street's demise, an eight-oared crew from Penn AC won the bid to represent the United States at the European Championships in Liege, Belgium. They were the first Americans ever to compete in these races, and on August 17, 1930, they not only beat all comers but also set a new world record by posting a phenomenal time of 5:18.2 over the two-thousand-meter course. The mark would go unequalled for decades to come.

When asked to comment, Jack Kelly simply laughed and replied, "Now fancy that. A bunch of out-of-work Irishmen beat the best in the world!"

The larger implication was that the Irish could do anything. On dry land, however, the situation for many of them continued to be much less optimistic. One day a former employee from Kelly Brickworks approached Jack for a $100 loan to make it through a dry spell. When Jack gave it to him, the man thanked him and then admitted under his breath that he might have done something foolish and desperate if Kelly hadn't given him the money. Times were tough, and it wasn't just the poor who needed assistance. Not long after this incident, another friend approached Kelly and asked if he would help him run his reelection campaign for Congress. The Republican political boss in his district, he explained, had refused to endorse his reelection, so he had decided to run as an Independent. Kelly naïvely agreed to help, and without thinking twice, he made a speech at a local gathering. People were instantly drawn to the tall, handsome athlete, the local boy from East Falls who had risen from nothing to become an Olympic champion. Like his brother Walter, Jack discovered that he had a natural gift for talking to people, and could shift easily from glib, joke-telling mode into a straight shooter, tell-it-like-it-is style that rang true with moral righteousness.

Not everyone who heard Kelly's speech liked it, however, and a week later Jack received a notice that the assessment on his Henry Avenue house had been raised $10,000. The Republican district boss, it turned out, was also the real estate assessor, and Kelly was now being punished for stepping out of line. The word on the street, soon relayed to Jack, was that he was now expected to apologize and say that he wouldn't do it again. After this mea culpa his real estate assessment would be restored to its original figure. It was Kelly's first taste of local politics, and it immediately offended his sense of fair play. He not only refused to visit the district boss, but he also began to poke around a little more to see how far the corruption of city government ran. He was shocked by what he found. In the city of Philadelphia, there were about two million people, and only thirty thousand of them were registered Democrats. Not only that, but Kelly discovered that the Republican city boss paid the bills of the Democratic leader, making him no more than a figurehead. It was a one-party system in all but name, with nothing to check internal corruption.

Like most Philadelphians, Kelly was a registered Republican, but he decided that he could no longer stick with a party that employed the dirty tactics he had experienced firsthand. As his Irish blood began to boil, he wondered what he could do to put an end to the injustice. J. David Stern, the publisher of *The Philadelphia Record*, had been calling for a stronger two-party system, and Kelly decided to pay a visit to the Democratic leader and offer him help to strengthen the party. This was the same man who was in the back pocket of the Republicans, however, and he had no wish to shake up the status quo. A fellow Irishman, he not only refused Kelly's offer to help but brushed it aside with an indignant laugh. Politics was no place for amateurs, he explained. Jack responded by telling the man to prepare himself for other employment, because he was going to take over the Democratic Party by force.

Kelly knew very little about politics, but he knew something about team building and winning. Little did he realize that in his newly chosen field of endeavor, hard work and good intentions didn't always result in victory. His friends tried to dissuade him from the takeover attempt, explaining that the Republican mob would probably try to ruin his bricklaying business. Kelly, however, had picked his next fight. Even though his days as a competitive athlete had ended, his instincts on dry land were still intact.

Within a few weeks, he had formed the Independent Democratic Party of Philadelphia with himself installed as chairman. The next step was to get a critical mass of committeemen elected, who could in turn elect enough ward leaders. These were the delegates in charge of the various townships, or neighborhood districts in Philadelphia, who could use their voting power to depose the old Democratic leader. Fortunately for Kelly, in addition to a critical mass of disgruntled Democrats, there were many within the Republican ranks who were also unhappy with the current political regime. These men, too, joined the Independent Democratic Party for the 1933 election.

That November, running on a coalition ticket of two Republicans and two Democrats, the Independent Democratic Party scored its first major victory, winning the elections for city treasurer, city comptroller, coroner, and registrar of wills. They had also succeeded in getting a few judges and magistrates elected, and more importantly, enough committeemen to get rid of the old Democratic leader. Kelly was now in charge, as he said he would be, only four months after he had set his mind to it. The only immediate problem for the former Olympic champion was to figure out exactly what his new job entailed.

A year earlier, with the election of Franklin D. Roosevelt, the Democrats had come into power on a national scale, and for the first time in many years, conservative-minded Philadelphians bristled as they witnessed a strong challenge to their seats of power. One of Kelly's first jobs was to serve as federal patronage dispenser for the city, a post that made him immediately popular among the masses of people who were still unemployed. The Depression continued, alleviated somewhat by the public works programs that Roosevelt established. But many were still struggling just to survive. Needless to say, Kelly's newfound political power didn't hurt his bricklaying business. During the 1930s, Kelly Brickworks received an abundance of government jobs, including post offices, schools, and railroad stations. Ultimately, over the next few decades, Kelly Brickworks would account for over 75 percent of the city of Philadelphia's public buildings. And as the young politician began to secure more ties to the federal government, his business would continue to expand, until it became the largest bricklaying company on the Eastern seaboard.

The following year was a gubernatorial election, an office that had not been held by a Democrat in fifty years. With his ascension to the Democratic chair, Kelly had inherited some of the old ward leaders, whose allegiance to the new party was in question, so he assembled a group of sixteen "young, smart, energetic fellows" and created "Kelly's flying squadron." Jack assigned them to the various wards around the city in order to keep an eye on things. Naturally, some of the old leaders didn't care for this arrangement, less so when they suddenly found themselves out of work. Kelly was slowly cleaning up the Democratic organization piece by piece, making it into a well-oiled machine that the Republicans began to fear. When Democrat George Earle was successfully elected governor, the next move was to try to capture the mayor's office. Kelly was strongly encouraged to run, but for the first time, Margaret objected.

Her husband's escalating involvement in politics had now become worse than his tenure in sports. He might indeed be the Democratic savior of Philadelphia, but he was sorely neglecting his duties at home.

"A family needs to have a father around it," Margaret reminded him. "It isn't right for me to have to raise children alone."

Jack agreed with his wife's assessment, but he felt obligated to see his political crusade through to the bitter end. Things were definitely getting more difficult and underhanded, just as his friends and family members had warned. Walter Kelly, in particular, reminded his younger brother that he had once lost his first real fortune running for political office, and he advised Jack to get out while he still could. Sure enough, as Kelly became more of a contender for the mayor's office, he began to experience the sharp edge of negative campaign tactics. When his supporters portrayed him as a Galahad who would clean up city politics, the Republicans retaliated by trying to dig up dirt on him. A detective agency was hired, his phones were tapped, and dictaphones were employed to try to catch him saying something unsavory.

Much to the Republicans' dismay, there wasn't much dirt to find on Jack Kelly. Despite his fiercely competitive background, he was generally regarded as a generous man who would go out of his way to help almost anyone in need, from an out-of-work husband to a kid trying to get into college. He had connections all right, but he used them for good purposes. Even his bricklaying business would frequently perform work at cost for those who could not afford to pay full price, including churches, synagogues, and chapels. In addition, he was running on a New Deal platform that promised to use federal WPA (Works Progress Administration) money to clean up the city slums, reduce local train fares, and promote an eight-hour day for city employees.

And then there was the other side of Kelly, the one that made his opponents equally wary of crossing the line with him. There were stories about how union bosses had tried to take care of Kelly with their thugs, only to have these tough guys return home with broken noses. Despite the fact that he was in his mid-forties, Kelly still knew how to use his fists if the situation called for it. In the end, Republican papers like the *Philadelphia Evening Ledger* had to be content with calling him puerile names like "Handsome Jack" or "the Adonis of Philadelphia." The implication was that the former athlete might have good looks and good intentions but very little substance. Then there was his Irish Catholic background to consider in a city still run by the Protestant elite. These were the

Main Line Philadelphians, who now lived on the other side of the Schuylkill River in wealthy suburbs west of the city that were strung out along the Pennsylvania Railway. Most of them cared little about the condition of the inner city. They had fled from it and were happily ensconced in suburban comfort.

Yet Kelly was making huge inroads with a larger audience. *Time* magazine ran a glowing article about him, listing his extensive athletic and business accomplishments and predicting that he was "virtually certain of victory." They labeled his come-out-of-nowhere effort as "the most stupendous political campaign in the history of the third city of this land," explaining to political outsiders that Philadelphia was historically controlled by Republicans. As the time drew closer to Election Day, Kelly's opponent S. Davis Wilson finally lost his composure and called Jack "an unmitigated liar" during a press conference. It was testimony to the growing strength of Kelly's campaign.

Asked to comment on this, Kelly calmly told a reporter, "I don't believe he said it. In the first place, he can't pronounce or spell unmitigated."

In the end, however, despite a historic campaign that garnered over 330,000 votes, Kelly came up short by 40,000. The Olympic champion had not been able to defeat the Republican machine, but he had certainly weakened it. The last Democratic candidate who had run for mayor had received only 31,000 votes in total. It was a moral victory, nonetheless, and Kelly took his defeat so well that even the Republican mouthpiece, *The Evening Ledger*, saw fit to devote an entire editorial page to him the following day:

Champion John B. Kelly

John B. Kelly persuades us to be a Democrat—his kind. For champion sportsmanship we commend to losers of all time Mr. Kelly's statement after Tuesday's election. The shining part of it is that he meant it. 'The Kellys,' he said, 'can take it.' And the rest was no stiff-lipped effort to put on a good front in the face of defeat. It was in keeping with his assurance that his philosophy of life is, 'Whatever is, is best.' With that he went on with a bit of verse that would be any real sportsman's creed:

Well, you are beaten to earth,
What about that?
Get up with a smiling face.
It's nothing against you to fall down flat,
But to lie there—that's disgrace.
The harder you're thrown, the higher you bounce;
Be proud of your blackened eye.
It's not the fact that you're licked that counts,
But how did you fight and why.

Kelly capped it off with his own words: "I do hope that I am giving you the impression that I am a good loser, as that is what I am trying to convey. I need not tell you I am disappointed, as I would like to have had a chance to show you what I could do, but you, the people, have willed otherwise, so I accept that with the knowledge that every disappointment that I have had in my life has been only the stepping-stone to a greater triumph."

Although Kelly had failed in his quest to deliver Philadelphia from the Republican machine, the majority of US citizens, including a large number of Irish Americans, had already thrown in their lot with Franklin Roosevelt, the Ivy League–educated Democrat who promised a "New Deal" for Americans suffering through the Depression. After leaving a comfortable post at Princeton, the wealthy Protestant had slowly come to be influenced by the doctrines of social justice being practiced by many American Irish Catholics. Roosevelt had been born into the life of an American aristocrat, but as he made his way up through the political ranks in New York, he came in contact with men like Father Charles Coughlin, an outspoken radio announcer who challenged him to face up to the discriminatory beliefs within his own character. Whether by political necessity or personal conviction, FDR emerged as an ardent proponent of the popular labor programs that put many destitute Americans back to work. His Irish supporters responded in turn, not only with their votes but also with valuable campaign funds. And when Roosevelt won his second election in 1936, Jack Kelly climbed to the top of the old Republican bastion in Philadelphia, the Union Club, and pulled down their flag, replacing it with an Irish one.

When Roosevelt came to Philadelphia for a victorious political rally in 1938, Jack was chosen as the speaker to introduce him at the banquet, and afterward the two men sat next to each other. Despite the difference in their backgrounds, they soon found they had enough in common to develop a mutual respect for one another. Roosevelt had been an occasional oarsman himself at Harvard University, but he had proven his real physical courage during his battle with polio, the debilitating disease that had suddenly

"The Big Eight" World Champion Penn AC Crew, 1930. Referred to as "a boatload of Philadelphia Irishmen," this eight trounced their European competition and posted a time that has never been equaled. COURTESY OF THOMAS E. WEIL

beset him at age thirty-nine. While Kelly was off winning Olympic medals, Roosevelt was learning to walk again, swimming every day to regain strength in his legs. No stranger to the challenge of overcoming physical adversity, FDR listened attentively when Jack began to express his opinion that the country that prided itself on physical strength was actually getting "soft."

Kelly told him that he had taken an informal survey of American males and estimated that 33 percent of the men currently eligible for a military draft would fail to pass a physical entrance exam. Roosevelt was dismissive at first and told him that the number would probably be closer to 25 percent. However, he promised to mull over Jack's concerns and give him a larger audience if he could come up with some real facts and figures. At the time, the president didn't care to discuss anything that referred directly to the growing tension in Europe. He had run his campaign on a platform of American military neutrality and economic isolationism. After all, it had been determined that part of the cause for the Great Depression had been the unpaid debts from World War I. Despite growing fears about Hitler and his plans for Nazi Germany, the American public by and large had no stomach for another military intervention that might once again leave them destitute.

Some even thought that Germany was on the right path to recovery, and many had been impressed by the 1936 Olympic Games in Berlin. The Germans had certainly proven their superior athleticism, dominating the Games and capturing the majority of the medals. Others, however, who actually participated in the Games were not impressed by this show of force and the intimidation that lay behind it. Jack Beresford, Kelly's old rowing rival, was now thirty-seven years old and competing in his fifth Olympics. He had been reluctantly put in the double scull that year with a younger partner named Dick Southwood. Many in the British rowing world thought that Beresford was too old, particularly to compete at such a high-level event. The Germans had hired two of the best professional coaches of the day, a Brit named Dan Cordery and Tom Sullivan from New Zealand. Cordery was coaching the double, and Beresford knew that he and his partner would need to row flawlessly in order to beat this well-trained boat. In the heats, however, they were quickly bumped off by the Germans and forced to fall back to the repechage, a consolation heat they needed to win in order to advance back into the finals. They went off the line with everything they had, bluffing their way to a comfortable lead, and then coasted in order to conserve their energy. Fortunately, no one challenged them during the second half of the race, and they advanced easily to the finals. To beat the Germans, however, they would have to use every tool at their disposal, not only their rowing ability but also their wiles.

When they pulled up to the line for the five-boat final, Beresford and Southwood deliberately false started, forcing all the boats to be recalled. As they were realigned for a second attempt, the British double proceeded to further delay the race by removing their sweaters just as the start was to be called. By now the Germans were entirely put out, and when the gun went off, they charged forward at full throttle. Beresford and Southwood were determined not to let them run away with the race this time and trailed along about a length and a half behind. At the halfway mark, they began to make their push, creeping closer and closer to the leaders. With two hundred meters to go, the boats were now dead level. Tom Sullivan could no longer contain himself as he watched from the stands. He snatched off his Berliner Ruderklub cap and cried out:

"The Englishmen have got them! The Englishmen to win, for 1,000 marks!"

The German boat proceeded to unravel right in front of Hitler's box, as Beresford and Southwood pressed their way through them, their lungs and legs screaming in pain. In the end, the British rowing victory was one of only two posted against their Olympic hosts, the second being awarded to the US eight from the University of Washington. When he was asked to comment on England's stunning, come-from-behind victory, Beresford admitted that a crew "must get a bit of hate into their racing."

Chapter Twenty

BERESFORD'S ENTIRE PERFORMANCE IN BERLIN, INCLUDING THE pre-race gamesmanship and the rowing from behind, had been a nod to his old rival Jack Kelly. The two oarsmen, in fact, had kept in touch over the years and had become close friends after their first encounter on the Grand Canal. Now it was 1940, two decades later, and a year into Hitler's conquest of Europe. France had fallen, and England stood virtually alone against Germany. Kelly wrote to Beresford, encouraging him to send his wife and family to Philadelphia, where he would look after them. Beresford declined, but the sentiments behind the offer would not be forgotten.

Meanwhile, now two years after their first meeting, President Roosevelt called Kelly to the White House. FDR had become more and more concerned about the war, and had requisitioned his own physical fitness survey. His findings had borne out Kelly's original estimates. America, indeed, was out of shape, and its citizens were in no condition to defend themselves, let alone to assist other nations. Would Kelly help him promote a national fitness plan, he asked him, and ready Americans for the possibility of war? The job would mainly entail giving speeches to various audiences around the country, suggesting programs that would benefit a broad range of the public. Kelly eagerly took on the job but soon discovered that not everyone appreciated being informed that they were unfit and unhealthy. Others didn't like to be told that they should walk up the stairs rather than take an escalator. After all, most Americans didn't have the time or the inclination to be as fit as Jack Kelly, who came off as a middle-aged Charles Atlas and insufferable do-gooder. After one of his motivational talks, a woman in the audience took particular offense to the tone of his remarks.

"You know what you are?" she said. "You're nothing but a destroyer!"

As Kelly went on the stump for physical fitness, he also turned his attentions back to his family and his four growing children, particularly young Kell. Now that the boy was getting older and bigger, it was time to supervise his athletic training. Kell was a blue-eyed, blond-haired youth who was all too happy to satisfy his father's wishes. One day, when he was about seven years old, Jack took him down to the Schuylkill River and put him in the stroke seat of a Swiss-made double scull. He placed Kell's small hands on the wooden oars, showing him how to hold them, left over right, and wrapped his thumbs over the ends of the grips. Then Kelly got in the bow seat behind his son and shoved the long boat free of the dock, pointing it upstream against the strong current.

The sight of the father and son out on the river elicited mixed emotions from passersby. People strolling on the banks who did not know the Kellys thought the two of them made a splendid pair. It was touching, after all, that a father would take such an interest in his son and introduce him to the sport that he so clearly loved. Even at age forty-five, Kelly Sr. cut a striking figure in a boat, wearing his white 1924 Olympic singlet. His muscular body was living testimony to the active lifestyle that he now preached. His son, by contrast, was an amiable towhead with straight bangs and broad cheekbones—more like his mother perhaps, but a sturdy boy nonetheless, who seemed to take readily to the sport. As the father and the son made their way past the line of other boathouses, however, a few veteran oarsmen watched in silence or even shook their heads. They knew that the scene in front of them was not as innocent as it might appear.

Nevertheless, out on the river, the sculling lessons began. Jack told Kell to go slowly at first and just follow his movements, while he demonstrated technique:

Bend from the hips . . . never overreach—like this—and avoid going back too far at the end of the stroke. Try to catch the water with your oars slightly inclined—like this—and pull the stroke through from beginning to end, bringing the blades cleanly out of the water with a snap—like this. Don't hang when the stroke is finished, but let the hands drop and shoot the arms forward fast. Now, do you think you can remember all that?

Kell nodded and gave it a try. Even though he was only seven years old, he had listened as his father discussed rowing at the dinner table, and most of the terms and concepts were already familiar to him. Not long into his first lesson, the young protégé was already stringing together full strokes and moving rapidly back and forth on the sliding seat. Slow down, his father repeated. Keep your oars in the water as long as possible when you pull through, and as near to the water as you can on the recovery. While Kell was busy rowing, Jack Sr. rested his oars on top of the water like training wheels, steadying the boat and making it easier to balance. Don't drop your shoulders, he corrected. Now take the kink out of your back.

It was a short session, perhaps only fifteen minutes long, but when the two Jacks finally returned home, Margaret asked her son how it went and whether he still wanted to be an oarsman.

"It was fun, Mom!" Kell replied.

Jack Sr. seemed pleased with the outing, too, and a secret smile played on his lips. "I think we have bred ourselves another champion," he finally admitted proudly. "He's a natural if I ever saw one."

"Well, he should be," Margaret smiled. "Look who his coach is!"

All three of them laughed. It was a lighthearted moment and a happy time in the young boy's life. Kell wanted nothing more than to please his parents, who were both demanding and strong-willed in their own ways. While "Pop" Kelly may have ruled the waters of the Schuylkill and local politics, his mother ruled the household. In addition to her volunteer work at the Women's Medical College, Margaret also served as the sergeant-at-arms at Henry Avenue and the day-to-day minister of justice. Her Teutonic authority was unrivalled in the Kelly clan, and she became known affectionately as "the Prussian General." The children were frequently enlisted to help her put on fund-raisers for the Women's Medical College, including an annual circus at the Kelly house. Kell got to be the strong man, Grace was a tightrope walker, and Lizanne and Peggy told fortunes.

Summer was Kell's favorite time of year, when he and his three sisters took up residence at Ocean City on the Jersey shore. It was here that Kell got to surf and row for fun, going out on the ocean in a little fixed-seat "midget boat," custom built for his small proportions. When his father joined them on the weekends, he would play with them for hours on the beach, holding young Grace by the arms and swinging her around like an airplane. On special occasions, Kell would get to go fishing with his father in a double dory lifeboat they named *The Two Jacks*. It was during one of these outings, as they rowed away from shore, that Jack took the opportunity to remind his eight-year-old son about the danger of the sea, explaining to him that it could take your life if you weren't careful.

Just a few days before, in fact, two boys had been reported missing in the local papers, last seen swimming out in the challenging surf. Suddenly, as Jack and Kell were rowing along talking, they spotted something floating in the water. As they drew closer, they realized that it was one of the missing boys. Kell watched silently as his father hauled the limp body out of the water and laid it down gently in the stern. Then he quickly returned to his seat and called over his shoulder,

"C'mon, Kell, let's row for shore!"

His father rowed as powerfully as he had ever seen, and Kell tried to match strokes with him, sensing his urgency. He was frightened now, and he did not understand exactly what was happening. He had never seen a dead body before. When they finally landed on the beach, his father quickly ordered him out of the boat and told him to run off to find a lifeguard. But even as he dashed toward the nearest lifeguard station, Kell realized that the boy was probably no longer alive. He hadn't moved at all from the bottom of the boat, and his face had a strange, bloated look to it. When he finally got to the station, he stammered out,

"T-there's a kid, a-a kid down there. He's drowned, I think!"

Things happened in a blur after that. An ambulance arrived and the boy's body was quickly taken away, surrounded by a group of curious onlookers. Kell couldn't remember much else after this, and he didn't want to talk about it with any of his friends. He was so stunned by the incident that he refused to go near the water for two weeks. The image of the dead boy would stay with him a lot longer, along with his father's words of caution: "See what happens when you get too fresh with the ocean. They didn't respect the ocean."

—◆—

Back home in East Falls, Kell began attending Penn Charter, a private boys' school only a few blocks uphill from his house. Penn Charter was the oldest Quaker school in the country, established in 1689 by William Penn himself, and it sat on a wooded forty-four-acre parcel that would have made its founder proud. The school's educational mission was to bestow upon its students academic excellence, respect for others, and the belief that there was "that of God in every person." More important than all of this, of course, it was a fine place to connect with the right people and eventually secure admission to a respectable college. Kell's three sisters attended the Ravenhill Convent Academy, a Jesuit-run elementary school that was imbued with strict Catholic traditions and administered by nuns. The schools were almost the same distance from the Kelly residence on Henry Avenue in opposite directions, and the girls often walked to Ravenhill by cutting through the private yards on Warden Street, unless it was raining and Fordie had to drive them. Despite their daily religious indoctrination, they often found that they could not suppress some of their father's entrepreneurial nature. On their way back from school in the spring, the girls frequently took it upon themselves to pluck flowers from various neighbors' gardens, without bothering to first secure permission. Later, they often sold the arranged bouquets back to the same people to raise money for the Women's Medical College.

Kell frequently bragged to his schoolmates at Penn Charter that his three sisters were superior athletes, as far as girls went at least, but he thoroughly enjoyed his uncontested position as the only male sibling. He built a tree fort in the backyard and organized a small gang of neighborhood boys who called themselves the "Tomato Men." Lizanne, Peggy, and Grace had their own elaborate clubhouse in the backyard, complete with fine curtains and a working stove. Often the boys would spy on them, and while each club was off limits to the opposite sex, pitched battles occasionally broke out between the two factions. The boys, despite their club name, weren't the only ones to employ rotten fruit as airborne weaponry. One day, however, when Margaret Kelly discovered why the tomatoes from her victory garden kept disappearing, she put an abrupt end to the children's war games.

On weekends and when time allowed, Kell continued to row with his father on the Schuylkill, and at age ten he made his competitive debut as a coxswain for a Penn AC intermediate eight. It was not a particularly memorable debut. For an active child, coxing was a bit of a letdown, not to mention an extreme challenge. To sit still and navigate a sixty-foot boat, negotiating strong currents and other crews, demanded far more concentration than most ten-year-olds could muster. But weighing a mere ninety pounds, Mr. Kelly's son was certainly worth the occasional mishaps.

The following year, due to a bout of scarlet fever, Kell went through a period of physical inactivity. As his stocky body began to accumulate extra weight, some of his classmates at Penn Charter began to call him "fat stuff." His father was not pleased, particularly when he learned that Kell was not excited to get back in a boat again. Like most boys, he now gravitated toward popular team sports like football, and clearly preferred physical contact with others to the lonely exile of a single scull. Jack Kelly, however, saw things differently. The boy simply needed a shot of discipline, just like the rest of America, so he sent him off to military school. When Kell returned, two years later, his baby fat was gone and he had grown into a handsome, broad-shouldered youth. At the military academy, he'd played football, boxed a little, and learned how to ride, physical pursuits that would have pleased most fathers. There was only one sport, however, that was absent from this repertoire.

Charley McIntyre, a junior Penn AC member who was four years older than Kell, was standing around the boathouse one day when he overheard Mr. Kelly talking in a stern voice to his son, telling him that he would not spend the summer with the rest of the family in Ocean City unless he rowed for "ninety straight days on the Schuylkill." From that day on, McIntyre observed that Mr. Kelly's son would dutifully arrive at the Penn AC boathouse every afternoon at 2:30 p.m., chauffeured by his older sister Peggy. The pair would pull up in front of the boathouse in an old paneled station wagon, and after Kell's two hours of practice out on the river, Peggy would reappear to retrieve her kid brother. McIntyre noticed their comings and goings with keen interest, not only because he rowed but also because the oldest Kelly daughter was a stunning beauty, by far the most attractive of the Kelly girls. As the warm spring days passed, McIntyre and his two brothers, Dick and Joe, would become intimate with the entire Kelly clan, close confidants to both Mr. Kelly and his son. Jack Sr. found Charley an easy job in the mailroom of a government office, and he and his brothers were frequently invited to the Kelly house on Henry Avenue.

As the ninety days of rowing servitude progressed, they turned out to be less of a punishment than either Charley or Kell imagined. In fact, when he took to the water again after his two-year hiatus, Kell was pleasantly surprised to discover how enjoyable the experience was and how easily the sculling motion came back to him. For someone like McIntyre, who was just entering the sport, the speed of Kell's progress was nothing less than inspiring. By rowing with his father at a very young age, Kell had developed a natural feel for rowing at a time when his body and his mind were most impressionable. Just as other child prodigies learn to play music or develop fluency with foreign languages, Kell had learned how to scull. As the Eastern European countries would soon prove to the rest of the world, training children from a very early age paid huge dividends at a future date. Their neurons were most receptive and would better remember a motion, sound, or image, and then store it in the subconscious. Even though Kell had moved away from rowing for a few years, a seed had been planted within him and it had continued to germinate, regardless of whether he wanted it to.

When Kell went out for a paddle with two veteran scullers one day, he not only found himself completely at ease in a boat but also faster than his older rowing comrades. He was, in every sense of the word, a natural, a precocious talent who rowed far better than men with many more years of rowing experience. As the two scullers paddled alongside Kell, and marveled at his rowing skill, they finally asked if he would like to try a short, five-hundred-meter race, just for fun. The amiable fourteen-year-old agreed, and much to everyone's amazement, he beat the two older men easily. In a year, no one on the Schuylkill River would be able to stay with him, except the man who had first introduced him to the water.

— ⁓ —

That summer at the Kelly summer residence in Ocean City, Kell also began to take an interest in the popular two-man lifeboat races that were held along the Jersey shore. These races were in the heavy, lapstrake rescue boats that Kell had rowed as a young boy with his father, with fixed seats and shorter oars that did not overlap. The wide, ocean-going skiffs demanded a different type of technique than the delicate sculls of the Schuylkill River, with a strong swing of the body toward the bow, held until the oarsmen were nearly lying prone. The workboats were a throwback to the early days of rowing and ironically were the same type of fixed-seat craft that had produced his father's British rival, Jack Beresford.

A strong back and arms were required for the fixed-seat rowing, and so when Kell went scouting along the beach for a partner, he looked for someone who looked as strong as he was, eventually ending up with another teenager named Joe Regan. They were the youngest team assembled among all the lifeguards, who would then compete against each other for the honor of going to the South Jersey Championships. The head lifeguard approved of the new pairing, but Kell informed Regan that his father would also have to see them row together. He was an Olympic rowing champion after all, Kell explained, and he knew everything about rowing and training.

When Mr. Kelly showed up at the beach, the first thing that Joe Regan noticed was how tall and muscular the middle-aged man was. He didn't say much at first, but looked Joe up and down and then had the two of them get in the boat. Originally, Regan's older brother Bobby had been Kell's pick, but he hadn't shown up at the beach when he was supposed to. Bobby was a great swimmer but didn't care much for rowing. Joe was, in a sense, the second string. He grew nervous as Kelly Sr. got right into the lifeboat with them, positioning himself in the stern, facing them. He didn't have to say anything to get the boys to start rowing as hard as they could, continuing on for a mile or so. All the while Mr. Kelly sat silently. Joe Regan noticed, however, that he was staring intently at the puddles of their oars, to see how hard their strokes registered in the water. Finally he motioned for Joe and Kell to stop rowing.

"Very, very good," he said. Regan breathed a sigh of relief. He knew he had passed muster.

Afterward, however, Kell informed Joe that he would have to cut back on his weightlifting, because his father thought his extra bulk would ultimately slow them down. Kell himself was now a trim, well-muscled fifteen-year-old, with an impressive physique that fell somewhere between a champion swimmer and a seasoned boxer. Regan immediately consented because he desperately wanted to row with Kell and win the Lifeguard Championships. He sensed something special about his rowing partner; he had an expectation of success. And if Regan wasn't sure exactly where this attitude came from, he would soon find out. On the day of the big race, Mr. Kelly pulled him aside, "You know Kell's blind; he can't see a damned thing so it's up to you to keep your eye on the buoy out there. Go straight and make the right return because you can lose the race otherwise. It's your eyes we're depending on."

Fortunately, Regan and Kell led the field of other lifeboats and won the race by a comfortable margin. It was the first competition that Joe Regan had ever won. It was a wonderful feeling, and he suddenly was caught up in the thrill of the moment and the infectious confidence of the Kelly clan. As the pair continued to train together in preparation for the South Jersey Championships, Regan slowly began to understand that confidence and how much of it was produced by the love between father and son. But he also realized that the pressure of Mr. Kelly's expectations constantly rested upon his son's shoulders. Kell venerated his dad, and much of his lifestyle was patterned after his advice, right down to the type of food he ate. After he worked all day as a lifeguard, Kell was in bed by 11 o'clock at the latest and seldom appeared at the summer parties along the beach.

Slowly, as the two teenagers grew closer, training day after day, Kell's lifestyle began to influence Joe. Kell affectionately called him "Atlas" because of his brawny weightlifter's body, and Joe in turn called the nearsighted Kell "Cyclops." But when Mr. Kelly discovered that Joe smoked cigarettes, he exploded and told Kell that he could no longer be in the boat with him. Regan promptly gave up smoking. As he was taken more closely into the family circle, Joe even began going on dates with Kell's kid sister, Grace. Mostly, however, the focus was directed toward the serious daily training required to win the South Jersey Championships, an open race for all comers. It was not a highly publicized event, but somehow Mr. Kelly began to draw attention to it, calling up the members of the press that he knew. On the day just prior to the race, Mr. Kelly called Joe aside again to give him a pre-race talk, reminding him that he was responsible for navigating.

Despite Kell's bad vision, this advice was appropriate given their positions in the boat; Kell sat at stroke, and Joe was the bowman. Traditionally in a double, the former set the cadence and the latter was responsible for steering. During the race, however, Regan's navigation was less than successful, and he ran the lifeboat into the wrong buoy heading out. The seas were exceptionally rough that day, and it took them an extra fifty yards to correct their course. Joe was certain that they had lost the race, and he imagined Mr. Kelly watching them with his binoculars, furiously pacing the beach. As they rounded the correct buoy, however, and began to row their way back toward shore, they suddenly found themselves in following seas. The surf was now pushing their boat from behind, and all at once they were lifted up in the air by a huge, accommodating wave and shot past the leaders in the final stretch.

Regan was relieved; Kell was ecstatic. Mr. Kelly just stood on shore and beamed for the photographers.

Many years later, Kell would admit to Joe that winning the South Jersey Championships was the most thrilling moment of his entire rowing career. That evening, in fact, both oarsmen felt so blessed by the victory that they walked over to the local church. Finding it locked, they knelt and prayed on the outer steps. For Jack Kelly's son, things would only get more and more challenging as time went by, and the waters he rowed on would seldom be so favorable. As for Joe Regan, Mr. Kelly would graciously employ him at the brickworks, and he would try his hand at boxing and other sports. Yet like so many others, he would eventually be relegated to the outer circle of Kelly friends, often forgotten in the swirling wake of their activities. But on that glorious day, Atlas and Cyclops had surfed into victory on a wonderful, lucky wave.

Chapter Twenty-One

CHARLEY MCINTYRE WAS SITTING ON THE STEPS OF THE PENN AC Boat Club one spring afternoon when Mr. Kelly suddenly drove up, got out of his black limousine, and walked straight over to him for a confidential chat. Kelly had a wonderful rapport with all the West Catholic High schoolboys who frequented the boat club, but to McIntyre he was nothing short of a surrogate father. Mr. Kelly had frequently given him jobs when he was out of work, and it was through his means that he and his brothers, Joe and Dick, and all the West Catholic schoolboys were able to enjoy the Schuylkill River.

As it turned out, that was what Kelly wished to speak to him about. Mr. Kelly wasn't someone to beat around the bush and he came right to the point. He was going to take Kell and leave Penn AC, in order to reopen the Vesper Boat Club. Internal political battles had begun to surface at Penn AC, as they frequently did at all clubs, and he was tired of having to fight to get his way. Vesper had lain virtually dormant since 1925, when Kelly and Paul Costello had staged their infamous walkout. Recently, the president, Doc Riegal, had approached Jack and asked him to take the reins. Now Kelly passed the question on to McIntyre. Would Charley and his two brothers want to join them and become the nucleus of the reconstituted club?

He didn't need to promise that it would be an exciting new venture; McIntyre knew that wherever Mr. Kelly went, an important entourage would follow. Of course he wanted in.

As with all of Jack Kelly's ventures, things moved rapidly once the decision had been made. At Vesper, the McIntyre boys along with several other chosen ones were immediately put to work, not only rowing and training but also helping to renovate the old building to turn it into a vital club again. Carpenters were brought in, new rowing shells were purchased, and there was constant cleanup work to be done. Mr. Kelly himself showed up at the boat club at 6:30 every morning and swept the front steps before he went off to work. No one ever sat idle, especially when Mr. Kelly's black limo pulled up, for if you were caught loafing around, you would be treated to a vicious tongue-lashing that would not soon be forgotten. Charley McIntyre knew, more than most, that underneath the well-tailored suit and the soft-spoken demeanor lay a tough Irishman who could cuss like a sailor, catching those who didn't know him completely off-guard.

While he seldom needed to resort to the tough-guy side of his character, it was there when he needed it, like a loaded gun. The polished, patrician façade was a recent addition, adopted by necessity during his political struggles. McIntyre's mother had once related to her son how, during Kelly's mayoral campaign, the East Falls native had been ridiculed after making a speech and labeled as a "dese, dat, and dose guy," uneducated and inarticulate. Kelly was so humiliated by the experience that he immediately sought out Monsignor Bonner, the superintendent of the Catholic schools in Philadelphia. Bonner often trained people in elocution, and he was the same priest who had been present at Mary Kelly's deathbed.

The Three McIntyres: Joe, Charley, and Dick, July 1947. A dedicated
trio of Vesper scullers who became close family friends of the Kelly clan.
Philadelphia People's Regatta. © CHARLEY MCINTYRE

After several weeks of coaching, Kelly emerged a different man,
almost effeminate in speech according to neighbor Gus Constant,
one of the other Penn AC boys who went with him to Vesper. He
had become more patrician, on the surface, but he never fully relin-
quished the other part of his character, and he never let you forget
that he had come from virtually nothing.

One time, as Charley McIntyre and the other boys were taking apart a decaying wall at the boat club, Mr. Kelly pulled up and
began to examine the boards. Inside the old lumber were dozens

of penny nails. Using a claw hammer, Kelly drew one out of a rotten piece of wood. The nail still looked to be in fairly good shape, despite the fact that it was over fifty years old. "There's nothing wrong with these nails," he announced. As the boys watched in disbelief, Mr. Kelly showed them how to straighten the old, bent nails with a hammer, and then told them to save as many as they could.

When Kelly wasn't around the boat club, a rough-edged acquaintance of his named Al Nino made sure that the boys stayed in line. Ostensibly, Nino was hired as the club manager, but he was actually rumored to be Mr. Kelly's bodyguard. An ex-boxer and a trainer at the Philadelphia Sports Club, he held the dubious distinction of having punched a speed bag for seventy-two hours straight. Supposedly it was recorded in the Guinness Book of World Records; at least that's what he told everyone. Around the boathouse, however, he behaved like a regular pit bull, frequently picking fights with the younger boys and taunting them to box with him. There were always boxing gloves lying around the boat club, and all the Irish kids learned how to use them. Nino was tough, but someone on the street might be even worse. And so, after many black eyes and at least one broken jaw, a few of the boys finally reached the age and skill level where they could turn the tables on their harsh tutor. Among them was Kell. In addition to Nino's "managerial" role at Vesper, he was also assigned to privately train Mr. Kelly's son, to "toughen him up."

Like many others, Nino assumed that Kell would be a spoiled rich kid, unable to tolerate the physical demands involved with bodybuilding and boxing. To test this theory, Nino did not hold back during sparring practice, and at the end of their sessions, he often left Kell's face badly swollen and bleeding. Kell, he figured, would quit soon enough. What reason did he have to stay? He was a hell of a nice kid, of course, but nothing like the old man. Yet after a few months of working out with him in the ring, Al Nino realized that he'd been wrong. The flat-footed, nearsighted, good-natured boy could indeed take a punch, and he was beginning to learn how to throw them, too. Soon, Kell was too much for Nino to handle and he passed him on to Tommy O'Keefe, a more experienced, lightweight contender.

On the water, Kell was also making rapid progress, guided by the steady hand of his father's old coach, Frank Muller. Paul Costello was entrusted with becoming the boy's rowing partner, now that Kell was fast enough to move a boat along well. Both Costello and Kelly Sr. kept their singles at Vesper hanging from the rafters, and everyone knew never to lay a hand on the long, delicate shells. A private single, after all, was almost like a man's soul. "Pop" Kelly himself rowed on occasion, but not with the regularity that his cousin had been able to maintain. Over the years, in fact, Costello's rowing had become as smooth and polished as a river stone, and equally hard at its core. Whenever Coach Frank Muller was at a loss for words to explain some subtle aspect of rowing technique, he would tell the boys to just go and watch Paul Costello, who had become the boathouse equivalent of the country club pro. After years of playing second fiddle, it seemed, Kelly's quiet cousin had finally gotten his due.

Everyone realized what a wonderful opportunity it was to be at Vesper during this time, to be around all of the various elements that led to the club's success. As the boys began to win their races, mostly in double and quadruple sculls, they appreciated this fact more and more. But it was not by luck alone that the boys received good coaching, a fine boathouse, and an inspiring group of master scullers whose example they could readily follow. Jack Kelly had made this happen; he was their patron saint. But anyone involved with the new Vesper program also knew that the reconstituted club had been created for one purpose alone: to foster his son's rowing career. Nino, Costello, and Muller worked with everyone, of course, but Kell was the protégé, the rising star.

His first race was to be the annual Schoolboy Regatta, an event held every May among the local Philadelphia high schools. Ever since Mr. Kelly had introduced the West Catholic program to Penn AC a decade earlier, other Boathouse Row clubs had followed suit, realizing that sponsoring a local school was an excellent way to feed their senior crews. A club, after all, would not survive without a constant influx of younger members, particularly with the rise of other organized team sports like baseball, football, and basketball. And so, as he had done with West Catholic High, Mr. Kelly now set up "feeder" programs at Vesper from Penn Charter and LaSalle High.

To the boys, it seemed like Mr. Kelly could do anything he wanted, for everyone knew him and seemed to owe him favors. On one occasion, a group of Penn Charter boys were driving down to the river on their way to practice when they were pulled over by a Fairmount Park guard on a motorcycle. The car was dangerously overstuffed with passengers. The officer walked up to the car and demanded to know where the boys were going and why so many of them were riding together.

"We're on our way to the Vesper Boat Club," they explained. "We're the rowing team."

"Oh," said the park guard. "That's Mr. Kelly's club, isn't it?"

The boys nodded, noticing the favorable change in his expression. "Well, in that case, follow me!" he said. He returned to his motorcycle, zipped ahead, and escorted them the rest of the way down to the Schuylkill River. For one brief moment, they felt what it was like to be in Kelly's entourage, given deferential treatment for the day.

— ◆ —

Tommy McCreesh, Kell's first opponent, was a skinny rope of an Irish kid who barely weighed more than a coxswain. Charley McIntyre was charged with escorting Kell upriver for his first race, rowing alongside him in a single. Even though it was clear that the race was a complete mismatch, McIntyre was surprised to see the anxious, jerky way that Kell executed his warm-up strokes. It soon became obvious that Jack Kelly's son was actually worried about losing to little Tommy McCreesh. He was wearing a replica of his father's famous green cap, perhaps for luck, yet McIntyre felt that he scarcely needed it. No one on the river could touch Kell. He was the golden boy, always tanned and smiling, as if nothing in the world could bother him.

"Relax," McIntyre told him.

"I'm not nervous," Kell said defensively.

After the first three strokes, the race was over. Kell shot out in front, a complete bundle of nerves, and Tommy McCreesh never saw him again. Although McCreesh would eventually develop into a fine lightweight sculler (and a state senator), he was no match for the young Hercules, who had just completed the first of what would become twenty-one straight victories. For Kell, however, finishing the race was more of a relief. After he'd retrieved his medal, he paddled back downstream where his father was waiting for him, along with a throng of local reporters and photographers. Even Paramount Pictures was on hand to record a short newsreel of the event. It was an historic moment, after all. Kelly's son had just won his first rowing competition.

Earlier that day, Kell had asked his father if he could wear the replica of his famous green cap, and it had obviously made the old man proud. But rowing up to the starting line with Charley McIntyre, he had begun to worry. What would happen if he lost, wearing the cap? But for now, at least, Kell had succeeded, and as far as Mr. Kelly was concerned, there would be nothing to stop him from further victory. He would make sure of that.

❦

For better or worse, there wasn't much competition for Kell on the Schuylkill in 1944, because most of the young men who could challenge him were now away at war. One of the few men who could have taught Jack Kelly's son a lesson or two was Joe Burk, a Penn AC sculler who had been the US National Champion for four years in succession from 1936 to 1940. A protégé of Frank Muller and Rusty Callow, the University of Pennsylvania varsity coach, Burk had also traveled to Henley twice, in '38 and '39, and had taken away the Diamond Sculls prize, setting a new course record and raising more than a few eyebrows with his high-stroking, unorthodox technique. But while Kell was beginning his series of easy victories on the Schuylkill, Burk was busy sinking Japanese submarines in the Pacific.

The rise of organized, professional team sports—football, baseball, and basketball—had also begun to lure more and more fine athletes from the rowing ranks. After all, there was no money in rowing. Even the devoted McIntyre brothers, who were always looking for a way to make an extra buck, played semi-pro football with the Philadelphia Flyers on the weekends, a mercenary effort that put $50 in their pocket for every game. Instead of using their real last names, which would have lost them their amateur status in rowing, they called themselves Joe, Dick, and Charley Kelly. Mr. Kelly was not altogether pleased by the honorific deception, for he worried that it might come back to haunt him. His son, after all, was nearly ready to make his bid to become the best amateur sculler in the world, and he did not want anything, or anyone, to interfere with that plan—not even a trio of loveable foster sons.

At Peggy's wedding later that summer, she and her two sisters, Grace and Lizanne, were having a wonderful time. People were dancing, big band music was playing, and it was a magical moment for the eldest Kelly girl. She scanned the room. Everyone seemed to be having a good time, except her father and brother. She spotted them standing off in a corner like two bored ushers, shifting about uncomfortably and looking anxiously at their watches. Finally, when she asked them what was wrong, her father replied that Kell had an important race tomorrow. He really needed to get a good night's sleep. Margaret and Peggy looked at each other in disbelief. Lizanne, who was only eleven years old, finally spoke up: "Listen, Dad, we want to stay and dance. You get your car and pack up your prize pup and take him home and put him to bed!"

The race was clearly an important one. Art Gallagher, another Penn AC member who had won the National Championships in

1943, was the biggest threat to Kell's ascension to the rank of king of the Schuylkill River. Nearly ten years older than Jack Kelly's son, when he finally came up against the seventeen-year-old, he pushed him harder than anyone had done before. When the race was over, Kell lay hunched over his oars for a long while, locking the handles into his belly, so that if he passed out and fell forward, the narrow scull would not flip over. His father had taught him this trick, and told him never to lie back in a boat, which was not only "bad form" but also potentially dangerous. If you lay back and passed out, you might capsize and possibly even drown. This time, however, Kell was okay, but he had driven himself right up to the edge of consciousness, very close to the point of blacking out from lack of oxygen. While his father had relished those moments when he had forced opponents into this state of utter collapse, he didn't much care to see it happen to his son. When Gallagher arrived back at the dock, beaten but satisfied with his performance, Mr. Kelly was waiting for him.

"You almost killed him!" he shouted, infuriated. "You almost killed my son!"

Chapter Twenty-Two

THE NEXT YEAR IN 1945 KELL WON ALL OF HIS SENIOR SCHOOL-
boy races, including the American and Canadian Junior National
Championships. He was now eighteen years old and ready to enter
"open" races as well. One day, just to test his son's speed, Kelly challenged him to a short race on the Schuylkill. Jack Sr. was rowing
in his British-made Sims, while Kell preferred an American-made
Pocock. Out on the water, there was not much difference between
their strokes. Kell was a little beefier in his upper body, but his
father sat up taller and looked more statuesque. When their boats
were more or less lined up, Kelly Sr. called out the start, and true to
form, he jumped ahead of his son a moment before he uttered the
final "Ready all—row!" For a brief length of time, perhaps twenty
or thirty strokes, Jack Kelly was the old Iron Man again, jumping
the start and then waiting for his opponent to catch up so that the
real competition could begin. But this time, when his son finally
closed the gap between them, Kelly stopped rowing; the test was
over. Despite his old racing tricks, Kelly was now fifty-six years old
and finally slowing down. Kell was only getting faster and faster. It
was time to pass the torch.

"I will never race you again," he called out to Kell as they paddled lightly back to the Vesper dock. It was a statement made casually, devoid of much emotion, but Kell knew that it was also an

Jack Kelly Sr. and Jack Kelly Jr. rowing on the Schuylkill, April 14, 1944.
© TEMPLE UNIVERSITY LIBRARIES, URBAN ARCHIVES, PHILADELPHIA, PA

important acknowledgment. In those few words his father had told him that he was now ready for any challenge.

That summer on July 4, Kell achieved his most impressive performance yet at the People's Regatta, winning five events in succession between the hours of 2:00 and 5:00 p.m., including the Junior Single, the Intermediate Single, the Association Single, and the Senior Single, plus the quarter-mile dash in the Senior Single. The feat had never been done before, not even by his father, and would never be repeated.

Turning eighteen also allowed Kell to do something else: fulfill his civic obligation to join the military.

Kell opted for the Navy and was assigned to a base in Bainbridge, Maryland. The war, for all practical purposes, was already over, and the eighteen-year-old spent his days training other rookies in "whaleboats," the wide rescue craft like the ones he had rowed since his childhood in Ocean City. Joe McIntyre, Charley's younger brother, was also at Bainbridge, along with another Philadelphia oarsman named Al Lawn. Mr. Kelly, who knew the admiral at the naval base, called him up and arranged for an eight to be delivered, just so that the boys could "keep in shape." After all, his own training had been interrupted by a year of military service, and he didn't want Kell's rowing to go stale. Before the boat arrived, Kell stayed in shape by boxing, just as his father had done during the war. His months of suffering under Al Nino's rough tutelage finally paid off when he became the heavyweight champion at Bainbridge.

But that spring, when it was announced that the Henley Royal Regatta would resume for the first time since the beginning of the war, Jack Kelly's heart skipped a beat. It was happening all over again, like a repeating film loop: the quest to become national champion, the intervention of the war, the announcement that Henley would reopen for all comers. This time around, however, the Jack Kelly who stood ready to enter the Diamond Sculls event was not a common laborer but a well-bred young man who had attended private schools and was on his way to the University of Pennsylvania. He had never laid his hands on a brick, and there could be no reason for his rejection by the Henley Stewards. Besides, the amateur rules had been altered now, and the manual labor exclusion had finally been removed.

Kelly Sr. was not alone in his desire to have Kell go to Henley, and a coterie of influential Philadelphia sportswriters began to write about the idea, petitioning the Navy to let young Kell go overseas and claim the coveted Diamond Sculls prize that should have gone to his father. As more and more pressure was applied, both in the papers and through political channels, the Navy finally responded favorably. Of course they would like to see a champion in their ranks. It certainly wouldn't hurt with recruiting. A Navy press agent was even dispatched to photograph the budding sports hero, who was set up on a bench holding two mop handles instead of oars. He was no Elvis Presley, who was drafted into the war effort after he had achieved fame, but he was definitely beginning to draw some attention. He had a big, toothy smile and a broad, open face. Along with his athletic ability, Kell had inherited the Kelly charisma, including the ability to get other people to do things for him.

During times of peace, special allowances were sometimes made for athletes in the military to compete in their sport. Early that summer, Kell was transferred to the Philadelphia Naval Yard, where he was given permission to resume his rowing training on the Schuylkill River in order to prepare for Henley. There wasn't much time for Kell to get back in a single and try to regain his speed, perhaps a month or so. By comparison, his father had trained for several years prior to his year of military service, and then spent two years afterward getting ready for his big debut. Kell was only nineteen, still a youngster in the rowing world, and his skills had not been tested against an international field. Art Gallagher, who also decided to put in an entry for the Diamonds, was the only one who had ever really challenged Kell in a race. Beyond that, the teenager had been completely untouched.

Al Lawn, who would soon become Kell's classmate at the University of Pennsylvania, also noticed that Kell had seldom needed to row a full two thousand meters during a race. He usually got so far ahead of his competition that he could virtually coast into the finish line. This was radically different from his father's racing strategy, the hold-back and then sprint-through tactic that had worked so well against formidable opponents. Kelly Sr. had tried in vain to teach this lesson to Kell, but the boy was less patient and often preferred to break out fast and try to capture the lead, even if it destroyed him.

~ ~

In England at the Henley Royal Regatta, the stage was set for the first official competition since the World War II. The expensive prize cups for the Grand Challenge, Thames, and Diamond Sculls events had been retrieved from J.P. Morgan in New York, and the Stewards' Cup had been brought back from Switzerland, where it had been stored for safekeeping. The booms and piles that delineated the straight, two-lane racecourse were reset; the swans removed; and the riverbank along the Berkshire side was cordoned off into the two sections that had existed since 1920: the Regatta Enclosure, open to all, and the Stewards' Enclosure, open for the Stewards, members of the Stewards' Enclosure and their guests. In the latter, proper attire was required, with men in suit coats and ties that showed their club colors and women in dresses that reached below the knee.

Also in Henley was the famous Leander Club. A membership in Leander was an exclusive privilege, often extended to those who had won a cup at Henley. The club mascot was a pink hippopotamus. To become one of the Stewards who oversaw the regatta, you had to be recognized as a stalwart soul so devoted to the perpetuity of the annual event that you would be personally liable for its success—both in financial terms and in committing to the post until death. Jack Beresford Jr. had recently been appointed as a Henley Steward, and it was through his hospitality that Jack Kelly and his son were now provided with an especially warm welcome both at the club and at Henley. Kelly Sr.'s offer of help during the war had not been forgotten.

Along the placid banks of the River Thames, excitement filled the air along with a feeling of trepidation. The war had held back the event for six years, and many wondered whether Henley would ever feel the same again or recapture the quaint, carefree atmosphere of a Sunday picnic. Huge canvas tents were erected on the Berkshire side of the upper Thames, each capable of holding sixteen eight-oared shells. There were smaller tents, too, which served as refreshment areas or changing rooms, and out on the river one could only hope that the usual assemblage of old picnic boats and punts would gather, occupied by natty gentlemen in straw hats and ladies holding aloft colored parasols, floating like lily pads amidst the rush of racing shells. The men were often more colorfully attired than the women, donning a garish assortment of lime greens, pinks, and other colors that identified them as members of the boat clubs of Eton, Oxford, or Cambridge.

As it turned out, the British sporting crowd and their guests needed the nostalgic event more than ever, to help them regain a sense that things could indeed return to normal. To acknowledge this on a national level, Princess Elizabeth and Princess Margaret were dispatched to Henley to help distribute the prizes. Their appearance would make this year's competition a rare occasion, for despite the "royal" billing of the annual regatta, the more important members of the royal family seldom patronized the event.

Even the Irish were sending a crew over from Trinity College to compete in an event known as the Ladies Plate. Ireland was one of the few countries that had remained neutral during the war, and the Trinity oarsmen wondered what sort of reception they would receive. As soon as they stepped off the train from London to Henley, however, they were met by a warm welcoming party, which helped them get installed at their rowing site halfway down the course at Remenham. Once there, several ladies emerged from their houses and provided the Dubliners with various cooking appliances. A spirit of goodwill was in the air.

Jack Kelly Sr., who arrived with his son about a week before the races began, had never actually been to Henley before, and he watched the elaborate preparations unfold with keen interest. He was dressed in a black suit and white spats, while Kell had on his navy whites with black shoes. As the two Kellys walked side by side along the river, they cut a striking image of polar opposites. The upper Thames, too, was nothing like the Schuylkill, and the town of Henley was far more provincial than East Falls. As the giant tents went up along the grassy banks, the whole affair took on a carnival-like appearance to the American millionaire. Despite the singular purpose of his visit, he was soon enchanted by his surroundings. He and his son checked into the Red Lion Inn, one of the old landmark hostelries often frequented by the rowing crowd. Well situated for those who liked to watch the races, it stood just along the finish line on the Buckinghamshire bank. It was doubtful whether there was anyone as excited and nervous about Henley as Jack Kelly, except perhaps his son.

Kell had just turned nineteen, two years younger than Jack Beresford Jr. had been when he first captured the Diamond Sculls. He had brought along his lucky green cap, and en route from London he and his father had stopped at the Sims Boatworks in Putney to pick up a brand-new racing shell. The boat had been special-ordered, just for the week's worth of racing. When the Kellys arrived at Putney, however, they discovered that the single scull had already been shipped along to Henley, so they took their hired car and headed northwest, reaching the riverbank with a few hours of daylight left to spare for Kell to take a quick spin. To Jack Kelly, everything was going along with great ease and expediency, for they had only left Philadelphia the afternoon before. Their plane made two stops to refuel, in Nova Scotia and Ireland, and they were able to sleep for most of the overnight flight. In his competitive rowing days, a trip overseas meant a weeklong journey across the forbidding Atlantic Ocean.

Trying to foresee all possible eventualities, Jack Kelly Sr. had even brought along special food and water for his son to eat during his training—Capon Springs bottled water and frozen steaks from his friend Toots Shore. He had remembered how inadequate his own post-war accommodations had been in Antwerp after World War I, and Kelly was concerned that his son might not eat well or have clean water to drink. Kelly Sr., in fact, had seen to nearly everything for his son, except the interference of another American. Almost immediately after the two Jacks arrived in Henley, they spotted Art Gallagher out sculling on the Thames, trailed by his Penn AC coach Tommy Mack. The pair had arrived a week before the Kellys, and they were as eager to claim the Diamond Sculls as their fellow Philadelphians. Not to be upstaged, Kelly Sr. hired a private launch and proceeded to coach his son through an electronic megaphone, a recent innovation. Tommy Mack was relegated to riding a rented bicycle along the towpath, shouting at Gallagher when he could get close enough to him.

That Saturday, however, Gallagher threatened to become a real thorn in Kell's side when the heat assignments were drawn up. The selections were made on Saturday morning at the Henley Town Hall, and Kell and his father waited impatiently for the draw, standing among the sixteen single-scull entrants. When the heats were finally announced, everyone pounced on the sheets like nervous undergraduates waiting to see to which dorm they had been assigned. The two Americans, for better or worse, had been placed in the same bracket together, along with six other scullers. That meant that if Kell and Gallagher both won their heats on Wednesday and Thursday, they would have to face each other in Friday's semifinal.

During the first few days of racing, Kell easily dispensed with his British opponents, beating W.H. Fullick of the Kingston Rowing Club on Thursday by four boat lengths. Gallagher had a more difficult time with his second opponent, William Jones from Uruguay, but the South American cracked in the last quarter and quickly fell eight lengths behind. Henley was a mano a mano competition, with two boats rowing side by side down a perfectly straight, eighty-foot-wide corridor of water. The distance was one mile, 550 yards. Many oarsmen and crews faltered in the final stretch, having miscalculated either the strength of the current, which could fluctuate daily, or their own physiological reserves. With floating wooden booms lining either side of the course and thousands of spectators lining the manicured banks, Henley was a pressure-cooker of a race with little room for error. While it was true that Joe Burk, the last American sculler to succeed in the Diamonds, in 1939, had run his boat into the booms during the final and still miraculously recovered to win, generally one slip like this meant total disaster.

Now that both Kelly and Gallagher had made it through to the semis, the local crowd began to lament the lack of an English champion and speculate about which American would have to face Jean Séphériadès from the Société Nautique de la Basse Seine. Before the war, the English rowing fans had been subjected to the unorthodox, awkward style of Joe Burk, who had nevertheless rowed largely unchallenged. It was hoped that whoever represented the United States this year would at least demonstrate better rowing form and provide some more dramatic racing.

They were not disappointed, for in the semifinals on the third day, the Henley crowd watched as the two Americans proceeded to row side by side over the first mile of the course. Art Gallagher clung to Kell as long as possible, forcing the favorite to push hard nearly the entire way. In the last quarter, Gallagher finally dropped back three lengths, but the effort to dispense with him had left Kell totally exhausted. His lack of proper training was beginning to show, and despite the steaks, he had lost ten pounds over the past three days of racing. The truth was, Jack Kelly's son wasn't prepared for another strong challenge. In physiological terms, "peaking" for a race was an art form, and it required weeks of planning out work and rest cycles. Kell had barely gotten back in a boat a month before the Diamonds, and he simply did not have the stamina to maintain his racing edge for the week's worth of racing that Henley required.

In the other heat bracket, Jean Séphériadès had proceeded through to the finals with considerably less effort, and had posted an even faster time than Kell in his semifinal. Séphériadès, who worked in Paris as a salesman for a postcard firm, was not an exceptionally large man, but he was an accomplished sculler, having won the European Championships earlier that summer. He was feeling confident coming into the final. The conditions the next day were ideal, with a slight cross-tail wind to help blow the two scullers up the course. At the same time, a cross wind made it challenging to get the boats pointed at the starting line. At the first fire of the cannon, Kell veered straight in toward the barrier along the Berkshire bank. The boats were called back, and the race was begun again. This time the scullers came off the line cleanly and rowed side by side for the first quarter mile, until Séphériadès surged forward to a half-length lead. He maintained the slight margin through the first mile, and then pushed himself farther out to a one-length lead. Kell had been waiting, trying to gauge the strength of his opponent, and now he responded, trying to come from behind. For a while at least, the late move seemed to be working. Wearing his silk green cap and rowing in his brand-new British shell, Kell soon pulled up even with the European champ, and then began to move through him, stroke by stroke.

Thousands of spectators lined the banks of the Thames, and as the oarsmen drew nearer, the cheering grew louder. During a close race like this, the normally subdued crowd became more attentive, rising up out of their lawn chairs for a better view. Jack Kelly Sr. was watching the race unfold from the official's launch, just astern of the two scullers. His son was going to win the Diamond Sculls at last; it was the moment he had anticipating for twenty-six years. Kell had rowed well, waiting for the French sculler to get a little bit ahead of him before making his final move. Jack Kelly was proud of his son. Part of him was rowing the race with Kell, stroke for stroke, experiencing the tension and elation of the close battle. Now was the time to strike at Séphériadès, and he wanted to shout this out at Kell, to urge him on. With only five hundred yards left, he felt his throat begin to tighten. No more than a quarter of a mile was left now, virtually the length of the Stewards' Enclosure, where everyone important would be watching his son.

Then suddenly, Kell seemed to falter. It was a subtle shift, barely perceptible, but it marked the moment when he had broken inside. He began to fade, slowly at first and then farther and farther back, until the distance between the two boats was nearly three lengths. Jack Kelly watched in disbelief from the umpire's launch, and his heart sank. To the man who prided himself on his violent closing sprint, Kell's sudden drop-off was particularly difficult to bear. He wanted to get out of the launch, to yell and curse. Instead he had to watch in silence as the two scullers crossed the finish line. They stopped rowing at once, and Séphériadès fell backward, lying flat and still like a corpse. Kell slumped forward over his oars, cradling them in his lap as his father had shown him.

Back at the dock, Kelly waited for his son. He had things to tell him, important things, about why he had lost the race. Kell had to realize his mistakes and learn from them, if he was going to be a true champion. Jack Sr.'s mother had taught him this, and he needed to pass the wisdom along (How many times did Caesar flunk? How many times was Nelson sunk?) But as Kelly stood there, trying to put his dark emotions into words, his son continued to float along on the Thames. His back was still hunched forward over his oars, the bill of his green cap pointed downward, defeated. He was completely spent, but his mind was still racing. It could not be over, he could not have lost, and what would his father and everyone back home think? While Séphériadès still lay back into the bow of his single, trying to regain his breath, the boy beside him continued to grow paralyzed with fear. His large hands, the same ones his father had been bragging about all week, now began to grip the oar handles so tightly that his knuckles grew white, matching the bloodless color of his face. He had never lost a race before.

After what seemed an impossibly long time, Kell managed to paddle back to the dock, but once he landed, he found he could not get out of his boat. His body suddenly became frozen again, his hands plastered to the oars, and finally his fingers had to be pried loose, one by one. With some help from British oarsman Richard Burnell who was standing on the dock, Kell was lifted out of his boat and carried to shore like a wounded soldier. Séphériadès, too, had to be helped from his boat, and both men were quickly brought into the medic's tent and laid out on tables beside one another. After a few minutes passed, and Kell finally regained full consciousness, he gazed up at his father and quickly asked, "Where's Séphériadès?" Kelly pointed over at the table where the French sculler was being revived by his two handlers. Kell sat up, against his father's protests, and quickly removed his racing shirt.

"I want you to have this, as I think you earned it," he said to Séphériadès, leaning over from his cot to pass him the shirt. Reluctantly, the French sculler took it, completely taken aback. He proceeded to remove his own shirt in trade. In American college racing, the losers often handed over their racing shirts to the victors, but an even trade like this meant that the feeling of admiration between the two oarsmen was mutual. Instead of bemoaning his loss, Kell had made an elegant gesture that Séphériadès would never forget, and it would mark the beginning of a lifelong bond. It was similar to the one shared by his father and Jack Beresford Jr., two men who had also rowed themselves to complete exhaustion.

Chapter Twenty-Three

WHILE KELL AND HIS FATHER HAD BEEN AT HENLEY TRYING TO capture the Diamond Sculls, the Kelly women were enjoying themselves at their summer house in Ocean City. Few people outside of the immediate family circle had heard the bad news yet. The day after Kell lost, however, Charley McIntyre and Paul Costello were walking along the boardwalk, wondering what had happened, when they spotted young Grace. The brown-haired seventeen-year-old was coming toward them, flanked by two male admirers, and she seemed to be in an awfully good mood as she flirted with her companions and ate an ice cream cone. Now that her older sister Peggy had gotten married, Grace had become the center of attention for all the single men whose path she crossed.

"How did Kell do?" Charley asked eagerly.

"Oh, he lost," Grace laughed, looking back over her shoulder. McIntyre suddenly felt sick to his stomach, as if he'd just been hit below the belt. It wasn't possible, he thought. No one could beat Kell. When Grace was out of earshot, Paul Costello turned to him and said, "If the old man heard her say that, he would have slapped her god-damned face!"

Charley agreed but also realized that Jack Kelly's middle daughter was growing more and more like her father every day, and more of a handful than anyone suspected. He wondered if Kell knew that she often sneaked off to the parties along the beach with the older kids. He also remembered how, at the Kellys' annual Christmas party, everyone had been drinking down in the finished cellar, including Grace and her two sisters. Neighbor Ike Levy was there, who owned the local radio station, along with his own daughters, who were good friends with the Kelly girls. Grace was laughing too loudly, and Fordie noticed it. In addition to being Mr. Kelly's chauffeur, he was also a bit of a snitch. Once he had caught Peggy smoking in the girls' playhouse and threatened to tell on her. Now, McIntyre watched as he approached Mr. Kelly and whispered something in his ear.

Grace Kelly with Jack Kelly Jr., circa 1942. © TEMPLE UNIVERSITY LIBRARIES, URBAN ARCHIVES, PHILADELPHIA, PA

"You're flagged!" Kelly suddenly shouted across the room, causing everyone to stop what they were doing. Grace, however, looked straight back at her father.

"What? But I only had one small glass!"

"You're flagged!" he boomed again.

And that was the end of it, at least for the moment.

—◦—

For the past few years, while Kell was being groomed for rowing glory, his sister Grace had been slowly making her own quiet plans. Unlike the rest of her siblings, she preferred acting to athletics, although she dutifully swam with the rest of the Kelly clan on Saturdays at the Penn AC's downtown pool. From an early age, Grace had been more interested in plays and the world of make-believe, and she possessed a quiet but remarkable level of self-reliance. Once, as a young girl, she had been locked in a cupboard by Lizanne, her kid sister, and left there for hours. Grace didn't complain or make a peep, however, and when the closet was reopened, Lizanne was dismayed to find her older sister babbling happily to herself, playing with her toys.

By age eleven, when Kell was sent away to military school, Grace had already begun to perform at a little East Falls theater called the Old Academy Players. Shy, chubby, and rather plain compared to her two sisters, Jack Kelly's middle daughter did exhibit unusual professionalism for her age. During one show, when an older actress forgot her lines, Grace improvised, dropping her handbag in order to distract the audience. Then she quickly turned her back to the crowd and artfully prompted the other actress. Her level of seriousness often fooled casting directors, and she once successfully lied about her age in order to play a role that called for a fourteen-year-old when she was twelve.

When she actually did turn fourteen, Grace commemorated the event by imprinting her birth date in the wet cement of the Kellys' new driveway. That fall, she transferred out of the strict confines of the Ravenhill Convent School and into the more relaxed atmosphere of the Stevens School in nearby Germantown. Kell was now back at Penn Charter, and some of his friends were beginning to express interest in Grace, having noticed that she had blossomed into an attractive young woman. Within a year or so, Jack Kelly Sr. found himself greeting so many young men on his doorstep, asking for his daughters, that he began to call them all "son" and quickly shake their hands before disappearing to watch his favorite TV show, *The Lone Ranger*.

Down at the Schuylkill River, both Grace and Kell attracted an equal amount of attention when she greeted her brother on the University of Pennsylvania dock. Kell had just enrolled there as a freshman, while Grace was beginning her junior year in high school. While she didn't quite know what she wanted to do, she saw that Kell's plans were all laid out for him. Their father, for the moment, did not want him to try out for the college eight, much to the dismay of the coach, Rusty Callow. While Kell was given some time to recuperate from his Henley loss, he was still directed toward sculling and encouraged to row in doubles and quads with the McIntyres. Charley, Joe, and Dick were like Kell's brothers, and if they couldn't help bolster his spirits, nobody could. Kell loved Joe in particular, who was closest to him in age and temperament. Both of them ate fast, talked fast, and were always on the lookout for the next fun thing to do. One of their favorite games that autumn was to row up to the top of the river in their quadruple scull and lie in wait for the University of Pennsylvania.

Rusty Callow knew exactly what they were up to, and he wasn't pleased. When his varsity eight turned around to head back downstream, the Vesper quad would ready themselves. "Run over those damn Irishmen!" Callow shouted angrily. It was bad enough that Jack Kelly's son wasn't rowing for him and his college team, but now this mischievous quartet, stroked by Kell himself, was purposefully getting in his way. Their next move was to shoot ahead of his finest varsity eight and row just hard enough to taunt them, laughing all the way down the racecourse. No matter how hard Callow instructed his crew to row, the Vesper quad would always win the mock scrimmage, and the game never ceased to amuse the spirited foursome. It was during these lighthearted moments, however, that Kell began to enjoy being on the water again. Compared to the unguarded loneliness of a single scull, the team boat provided a welcome sense of camaraderie and shared burden. Charley McIntyre couldn't help but notice the change in Kell, how relaxed he became, almost like a different person. For the McIntyres, it was a pure delight to row behind Jack Kelly's son. When he was in the stroke seat, they simply could not lose.

Joe decided that he wanted to be just like Kell, to have a lot of money, be popular, and ride around in a powder blue Buick convertible. "You can't compete with inherited wealth," his brother Charley warned him. Others knew, too, that there was a price to be paid for the summers on the beach, the cars, and the private school. "I wouldn't trade places with Kell for all the money in the world," said another Vesper member. Back at the boathouse, when Mr. Kelly appeared, things instantly became more serious again.

Kell needed to check everything with his father, whether it had to do with rowing or life in general. Everyone at Vesper did, for they were all indebted to him. And when Charley's brother Joe asked "the boss" if he could challenge Kell for the bid to row the Vesper single entry at the US Nationals that year, he was crestfallen when Mr. Kelly turned him down. The very democracy of rowing that Kelly had once symbolized now stood at odds with his plans for Kell. He was acting more like a local despot who wanted his son to ascend to the throne so badly that he would not let anyone challenge his birthright.

❧

The summer following his freshman year in 1947, Kell was ready for a second try at Henley. He'd won the US Nationals again and put in a full year of training. On June 20 the entire Kelly clan, except for Peggy, boarded a steamship in New York. They were optimistic, and the four-day ocean voyage allowed them to enjoy the wonderful anticipation leading up to the grand event. It was wonderful, of course, if you were not competing and not expected to win. As they stepped off the boat on British soil, Grace and Lizanne Kelly, at ages seventeen and fourteen, looked like twins in full blossom. They were certainly thrilled to be given the opportunity to dress up and the chance to catch a glimpse of royalty.

The British sporting press, which was naturally inquisitive about any foreigners competing in their national pastimes, took a particular interest in the Kellys during their second visit. The whole of England at this time, including its athletes, was still under a policy of meat rationing due to the war, and the rich American interlopers made for excellent copy. Back in New York, Jack Kelly Sr.

had accepted Toots Shore's annual offer of frozen steaks and spring water, and this time Kell had brought over his boat, an American-made Pocock. While the practice of bringing one's own provisions wasn't anything new or unwarranted, the reporters had a field day with it. In Kell's rented rooms above the Red Lion Inn, photographers lined up empty bottles of Capon Springs water and portrayed the naïve twenty-year-old as a spoiled rich man's son who fed on thick steaks but was lacking in the social graces. "Gum-chewing, green-capped Kelly" ran one headline in the *Manchester Guardian*. The muscle-bound American was also reported dashing around the quaint little British village looking very conspicuous with an attractive bottle-blonde on his arm. The young woman, of course, was Kell's sister Grace, who seemed to be enjoying her role as belle of the Henley festivities, along with her little sister, Lizanne.

In the first heat against Ben Piessens, a Belgian sculler, Kell crossed the finish line four boat lengths ahead, with a time of 9:06. After the race, he realized that the strong current and the slight headwind pushing against him probably meant that few records would be set at the 91st event. On the Schuylkill, the racecourse always ran in the same direction as the strong current, giving the water a completely opposite feel. Rowing against the forces of nature, however, did favor bigger, heavier men who could better shoulder the added load. And Kell, as the British press had pointed out, was one of the biggest athletes in attendance, weighing fourteen British stone, or two hundred American pounds. The stocky American could certainly muscle his way against the conditions if they called for it.

Bert Bushnell of the Maidenhead Rowing Club was England's best hope of beating Kelly. At six feet four inches, he was not a small man himself, and during his heat on Thursday, he trounced his fellow countryman, J. B. Brown, by fifteen lengths of open water. In rowing terms, this wasn't much of a boat race, and it was graciously registered on the Henley scoreboard as won "easily." Brown, who hailed from the Loughborough Boat Club, had gotten through his first heat on Wednesday by sprinting off the starting line at fifty-two strokes a minute, about ten beats higher than any normal sculler would consider rowing.

Affecting such a high stroke rating generally led to disaster, either in the form of a technical mistake, such as a crab or misplaced oar, or simply physical exhaustion. Of course, if you got far enough ahead of your opponent, as Brown managed to do, you could then drop the stroke rating to a more manageable pace. Nearly everyone at Henley tried to sprint and then "settle" down to some degree, but the first twenty strokes of the race had to be managed judiciously, like one's initial bet in a poker game. Going out extremely high, as Brown liked to do, was somewhat akin to bluffing in a big game, and then hoping that the other man didn't call your bluff. This, unfortunately, was exactly what Bert Bushnell had done, holding Brown off by rowing only thirty-nine strokes a minute. Even up at a fifty-two, Brown hadn't been particularly effective at creating real boat speed; instead, he looked more like a drowning swimmer, flapping his oars wildly in and out of the water.

Even in the face of a stiff headwind and a medium current, Bushnell had posted a time of 9:13, which was thirty-one seconds faster than Kelly in his next heat against Arthur Holloway. Comparing times between heats, of course, was a risky business, for you had to know the conditions under which each race had been conducted. In Kell's heat against Holloway, which went off just fifteen minutes before the Bushnell–Brown matchup, the American had gotten out to nearly a two-boat-length lead by the half-mile mark. Sensing defeat early on, Holloway had virtually folded, taking his stroke rate down from a thirty-eight to a twenty-four. On the full spectrum of possible stroke ratings, anything that fell below a twenty-five during a race usually indicated one of two things—either total exhaustion or willful abdication. When Kell looked back at Holloway and saw him wilting, he wisely decided to take his own rating down to a mere twenty, conserving his energy for the next race.

If you were an English betting man, comparing Kelly's heat to Bushnell's that day, you might conclude that Bushnell was the slight favorite for the semifinals. At least his times through all of the recorded posts were noticeably faster. Even Bushnell, however, was wary that his American opponent had not shown the Henley crowd what he could really do.

"I haven't seen Kelly row yet this year," he admitted to the press. "I think it's unlucky, and I might be unduly frightened."

The following day on July 4, his anxious words proved to be prophetic. Going off the line at a forty, compared to Kelly's thirty-nine, Bushnell soon found himself a full length behind the American. At the quarter mile, Kell registered a 2:22—five seconds faster than Bushnell's time the previous day. At Fawley station, the three-quarter-mile mark, Kell increased his lead to one boat length, while dropping his stroke down to a comfortable twenty-eight. Bushnell was struggling along behind him, rowing four beats higher, an almost certain sign that he would never be able to catch up. In rowing terminology, Kell was under-stroking his British opponent and still gaining more distance on him. He was, in a sense, "striding" down the course, taking fewer strokes to cover just as much water as Bushnell. The race quickly became another easy victory for Kell, who finished at the Stewards' Enclosure four lengths ahead. Now there was only one more day, and one more opponent left for him to master.

Chapter Twenty-Four

THE STARTING LINE AT HENLEY WAS A BEAUTIFUL STRETCH OF eddy water, wedged between Temple Island and the Berkshire bank. Here the river was narrow and partly shaded from the sun, protected by the tall trees that rose from the island. The trees also helped shelter the course from the prevailing winds, and the shade turned the still water dark and olive-colored. An old British punting boat lay still between the two lanes, and an elegant umpire's launch idled just astern. In the bow of the launch stood a well-dressed umpire, wearing a blue coat and white pants. He held aloft a small red flag. A cannon would boom when the race had begun, indicating the start to everyone waiting at the finish line. There were several other launches of the same sleek design, gliding up and down the course and leaving little wake. Their names were *Empress, Magician,* and *Amaryllis,* and they served as the workhorses that kept the races running on time.

As the launches followed the boats upriver, the course widened and was eventually flanked on both sides by a variety of spectators, some in boats, some on land, thickening in number toward the finish line. Once, before the Temple Island reach had been created, effectively backing up the course two hundred yards, the oarsmen had to race right to the Henley Bridge itself, making for more dramatic, if more dangerous, endings. The little island and the

Beresford leading G. S. Goddard along Temple Island at the final of the Diamond Sculls, 1926. © JOHN BERESFORD COLLECTION, COLD ASTON, GLOUCES-TERSHIRE, ENGLAND

man-made eddy beside it were not only a practical improvement but also an aesthetic delight. The island itself was considered the "jewel in the crown" of the Henley real estate, complete with a miniature replica of an Etruscan temple at its headland, constructed as an architectural folly in 1771 by James Wyatt, the surveyor of Westminster Abbey. Everything about Henley was grand and ritualized and smelled of manicured power, but the Kellys had brought along their own symbolic tokens this time, to remind themselves of who they were and why they were here in England.

Kell had on his green cap, a silk replica of the one his father had always worn and sent off to King George V after the 1920 Olympics. Around his neck he wore a medal of Saint Christopher. Before he left for the racecourse that morning, his Protestant-born mother had even made the sign of the cross on his back, just as Mary Kelly used to do when her son left the house for an important race. And at the dock, as he shoved off to row down to the starting line, his father had kneeled down and scooped up a handful of water from the Thames, splashing it over Kell for good luck, just as his coach, Frank Muller, had once done for him. The entire pre-race ritual was a reenactment of his father's most dramatic race—the green hat, the mock baptism, the blessing of the cross upon his back. They were old customs that now served as sympathetic magic, bridging the two generations of Jack Kellys together and symbolically binding their fates.

"This is the big one, son," his father had said to him as he finally pushed him away from the dock.

As he slowly made his way downstream to the starting line, Kell mused that his father must have been pleased that the program listed him as "J. B. Kelly," dropping the diminutive "Jr." and thereby erasing any difference between their two identities. In other ways, too, the press had begun to mix up their stories. In one article, Kelly Sr. was listed as having "worked as a bricklayer one summer during his college days," while another claimed that Kell was wearing the very same cap that his father had worn at the 1920 Olympics, and referred to it as "his family flag of revenge." His father, he noticed, did little to correct these bits of misinformation, which seemed to make for lively controversy. Other coverage, however, had been less satisfactory.

The center of the controversy was, of course, the original story of Jack Kelly's Henley rejection. By now, it was a moth-eaten tale that few people in England wanted dragged out of the closet. But Kell's appearance at the regatta, along with his father, made it unavoidable. At best, it was called a falsehood, a family myth invented to cover up the real truth about the 1905 Vesper eight; at worst, it was an embarrassing historical moment. And so each time Kell rowed past the Stewards' Enclosure on the way to winning his heats, he had been booed by a small but vocal contingent of British spectators. Whether it was the steaks he ate or his grandstanding father, he was seen as another Edward Ten Eyck, another American "pro."

Now, however, as Kell sat at the starting line, there was only nerve-racking silence and the overwhelming reality of the race. On the surface of things, everything looked remarkably controlled and well-orchestrated. He had carefully backed his honey-colored boat into the tiny starting platform, where it was grasped and held firm by a prone attendant. There was no escape and nowhere to hide in a single scull, and certainly no opportunity to enjoy the scenery. At Henley, more so than at any other race, you felt like a racehorse corralled at the starting gate. Many scullers "cracked" for this reason, losing their nerve and going down the course looking like they'd never been in a boat before. Others flipped, or ran up against the booms. Last summer, he remembered, when he'd raced against Jean Séphériadès, he'd gone off the line such a bundle of nerves that he'd run his boat up against the Berkshire bank. He could not think about this, however, nor about his father behind him, watching expectantly in the umpire's launch. He could not even focus too much on the man beside him, but simply concentrate on one thing now: to make his boat go as fast as it could. In rowing you had to put on mental blinders and not allow yourself to be distracted by the world around you. It was a part of the sport that most outsiders didn't understand. Of course, there was also the extreme amount of pain, and Kell had the added pressure of his father's legacy. Despite his happy-go-lucky exterior, Kell had once admitted to his friend Charley McIntyre, "Every time I race in a single, I sweat blood."

"Are you ready?" the starter called out.

—◆—

It was impossible to say whether Kell jumped the start on purpose. He was certainly unlike his father in this tendency, trying to irk his opponents before the race began. And Carl Fronsdal of Norway, sitting in the lane next to him, hardly merited such concern. The day before, rowing against Bert Bushnell, Kell had posted a time of 8:57, far better than Fronsdal, who won the other heat in 9:24. The Norwegian, however, had won easily by six lengths, which meant that he hadn't been pushed to his maximum effort. Many of the preliminaries, in fact, had been "row-overs" like this, so it was impossible to say who had pushed hard and who had not.

As the boats were realigned, Kell tried to block out all of these useless calculations and other random thoughts. Previous races were irrelevant. Besides, it wasn't about Fronsdal, or any other opponent. It was about his father. He knew this much. Kell uttered a small prayer, trying to regain his focus. Everything leading up to this moment had been laid out for one purpose. He had to win this one, or else. There was family pride involved, but something much deeper. Even his boat, the *V-Grace,* was named after his departed aunt, not his living sister. Kell realized that he was rowing for those who had gone before him, those who had lost something that only he could redeem.

Suddenly the cannon went off, and the boats shot forward in a fury of oars churning the still water. For both scullers, instinct now took over. Breathe, breathe, Kell told himself. Hands away, hands away. Drive the legs. It was his father's voice inside him, but it was also his own. After four hundred yards, he took a quick look to his right, and noticed that he had already gone through Fronsdal by two lengths. Push harder, he said. Now lengthen out. Even with the early lead, he did not slow down, but with each stroke he took, he seemed to gain a little more confidence and a little more distance. By the halfway mark, he had gained three lengths. Inside Kell's head, however, a growing feeling of elation was mixed with fear. Any number of things could still go wrong. He could break an oarlock or "jump the slide," lifting his rolling seat out of its slender tracks. As he moved closer to the one-mile mark, he also realized that his entire family could now see the race, and his father's eyes were trained upon him. The coveted Henley victory was finally in hand, and to his father it was no less important than the Holy Grail, an elusive prize that promised to erase twenty-seven years of pain. "This is for you, Dad," he began to chant, coxing himself down the course.

Instead of slowing down as he approached the stands, he went faster and faster, until he was nearly eight lengths ahead of Fronsdal. He glanced over his right shoulder, gauging the distance between himself and the finish line. As he rowed past the Stewards' Enclosure, he felt the eyes of the crowd upon him, studying every stroke he took. "Well sculled, Kelly," a nameless spectator called out. Several others began to clap as Kell made his way by; otherwise, there was an almost deferential silence. Kell's strokes were seamless, with the smooth reverse swing of his rounded shoulders around the end of the stroke that was so different from the classic, English style, which featured an upright back, and the quick pulse through the water. There was no struggle or battle for the crowd to behold, and as Kell crossed the line, his lightweight opponent was nowhere in sight. When the race was over, Kell came to a slow, graceful stop, and then he circled back to the press dock to greet Fronsdal.

"Kelly is so far ahead that he is turning around to hear the applause from the bank," said the announcer on the PA system.

The sky was overcast now and the Thames was a calm gray mirror. It was a little cool for July, with the threat of rain. Too much could turn the pleasant grassy banks into a muddy barnyard, suitable only for knee-high Wellies. He made his way over to Fronsdal, and the two had their photos taken. Then he got back in his boat and paddled back to the competitor's dock. There, waiting patiently, was the only person whose approval he really needed.

"We did it, Dad!" Kell called out, landing on the dock as the photographers quickly descended on him. As the flashbulbs ignited and the newsreels ran, Kell stood up and grinned like a young boy who had just caught his first big fish. He gave a toothy "aw-shucks" grin and looked uncomfortably from side to side as he smiled at the cameras, with none of the straightforward intense stare that characterized his father.

"You could have won by five more lengths!" his father said, beaming, as a news cameraman set up his tripod and announced, "A gentleman from the University of Pennsylvania simply rowed away with the Diamonds this year. His name—J.B. Kelly." Margaret, Grace, and Lizanne now joined Kell, crowding onto the small landing. It was a picture-perfect victory, except for the sound of scattered booing that now issued from the Berkshire bank. Among the twenty thousand spectators in attendance, there were many true rowing aficionados who were clearly disappointed by the American's win. They were disgruntled, too, by the orchestrated scene in front of them, the entire Kelly clan having their photos taken. Mr. Jack Kelly was now holding court among all the reporters, and altogether too much fuss was being made over the overrated youngster, who had yet to really prove himself in a strong, international field. Added to the whole picture, of course, was the lingering feeling of resentment in the air, the suspicion that the Kellys had only come to Henley to fulfill a personal grudge against their hosts.

"In your imagination," one reporter said, "I suppose you thought of how you would gloat when this day came."

"I felt that way at times," Jack Kelly admitted, "but now that it's here, I only have a tremendous feeling of pride for Kell. He is the one that really matters, not the thwarted ambition of an old guy who once got his fingers publicly slapped over here because he was born without a silver spoon in his mouth."

Later that day, showered and dressed in a gray woolen suit, Jack Kelly Jr. ascended the steps of the Henley grandstands and received his prize from Viscountess Hambleden, the Queen's lady-in-waiting. He needed both hands to hold the Pineapple Cup and the Diamond Sculls, and he tucked the leather case firmly under his arm, in order to shake her hand. It was a quick, perfunctory exchange of greetings, for there were many other awards to be distributed that day. But there were none so long in the making. When Kelly rejoined his family, they gathered around him for one last photo, holding his prizes. After so many long years, it all seemed too good to be true. Kelly Sr.'s left hand rested lightly on his son's shoulder, as if to signal that he shared in the victory, and everyone's eyes fell upon the beautiful golden chalice known as the Pineapple Cup. He balanced the Diamond Sculls case on his lap, with its miniature crossed oars and silver plaques containing the names of past winners. The name Jack Kelly Jr. would soon be inscribed on one.

"I won this for you, Dad," he said, looking over his shoulder. His father was sitting behind him, looking at the prizes with pride and a tinge of envy. Kell noticed that his father had now started to become more relaxed and benevolent to everyone around him, even in the face of the inhospitable booing. It was almost as if, now that Kell had won, his father didn't want anything or anyone to take away from the victory, whether it was a few sore losers in the British crowd or his own feelings of revenge.

"Mr. Kelly," one American reporter had asked him, "what your boy did this afternoon is a definite victory over snobbery." When Kelly failed to respond, he added, "Was that little green hat your son wore the same as the one you wore when you raced?"

Kelly shook his head, explaining that it was merely a reproduction. "I wanted something of mine to ride across the Henley finish line today to make up for the heartbreak I felt in 1920. But

Kell waves his signature green cap to the crowds after winning the
National Championships in 1956. Kell made his last, and best, attempt
for an Olympic gold that year in Melbourne, Australia, but he came up
short, with a third place finish. He gave the bronze medal to sister Grace
as a wedding present. © TEMPLE UNIVERSITY LIBRARIES, URBAN ARCHIVES, PHILA-
DELPHIA, PA

I now know that the replica of the green cap wasn't of the slightest importance at the showdown. That was my son out there—to me the greatest single sculler that ever lived. For all of me, he couldn't have changed that if he wore a beret!"

For Jack Kelly, Independence Day had come at last, twenty-seven years and one day late.

Epilogue

When the Kellys arrived back in New York on the *Queen Elizabeth*, they were met by a small army of reporters who eagerly pushed their way onboard. Many of them had received conflicting stories from overseas, and they wanted to confirm the alleged reports of booing crowds. To their immediate dismay, Jack and Kell informed them the British had been perfect hosts. "I never was treated better in my life," Kell stated, looking surprised and acting almost indignant when he was questioned otherwise. The well-groomed twenty-year-old was dressed in a navy blue flannel suit and gray trousers, identical to his father, who gave a similar report. "I didn't hear a single boo all the time I was in England," he said. "How anyone could have been treated better than the Kelly family, I don't know." It was complete and unequivocal denial, leaving several reporters at a sudden loss for words.

"We were entertained by Lord and Lady Hambleden," Kelly Sr. added, emphasizing their acceptance by members of the Royal Court. Kell proceeded to compliment the British rowing style, claiming that it was superior to American form and that the English oarsmen were only lacking in size and a better training diet. When his father was asked to comment about his 1920 rejection, the former politician now became gracious and circumspect, framing the old denial as a simple misunderstanding. "They refused to let me row because my father gave me a wheelbarrow and told me to catch up with the wheel," he joked. Then he shrugged it off. "They told me they made a big mistake."

Philadelphia parade car after Kell's return home from Henley, 1947. Margaret, Kell, and an unidentified friend in the back seat; Jack Kelly Sr. sitting in front next to Mayor Bernard Samuel. © TEMPLE UNIVERSITY LIBRARIES, URBAN ARCHIVES, PHILADELPHIA, PA

Soon afterward, when William O'Dwyer, the mayor of New York, stormed onto the *Queen Elizabeth* with his own entourage and escorted the Kellys to City Hall, Jack Sr. still refused to sour the affair by speaking ill of the English. During a speech he made in front of City Hall, Kelly even confessed to the group of politicians and policemen that if he had been allowed to compete at Henley back in his heyday, he probably would have had an unfair advantage. This was a complete shift in Jack Kelly's sentiment, and perhaps a conscious effort not to spoil his son's victory with any mention of past ill treatment. The self-effacing admission, of course, did nothing to lessen his son's stock. "Where can I get one of those green hats?" one policeman inquired.

Back home in Philadelphia, the Kellys met with more un-qualified praise and an organized parade, just like the one Jack Sr. had received twenty-seven years earlier. Thousands of well-wishers lined the city streets, now adorned with countless banners, flags, and streamers embossed with the word Kell. Green caps were in great abundance and said it all. It was Irish-American pride on display, and there was nothing demure or restrained about it. Kell sat up on the backseat of the lead car with his mother, tipping his cap as he passed through the city streets. His father shared the front seat with Mayor Bernard Samuel, dressed impeccably, while Charley McIntyre followed on foot, leading a rag-tag squadron of Vesper oarsman. Several of them carried long oars that they held aloft, as they tried to walk in step to a brass band that played loudly.

A week later, an awards banquet was held at the Bellevue Stratford where endless toasts were given by those in attendance, including Jack and Margaret Kelly, Mayor Samuel, and Kell himself. In the interim between the parade and the banquet, he had flown to Detroit to compete in the US National Championships, and then traveled to Canada to row in their Nationals as well. He capsized his shell in the first race, battling extremely rough conditions, and then redeemed himself in the second outing, winning handily. At the awards banquet later, his father chided him for flipping but finally admitted, "No picture looks good with total sunshine or total shade."

Although many at Henley had made light of Jack Kelly Jr. and his easy victory at the 1947 regatta, in his own country he was honored with the prestigious James L. Sullivan Award, given annually to the best US amateur athlete. Expectations for him were running higher than ever, and he returned to England the following year for his first of four Olympic Games. In a spectacular semifinals battle against Eduardo Risso of Uruguay, Kell lost by a photo finish in driving rain. The dramatic finish line photo became widely distributed, for the camera angle favored Kell and clearly showed the agony on his face. Despite the loss, however, in this one brave effort he finally began to win over the hearts of the English rowing crowd. As had happened in his race against Jean Séphériadès in 1946, Kell was barely able to make it back to the dock, and once there he had to be carried from his boat. After that performance, few questioned the conviction of Jack Kelly's son. If anything, they began to feel more sympathy for the young man, who had been tasked with the near impossible duty of living up to his father's legacy. Having won Henley, he was now expected to win an Olympic gold medal, just as Jack Sr. had once done.

In 1949 he won the Diamond Challenge Sculls for a second time, proving that his first victory had not been a fluke. By now, he was a sought-after rowing star, signing autographs for young acolytes and shaking many hands on shore. After Henley, he and his Philadelphia friend Joe Flanagan took a rowing tour of the continent, capped off by a victory at the European Championships in Amsterdam. It was probably the best summer of rowing that Jack Kelly Jr. would ever have, away from his father's watchful eye. During the first part of his journey, Kell even visited Eton, the cradle of English schoolboy rowing. As he strode around, surveying the school grounds, he marveled at the evenness of the grassy playing fields. Locating a landscaper, he asked the man innocently how he managed to get the lawn so perfect, explaining that he'd like to get his own lawn that way.

"Roll it out for two hundred years," the English gardener told him.

〜

It was a decade later that Kell and his father would admit, when pressed, that they had indeed been booed at Henley in 1947, and that it had bothered them more than they cared to admit. They didn't want to acknowledge it at the time, not only out of fear that it would make them seem like bad winners but also that it would take something away from the victory. Slowly, too, as Kell's reputation as a world-class sculler became more established, his acceptance by the English improved, aided by the growing popularity of his sister Grace. KELLY FOR BRICKWORK T-shirts became a valuable commodity at Henley each year, worn by underdogs of all nationalities, including a rebellious young Australian named Stuart MacKenzie, and even some members of the Thames Rowing Club, Jack Beresford's old alma mater. The long-standing rift was finally beginning to heal.

During one of Kell's trips to Henley, the English oarsman Bert Bushnell succeeded in getting a date with Kell's sister, Grace. As the two strolled along the banks of the Thames, she spoke at length to him about her wish to become a model and a dancer against her parents' wishes. Not long after, she would become more famous than her father and brother combined, as an international movie star and later as royalty. Many years later in 1981, she was invited back to the Henley Royal Regatta, this time to

Kell and family looking over the Henley Diamond Sculls trophy known as the Pineapple Cup, 1947. Grace, Jack Sr., Jack Jr., Lizanne, and Margaret Kelly (left to right). © TEMPLE UNIVERSITY LIBRARIES, URBAN ARCHIVES, PHILADELPHIA, PA

hand out the prizes as the Princess of Monaco. It was a symbolic peace offering by the Henley Stewards, and an attempt to finally put the long conflict to rest.

Afterword

As one of my sources put it, the story of the Kellys is an epic saga that could go on for years. I chose to end here, with Kell's victory at the 1947 Henley Royal Regatta, for a variety of reasons. First, it was the endpoint of Jack Sr.'s original autobiography, a source to which I have tried to stay true. Next, it was one of the high points of Kell's illustrious rowing career, after which he struggled to get an Olympic gold medal that always seemed to elude him.

The closest he came was a bronze in the 1956 Games in Melbourne, a medal that he gave to his sister Grace as a wedding present. Some rowing critics claim that Kell burned himself out in the preliminary heats at Melbourne, while others point out that the competition in world rowing had deepened since his father's day, and a slight fall-off in training, or a bad day, could cost any of the top contenders a medal on any given outing.

Jack Kelly Sr. continued to play the role of the benevolent patriarch to hundreds of people and their causes, extending his influence on both a local and national level. In the 1950s, as he had once done for FDR, Kelly became the National Physical Fitness Director for President Eisenhower, and he remained an impressive example of an athletic lifestyle. He also continued to serve as a patron saint for many struggling oarsmen, often handing them cash outright when he could not secure them employment. After a brave battle with stomach cancer, Kelly passed away at age seventy-one, leaving a long, humorous will that began, "This is my Last Will and Testament and I believe I am of sound mind. (Some lawyers will

"Have shell, will travel." Jack Kelly Sr. and Jack Kelly Jr. return home from their victorious boat races at St. Catharines, Ontario, Fairmount Park, July 30, 1945. © TEMPLE UNIVERSITY LIBRARIES, URBAN ARCHIVES, PHILA-DELPHIA, PA

question this when they read my Will; however, I have my opinion of some of them so that makes it even...") The giant bronze statue of him, sitting in his single, was commissioned the year after his death in 1960. It still rests at the grandstands of the Schuylkill rowing course, facing upstream.

Kelly Sr.'s English rival, **Jack Beresford Jr.,** continued to win numerous medals and accolades in rowing until his death in 1977 at age seventy-eight. He was one of the finest oarsmen ever to come out of England, and his overall rowing accomplishments were equaled only by another Englishman of more recent times, Sir Steven Redgrave. Beresford Jr. competed in five consecutive Olympic

Games (1920, 1924, 1928, 1932, and 1936), and in this period he won three Olympic gold medals and two silvers in various boats. At the Henley Royal Regatta, he won the Diamond Challenge Sculls four times (1920, 1924–26); the Silver Goblets and Nickalls' Challenge Cup for coxless pairs with Gordon Killick in 1928 and 1929; the Stewards' Challenge Cup for coxless fours in 1932; and the Grand Challenge Cup for eights in 1923 and 1928. He also rowed a dead-heat, together with Dick Southwood, in the Double Sculls Challenge Cup final against an Italian duo in its inaugural year, 1939. Beresford Jr. was also a noteworthy coach and managed many elite British crews. In 1947 he was awarded a gold medal by the International Rowing Federation for his long contribution to rowing. The following year he was a member of the organizing committee for the Olympic rowing at Henley, and in 1949 he received an Olympic diploma of merit. In 1960, he was appointed CBE (Commander of the British Empire).

Like his father, **Jack Kelly Jr.** learned the bricklaying business and eventually entered the world of local Philadelphia politics. He served on the City Council in Philadelphia for many years. His mother, Margaret Kelly, effectively derailed a short-lived run for mayor, fearing that the details of her son's colorful social life would not hold up well under public scrutiny. After his father's death in 1960, Kell had effectively hung up his oars, gotten a divorce, and become something of a playboy socialite. As Grace aptly observed of her brother, "He lived the first part of his life thinking he was Dad, and the second part of his life trying to be like James Bond."

In addition to his numerous rowing accolades (eight times the US Singles Champion between 1946 and 1956; six-time Canadian champion; Pan American Champion in the single, 1955, and the doubles, 1959, with Bill Knecht), Jack Kelly Jr. also served as president of the NAOO and the AAU, and was elected president of the US Olympic Committee in 1985. Unfortunately, he would never realize this dream job come true. Two weeks after the post was announced, Kell died of a heart attack while jogging back from his daily morning row. He was only fifty-seven years old.

Although he may have failed to cap off his Henley victories with an Olympic gold medal, Kell did share an Olympic gold medal victory by organizing a famous Vesper crew who represented the United States at the Tokyo Olympics in 1964. Many of the members of that boat who are still alive recall how he helped put the crew together, seat by seat, in much the same way his father had done with the famous Penn AC crews of the 1930s. He recruited many of them from outside the Philadelphia area, found them housing and employment, and fought various political battles for the crew. The 1964 US Olympic eight was, in a way, the first orchestrated effort to create a US national team boat, and it is one of Kell's greatest accomplishments.

Grace Kelly went to acting school in New York the autumn following Kell's Henley victory in 1947, gaining admittance at the last minute because of her Uncle George's connections. Her sudden rise to Hollywood fame and fortune began with the western *High Noon* in 1952, and finished with *High Society* in 1956. Ironically, this last film was a satire of American class prejudice, originally called *The Philadelphia Story*. In it Kelly played Tracy Lord, a spoiled, rich socialite from Main Line Philadelphia, the one group to which the Kelly family never gained admittance. On the silver screen, however, Grace was able to fulfill one of her childhood dreams, to come out as a Philadelphia debutante.

A year earlier, on a shoot for the movie *To Catch a Thief* in Monaco, she met Prince Rainier and their curious courtship began. Grace's marriage to the prince would provide a final bit of irony to the Kelly saga, particularly when Rainier asked Jack Kelly Sr. for a dowry of $100,000. To the man who had worked his way up from nothing, the prince reeked of charm without substance. The enormous press coverage, however, and the prestige of marrying into royalty seemed to balance Kelly's frustration with the affair. Besides, as he and Margaret slowly began to realize, their middle daughter always seemed to get her way, a skill her father had once held exclusively.

Grace and Kell remained close right up to the moment of her untimely death in 1982, in a tragic car accident on the same scenic drive featured in *To Catch a Thief*. To memorialize her, Henley Royal Regatta changed the name of the Women's Quadruple Sculls to the Princess Grace Challenge Cup in 2003, and the following year her son Prince Albert gave out the prizes.

ACKNOWLEDGMENTS

Without the following "crew" of people, who helped me uncover and make sense of the vast amount of material involved with this book, I would have been unable to complete the task:

Ellen Sheehan and Wendy Moody from the East Falls Historical Society, John Pettit, assistant archivist, Jean Arnone and Thomas Manson, at the Temple University Urban Archives, and Jean Longo, from the Friends Library, Philadelphia, who helped track down many old Kelly family photos and articles; Matthew Struckmeyer and Murdo McGrath, who helped with library research; John B. Kelly III, grandson of Jack Kelly Sr., who entrusted me with his grandfather's memoir and generously provided family photos; John Beresford, for sharing photos from his family collection; Göran R. Buckhorn, my editor at Mystic Seaport; my wife, Karen Barss, who batted editorial "cleanup"; Edward ("Ned") Thomas, Jack Galloway, Gus Constance, Allen Rosenburg, and Al Lawn, who lent their stories about Jack Kelly Sr. and Jr.; the late Hart Perry, Bill Miller, William Lanouette, and Tom Weil, the four "deans" of American rowing; Tim Wilson, historian from the Thames Rowing Club; and Michael Rowe from the River and Rowing Museum in Henley. Special thanks to Charley McIntyre, whose many anecdotes about the Kellys helped bring this book to life, and to Connie Stein, Mary Anne Stets, and Louisa Alger Watrous at Mystic Seaport for tending to all the little details that helped to ensure its well-being.

NOTES AND SELECTED BIBLIOGRAPHY

The information for this book was collected from an eclectic variety of sources, including interviews, newspaper articles, and previous books written about the Kelly family. I was also fortunate enough to have obtained a few pieces of writing from J. B. Kelly Sr., including a short autobiography and a lengthy last will and testament. The latter begins in a characteristic Kelly vein: "For years I have been reading last wills and testaments, and I have never been able to clearly understand any of them at one reading."

At times, sifting through the various sources and stories about Jack Kelly Sr., I was faced with some difficult choices. Many anecdotes and articles were contradictory in nature and had to be cross-referenced against other accounts. Even simple items, like the spelling of names or the times of various Olympic races, were not always recorded accurately. And then, of course, there were the endless Kelly anecdotes, often colorful in nature, which had to be questioned for their veracity. Having some amount of Irish blood running through my veins, I feel qualified to note that the oral tradition of the Emerald Isle has a general tendency toward embellishment. While this may be an acceptable literary technique, it presents a problem for an author seeking to write a work of nonfiction.

Needless to say, there are many Kelly legends that have been handed down over the years that may be true in spirit without being grounded in fact. In the end, I believe an author must act more like a judge than a mathematician in deciding how to make sense of the information at hand, sometimes relying on gut instinct when faced with conflicting sources. I can only hope that I have applied a moderate hand to the material, and neither censored too much nor passed along too many yarns.

Periodicals

"Jack Kelly Within Reach of National Rowing Crown," *The North American,* Philadelphia, August 6, 1916.

"Athletes of Note to Train Soldiers," *New York Times,* April 7, 1918.

"Kelly May Enter Diamond Sculls," *New York Times,* April 28, 1920.

"Kelly to Row in Olympics: Wants to Meet Diamond Sculls Winner," *Philadelphia Free Press,* June 1920.

"Jack Kelly Misses Mother's Custards," *Philadelphia Evening Bulletin,* August 30, 1920.

"Mrs. Kelly Happy at Son's Triumph," *Philadelphia Evening Bulletin,* August 30, 1920.

"No Rival in Sight for Jack Kelly," *Philadelphia Evening Bulletin,* August 15, 1921.

"Democratic Candidate for Mayor Gets Present," *Philadelphia Evening Bulletin,* August 30, 1935.

"Philadelphia Primary," *Time* Magazine, September 18, 1935.

"Kelly Gains Final in Diamond Sculls," *New York Times* (AP), July 5, 1946.

"Sephariades of France Defeats Kelly by Three Lengths at Henley," *New York Times,* July 7, 1946.

"Kelly Gains Final in Henley Regatta," *New York Times* (AP), July 4, 1947.

"Kelly Easy Victor in Diamond Sculls," *New York Times* (AP), July 5, 1947.

"Jack Kellys Return Home Denying Boos at Henley," *Philadelphia Evening Bulletin,* July 15, 1947.

"The Philadelphia Princess," *Time* Magazine, January 16, 1956.

"The Girl in the White Gloves," *Time* Magazine, January 31, 1956.

"What Makes Jack Kelly Run?" *The Philadelphia Inquirer,* January 19, 1975.

"An Olympian, City Councilman, and Bricklayer," *The Philadelphia Inquirer,* March 4, 1985.

"A Stroke of Genius in the Racing Shell," *Sports Illustrated,* July 27, 1996.

"At His Fifth Olympics Jack was the Master," *The Guardian,* September 2000.

"Hitler was enraged by my father's Olympic feats," *The Daily Telegraph,* September 22, 2006.

BOOKS

Burnell, Richard. *Henley Royal Regatta: A Celebration of 150 Years.* London: William Heinemann, 1989.

Burt, Nathaniel. *The Perennial Philadelphians: The Anatomy of an American Aristocracy.* Philadelphia: University of Pennsylvania Press, 1999.

Cleaver, Hylton. *A History of Rowing.* London: Herbert Jenkins, 1957.

Cleaver, Hylton. *Sporting Rhapsody.* London: Hutchinson's Library, 1951.

Cooper, Helen A. *Thomas Eakins, The Rowing Pictures.* New Haven: Yale University Press, 1996.

Dodd, Christopher. *Henley Royal Regatta*. London: Stanley Paul & Co., 1981.

Dodd, Christopher. *The Story of World Rowing*. London: Stanley Paul & Co., 1992.

Heiland, Louis. *The Schuylkill Navy of Philadelphia*. Philadelphia: The Drake Press, Inc. 1938.

Kanin, David B. *A Political History of the Olympic Games*. Boulder, CO: Westview Press, 1981.

Kelly, Walter. *Of Me I Sing: An Informal Autobiography*. New York: The Dial Press, 1953.

Lacey, Robert. *Grace*. New York: G.P. Putnam and Sons, 1994.

Lewis, Arthur H. *Those Philadelphia Kellys*. New York: William Morrow and Co., 1977.

Mallon, Bill. *The 1920 Olympic Games: Results from all competitors in all events, with commentary by Bill Mallon and Anthony Th. Bijkerk*. London: McFarland & Co. Inc., 2003.

McCallum, John. *That Kelly Family*. New York: A.S. Barnes and Co., 1957.

Mendenhall, Thomas C. *A Short History of American Rowing*. Boston: Charles River Books, 1980.

Taraborrelli, J. Randy. *Once Upon a Time: Behind the Fairy Tale of Princess Grace and Prince Rainier*. New York: Warner Books, 2003.

Vamplew, Wray. *Pay Up and Play the Game: Professional Sport in Britain, 1875–1914*. Cambridge: Cambridge University Press, 1989.

INDEX

Page numbers in italics refers to illustrations.

Henley Royal Regatta,
80–81, 115–18, 119–26,
190, 235, 237–46, 247,
252–53, 257–67, 272, 273
in the Army, 2–5, *3, 7,* 8–10,
94–95, 98–104, *103,* 109–
10, 111
KELLY FOR BRICKWORK, 110,
191, 272
Olympic Games, 116, 127,
138–42, 140, 144, 146–47,
148–58, 159–61, 181, 184,
other sports, *7,* 28–32, 57,
111–12
political career, 196–203
Kelly, John Henry (father), 13,
19, 20, 25, 29, 30, *121*
Kelly, Margaret "Peggy"
(daughter), 189–93, *192,*
213–16, 231, 247, 249,
252, 264
Kelly, Margaret Majer "Ma"
(wife), 164–67, 171, 177–
180, *178,* 189–93, *192,*
200, 212, 215, *269,* 270,
273, 276, 278
Kelly, Mary (sister), 13, *20*
Kelly, Mary Costello "Ma"
(mother), 9, 13, 17–22,

20, 23–30, 37, 41, 57, 61,
65–67, 93–96, 101–2,
104–6, 110, 111, 113, 117,
120, 125, 157, 166, 188–
89, 224, 244, 259
Kelly, Patrick "P.H." (brother),
13, 19, *20,* 24, 25, 26, 33,
34, 65, 94, 109, 112, 117,
118, *121,* 188, 194, 195
Kelly, Walter (brother), x, 13,
20, 27, 62–71, *63,* 72, 81,
94, 95, 102, 110, 117, *121,*
121, 186, 187, 188, 197,
200
Killick, Gordon, 276
Knecht, Bill, 277

Lawn, Al, 235, 237, 279
Levy, Ike, 248
Ljunglöf, Nils, 146

Mack, Tommy, 240
MacKenzie, R. Tait, 180
MacKenzie, Stuart, 272
Margaret, Princess of England,
238
McCarthy, Pat, 6, 59–61
McCoy, Kid, 70
McCreesh, Tommy, 229

Sheppard, Fred, 15, 44, 53, 54
Shore, Toots, 240
Sloak, Joe, 173–76
Southwood, Dick, 206, 207,
    208, 276
Stern, J. David, 198
Sullivan, Tom, 207

Ten Eyck, Edward H., 122,
    123, 260
Tilden, Bill, 163
Tunney, Gene, 105, 109

Uhl, Eleanor, 163

Veth, Bastian, 146

Walsh, "Monsignor", 22
Washington, George, 14, 70
Whitlock, Brand, 148
Whitman, Walt, 18
Whitney, Casper, 77
Willis, Cecil, 78
Wilson, S. Davis, 207
Withington, Dr. Paul, 116
Wyatt, James, 259

Zahn, George, 111
Zinke, Gustav, 144

About the Author

DANIEL J. BOYNE is the author of *The Red Rose Crew: A True Story of Women, Winning and the Water*, and *Essential Sculling* (both from Lyons Press). He has also written articles for *The Atlantic Monthly, Harvard Magazine, Double Take, WoodenBoat,* and *Gray's Sporting Journal,* among others. He currently lives in Cambridge with his wife and daughter, and works at Harvard University.